CAMBRIDGE LIBRARY COLLECTION

Books of enduring scholarly value

Art and Architecture

From the middle of the eighteenth century, with the growth of travel at home and abroad and the increase in leisure for the wealthier classes, the arts became the subject of more widespread appreciation and discussion. The rapid expansion of book and periodical publishing in this area both reflected and encouraged interest in art and art history among the wider reading public. This series throws light on the development of visual culture and aesthetics. It covers topics from the Grand Tour to the great exhibitions of the nineteenth century, and includes art criticism and biography.

First Additional Supplement to the Encyclopaedia of Cottage, Farm, and Villa Architecture and Furniture

After the success of his richly illustrated *Encyclopaedia of Cottage, Farm, and Villa Architecture and Furniture* (1833), which is also reissued in this series, the landscape gardener John Claudius Loudon (1783–1843) received a great deal of correspondence from interested readers. This prompted him and the *Encyclopaedia*'s contributors to publish this supplement in 1842. Loudon and his colleagues had continued to study a range of rural buildings – from homes to farms and schools – in England and Scotland, while at the same time receiving architectural designs and detailed letters from North America and Australia. The supplement draws on this wealth of material to discuss developments in the use of building materials as well as innovations in design. The focus is on cottages, farms, pubs, schools and almshouses. Construction methods and furnishings are also discussed. As with the volume it supplements, this work contains a plethora of detailed illustrations.

T0384641

Cambridge University Press has long been a pioneer in the reissuing of out-of-print titles from its own backlist, producing digital reprints of books that are still sought after by scholars and students but could not be reprinted economically using traditional technology. The Cambridge Library Collection extends this activity to a wider range of books which are still of importance to researchers and professionals, either for the source material they contain, or as landmarks in the history of their academic discipline.

Drawing from the world-renowned collections in the Cambridge University Library and other partner libraries, and guided by the advice of experts in each subject area, Cambridge University Press is using state-of-the-art scanning machines in its own Printing House to capture the content of each book selected for inclusion. The files are processed to give a consistently clear, crisp image, and the books finished to the high quality standard for which the Press is recognised around the world. The latest print-on-demand technology ensures that the books will remain available indefinitely, and that orders for single or multiple copies can quickly be supplied.

The Cambridge Library Collection brings back to life books of enduring scholarly value (including out-of-copyright works originally issued by other publishers) across a wide range of disciplines in the humanities and social sciences and in science and technology.

First Additional Supplement to the Encyclopaedia of Cottage, Farm, and Villa Architecture and Furniture

Bringing the Work Down to 1842

JOHN CLAUDIUS LOUDON

CAMBRIDGE
UNIVERSITY PRESS

CAMBRIDGE
UNIVERSITY PRESS

University Printing House, Cambridge, CB2 8BS, United Kingdom

Published in the United States of America by Cambridge University Press, New York

Cambridge University Press is part of the University of Cambridge.
It furthers the University's mission by disseminating knowledge in the pursuit of
education, learning and research at the highest international levels of excellence.

www.cambridge.org
Information on this title: www.cambridge.org/9781108071635

© in this compilation Cambridge University Press 2014

This edition first published 1842
This digitally printed version 2014

ISBN 978-1-108-07163-5 Paperback

AN

ENCYCLOPÆDIA

OF

COTTAGE, FARM, AND VILLA

ARCHITECTURE

AND

FURNITURE:

CONTAINING

NUMEROUS DESIGNS FOR DWELLINGS,

FROM THE COTTAGE TO THE VILLA,

INCLUDING FARM HOUSES, FARMERIES, AND OTHER AGRICULTURAL BUILDINGS;

SEVERAL DESIGNS FOR

Country Inns, Public Houses, and Parochial Schools,

WITH THE REQUISITE FITTINGS-UP, FIXTURES, AND FURNITURE, AND
APPROPRIATE OFFICES, GARDENS, AND GARDEN SCENERY;

EACH DESIGN ACCOMPANIED BY

ANALYTICAL AND CRITICAL REMARKS,

ILLUSTRATIVE OF THE PRINCIPLES OF ARCHITECTURAL SCIENCE AND
TASTE ON WHICH IT IS COMPOSED.

BY J. C. LOUDON, F.L.S. H.S. &c.

CONDUCTOR OF THE GARDENER'S MAGAZINE, ETC.

Illustrated by more than Two Thousand Engravings:
The Designs by upwards of fifty different Architects, Surveyors, Builders, Upholsterers, Cabinet-makers,
Landscape-Gardeners, and others, of whom a List is given.

A NEW EDITION:

WITH A SUPPLEMENT

CONTAINING

ABOVE ONE HUNDRED AND SIXTY PAGES OF LETTER-PRESS, AND
NEARLY THREE HUNDRED ENGRAVINGS,

BRINGING DOWN THE WORK TO

1842.

LONDON:

LONGMAN, BROWN, GREEN, AND LONGMANS;

AND SOLD BY

JOHN WEALE, AT THE ARCHITECTURAL LIBRARY, HIGH HOLBORN.

1842.

☞ *The Author may be consulted, either personally or by letter, on any of the subjects treated of in this Volume, at the rate of One Guinea per hour; or, if required to go from home, at the rate of Five Guineas a day, with travelling expenses. The charge for Plans and Reports may be ascertained by previous agreement.*

LONDON:
Printed by A. SPOTTISWOODE,
New-Street-Square.

FIRST

ADDITIONAL SUPPLEMENT

TO

LOUDON'S ENCYCLOPÆDIA

OF

COTTAGE, FARM, AND VILLA ARCHITECTURE AND FURNITURE.

1842.

CONTENTS.

6 T

ADDITIONAL LIST OF BOOKS QUOTED.

Arch. Mag., 2433. The Architectural Magazine. By J. C. Loudon, F.L.S., H.S., &c. London, 5 vols., 1839.

Brit. Farm. Mag., 2534. The British Farmer's Magazine. London, 1842. Continued.

Combe's Principles of Physiology applied to the Preservation of Health, 2475. 1841. 12mo.

Dict. of Arts, &c., 2447. A Dictionary of Arts, Manufactures, and Mines. By Andrew Ure, M.D. London, 1839. 8vo.

Donaldson's Treatise on Manures, &c., 2233. A Treatise on Manures, their Nature, Preparation, and Application. With a Description and Use of the most approved British Grasses. To which is added a Miscellaneous Article on Farming. By John Donaldson, Land-Steward. London, 1842. 8vo.

Gard. Chron., 2349. The Gardener's Chronicle. A weekly Journal. 4to. London, 1842. Continued.

Gard. Mag., 2327. The Gardener's Magazine. By J. C. Loudon, F.L.S., H.S., &c. London, 1842. 17 vols. 8vo. Continued.

Gilly's Peasantry of the Border, &c., 2233. The Peasantry of the Border. An Appeal in their Behalf. By the Rev. Dr. Gilly, Canon of Durham. 1841. Pamph., 8vo, 5 plates.

Gilpin's Cumberland, p. 1254. Observations on several Parts of England, particularly the Mountains and Lakes of Cumberland and Westmoreland. By William Gilpin, A.M. London, 1808. 2 vols. 8vo.

The Grainer's Guide, 2520. By Charles Moxon. Edinburgh, 1842. fol. 2l. 2s.

Hakewell's Attempt to determine the exact Character of Elizabethan Architecture, 2308. 1835. 8vo.

History of Cassiobury Park, 2313. The History and Description, with Graphic Illustrations, of Cassiobury Park, Hertfordshire. The Seat of the Earl of Essex. By John Britton, F.S.A. London, 1837. folio.

Minutes of the Committee of Council on Education, p. 1241. London, 1840. folio.

Parker's Villa Rustica, p. 1241. 1842. 4to.

Proceedings of the British Association for 1838. 2442. 8vo.

Pugin's Christian Architecture, 2327. The true Principles of Pointed, or Christian, Architecture. By A. Welby Pugin, Architect. London, 1841. 4to.

Railway Stations, 2299. By Francis Thompson, Architect. London, 1842. folio. 25s.

Ricauti's Rustic Architecture, 2278. By T. J. Ricauti, Architect. London. 4to. 1840.

Sanitary Report of the Poor-Law Commissioners, 2233. London, 1842. 8vo.

Stuart's Dict. of Arch., 2283. A Dictionary of Architecture. By Robert Stuart, Architect and Civil Engineer. London. 3 vols. 8vo.

Suburban Architect, &c., 2474. The Suburban Architect and Landscape-Gardener. By J. C. Loudon, F.L.S., H.S., &c. London, 1838. 8vo.

Suburban Horticulturist, 2297. The Suburban Horticulturist. By J. C. Loudon, F.L.S., H.S., &c. London, 1842. 8vo. 15s.

The London Farmer's Magazine, p. 1234. London, 1839. 8vo. Continued.

Trans. Ent. Soc., 2528. Transactions of the Entomological Society. 1839. 8vo. Continued.

Trans. Inst. Brit. Arch., 2446. Transactions of the Institution of British Architects. London. vol. i. 4to. Continued.

LIST OF CONTRIBUTORS.

A—, C—, p. 1179.

Curtis, John, Esq., West Rudham, near Rougham, Norfolk. p. 1258. and 1263.

Dobson, John, Esq., Newcastle upon Tyne. p. 1186, 1187, 1188.

Donaldson, John, Land-Steward, Genwysk, Pont Lenny, near Brecon. p. 1234.

Eales, C., Esq., Architect, London. p. 1249.

E. B. p. 1269.

Elliott, John, Esq., Architect, Chichester. p. 1252.

F. H. p. 1161.

G. B. W. p. 1178.

Gorrie, Archibald, F.H.S., &c., Land-Steward, Annat, near Errol, Perthshire. p. 1199. and 1269.

Hay, D. R., Esq., George's St., Edinburgh. p. 1215.

Henderson, John, Esq., Architect, 16. London Street, Edinburgh. p. 1172.

Hunt, Mr. Joseph, Ironmonger, Derby. p. 1288.

J. M. p. 1279.

J. R. p. 1268.

Lamb, *Edward Buxton*, Esq., F.I.B.A., Architect, 10. Burton Crescent, London. p. 1170, 1171. 1173. 1183, 1184. 1195, 1196, 1197. 1203, 1204, 1205, 1206. 1215. 1217. 1223. 1229.

Liddell, Hon. *Thomas*, Ravensworth Castle, near Durham. p. 1163.

Menteath, *James Stuart*, Esq., Closeburn, Dumfriesshire. p. 1151.

Milne, *John*, Esq., Architect, Princes Street, Edinburgh. p. 1207.

Parker, *Charles*, Esq., F.I.B.A., Architect, Tavistock Street, Bedford Square, London. p. 1241.

Ricauti, *T. J.*, Esq., Architect, 22. Duke Street, Portland Place, London. p. 1155.

Robertson, *John*, Esq., Architect, Chatsworth, p. 1162. and 1200.

S. p. 1284.

S. T. p. 1263.

Thompson, *Francis*, Esq., Architect, Market-Place, Derby. p. 1164, 1165, 1166, 1167, and 1168.

T. W. p. 1268.

Varden, *R.*, Esq., Architect, Worcester. p. 1158.

Wild, *J. W.*, Esq., Architect, 130. Piccadilly, London. p. 1253.

Wilds, *W.*, Esq., Architect, Hertford. p. 1261.

Wilson. *Thomas*, Esq., The Banks, near Barnsley. p. 1145.

Wood, *Frederick*, Esq., Architect, Rugby. p. 1243.

W. T. p. 1263.

INTRODUCTION.

Since the publication of this Encyclopædia, in 1833, we have carefully watched the progress made in the knowledge and practice of the subjects of which it treats, in order to add to our stock of ideas with a view to a new edition, or a Supplement. For this purpose we commenced the *Architectural Magazine* in 1834, and continued it for five years, recording in it a variety of information, not only on the subjects embraced by this Encyclopædia, but on every other department of architecture, public as well as private, with the view of rendering architecture a popular study. Though we gave up the *Architectural Magazine* in 1839, yet we have been ever since not less eager in collecting materials for this Supplement. We have examined all the recent publications which bear on the subject, including the *Sanitary Report of the Poor Law Commissioners* just published; and we have inspected a great many cottages, villas, farmeries, and schools, in different parts of England and Scotland. We have had designs of cottages and villas submitted to us for criticism and amendment from all parts of the country, and even from North America and Australia; and we have been in the constant habit of receiving architectural communications from professional friends and correspondents, more especially since we announced, above a year ago, our intention of bringing out this *Supplement*. From the great abundance of materials thus brought before us, we have made a careful selection, which we have arranged under the heads of— 1. Cottages for Labourers and Mechanics; 2. Cottage Villas and Villas; 3. Farmeries; and 4. Schools, Public-houses, Union Work-houses, and Alms-houses. We have added, 5. a chapter on Construction and Materials; 6. one on Fittings-up, Finishing, and Furniture, generally applicable; and 7. one containing Hints to Proprietors desirous of improving the Labourers' Cottages on their Estate; and we have given a new General Index, including in it the body of the work as well as the Supplement.

We have numbered the paragraphs in continuation from the last paragraph in the Encyclopædia, for the sake of uniformity both in the text and the Index; and we have frequently referred to paragraphs and pages in the body of the work, in which the same subjects are treated of, for details which it would have been superfluous to repeat.

CHAP. I.

Cottages for Country Labourers and Mechanics, and for Gardeners, Foresters, Bailiffs, and other upper out-of-door Servants in the Country; including Gate-Lodges and Gates. (Encyc. of Cott. Arch., p. 8.)

2233. (1336. to 1341.) *Present State of Labourers' Cottages.* Instead of adding any remarks of our own to those already given in the Encyclopædia, òn the present state of labourers' cottages, or the benefits to labourers and to the country generally from improving them, we give the following extracts from a recent pamphlet, entitled *The Peasantry of the Border*, &c., by the Rev. Dr. Gilly, Vicar of Norham, in Northumberland (1841), from the *Sanitary Report of the Poor Law Commissioners* (1842), and from a recent work on *Manures and Farming* by Mr. Donaldson. We give these extracts to prove to the reader the great necessity of improvement in the cottage of the labourer, and more especially of the agricultural labourer.

" The general character of the best of the old-fashioned hinds' cottages in this neighbourhood [Norham, on the banks of the Tweed, not far from Berwick] is bad at the best. They have to bring every thing with them; partitions, window-frames, fixtures of all kinds, grates, and a substitute for ceiling; for they are, as I have already called them, mere sheds. They have no byre for their cows, no sties for their pigs, no pumps or wells, nothing to promote cleanliness or comfort. The average size of these sheds is about twenty-four feet by sixteen feet. They are dark and unwholesome. The windows do not open, and many of them are not larger than twenty inches by sixteen inches. And into this space are crowded eight, ten, and even twelve persons. How they lie down to rest, how they sleep, how they can preserve common decency, how unutterable horrors are avoided, is beyond all conception. The case is aggravated when there is a young woman to be lodged in this confined space, who is not a member of the family, but is hired to do the field-work, for which every hind is bound to provide a female. It shocks every feeling of propriety to think that in a room, and within such a space as I have been describing, civilised beings should be herding together without a decent separation of age and sex. So long as the agricultural system, in this district, requires the hind to find room for a fellow-servant of the other sex in his cabin, the least that morality and decency can demand is, that he should have a second apartment, where the unmarried female and those of a tender age should sleep apart from him and his wife." (*The Peasantry,* &c., p. 20.)

The agricultural labourers' cottages in Bedfordshire, according to the *Sanitary Report*, are not much better. " If we follow the agricultural labourer into his miserable dwelling, we shall find it consisting of two rooms only. The day-room, in addition to the family, contains the cooking utensils, the washing apparatus, agricultural implements, and dirty clothes, the windows broken and stuffed full of rags. In the sleeping-apartment the parents and their children, boys and girls, are indiscriminately mixed, and frequently a lodger sleeping in the same and only room ; generally no window, the openings in the half-thatched roof admit light, and expose the family to every vicissitude of the weather: the liability of the children so situated to contagious maladies frequently plunges the family into the greatest misery. The husband, enjoying but little comfort under his own roof, resorts to the beer-shop, neglects the cultivation of his garden, and impoverishes his family. The children are brought up without any regard to decency of behaviour, to habits of foresight or self-restraint ; they make indifferent servants. The girls become the mothers of bastards, and return home a burden to their parents or to the parish, and fill the workhouse. The boys spend the Christmas week's holiday and their year's wages in the beer-shops, and enter upon their new situation in rags. Soon tired of the restraint imposed upon them under the roof of their master, they leave his service before the termination of the year's engagement, seek employment as day-labourers, not with a view of improving their condition, but with a desire to receive and spend their earnings weekly in the beer-shop ; associating with the worst of characters, they become the worst of labourers, resort to poaching, commit petty thefts, and add to the county rates by commitments and prosecutions." (p. 178.)

The same writer gives the following picture of an improved cottage : —

" On entering an improved cottage, consisting, on the ground floor, of a room for the family, a wash-house, and a pantry, and three sleeping-rooms over, with a neat and well cultivated garden, in which the leisure hours of the husband being both pleasantly and profitably employed, he has no desire to frequent the beer-shop, or spend his evenings from home; the children are trained to labour, to habits and feelings of independence, and taught to connect happiness with industry, and to shrink from idleness and immorality: the girls make good servants, obtain the confidence of their employers, and get promoted to the best situations." In short, as another Bedfordshire writer observes, in the same *Report*, the cottager feels that he is somewhat raised in the scale of society. He sees his wife and family more comfortable than formerly ; he rises in respectability of station, and becomes aware that he has a character to lose. Having acquired these important advantages, he is anxious to retain and improve them. (p. 177.) On the other hand, " a man who comes home to a poor comfortless hovel, after his day's labour, and sees all miserable around him, has his spirits more often depressed than excited by it. He feels that, do his best, he shall be miserable still, and is too apt to fly for a temporary refuge to the ale-house or beer-shop. But give him the means of making himself comfortable by his own industry, and I am convinced, by experience, that, in many cases, he will avail himself of it." (p. 178.)

Speaking of the cottages in the improved districts of Scotland and the North of England, Mr. Donaldson, in his excellent work on *Manures and Farming* (London, 8vo, 1842), expresses a hope that improvement, now so general in every department of rural economy, will soon be extended to them. " The square space," he says, " forming one apartment, huddling together a numerous family as in a penfold, constitutes a blot of no small magnitude in the social economy of those northern counties where the genius of agriculture has been truly said to have fixed its chosen residence. The accommodations provided for the farmer and the farm stock have formed a most marked, and it may be added, a very discreditable contrast with the habitations provided for the labourers, without whom the former could not exist. The arrangement of the dining and the drawingroom has engaged the attention of the farmer; the skill of the architect has been employed in erecting convenient accommodations for the poultry and the pigs, the gig and the saddle horse, while any hovel is reckoned sufficient for the labourer; the moving power, the sinew and strength of every active employment. Any improvements in cottage accommodations have mainly arisen from the manufacturing class; and wherever the number of that class is greater, there the country is richer, and the social condition improved in every respect; for a purely agricultural district is ever a poor one for the labourers. Payment of wages partly in produce is preferable for resident country labourers; and a garden, and accommodation for cow and pig, will add much to their comfort." (*Treatise on Manures, &c.*, p. 384.)

Though we are convinced that the only permanent security for the amelioration of the lowest classes is to be found in enlightening and elevating their minds by education, yet, as this can only apply to the rising generation, or rather perhaps, in this country at least, to a generation yet unborn, the existing race can only be benefited by the humanity and kindness of those of their employers who are men of wealth. The unhappy unsettled habits of common British labourers, whether in agriculture or in manufactures, which, we believe, far exceeds anything of the kind which exists in any other country, can only be changed by something which will induce them to forego a present enjoyment for a future good; and, in the present state of things in this country, we know no way in which this can be so easily done, as by arranging so as that every married country labourer may occupy a comfortable cottage and garden.

We shall arrange this chapter under the heads of—1. Designs for Model Cottages. 2. Select Cottages erected. 3. Miscellaneous Designs partly erected. 4. Details of Construction. 5. Cottage Fittings-up and Furniture; and 6. Villages.

Sect. I. *Designs for Model Cottages.* (Encyc. of Cott. Arch., p. 8.)

2234. (13.) The model cottages given in the body of the work are to be regarded as exhibiting the beau-ideal of the accommodation and comfort which a building of the humblest class may be made to supply: those which we are now about to submit are progressive in accommodation; and in the lowest of them there is absolutely nothing that can be omitted without destroying the comfort of the occupant, and, in short, reducing the accommodation to that afforded by those wretched Northumbrian hovels, so feelingly described by the Rev. Dr. Gilly. We have given two fundamental models: one calculated for agricultural labourers, and especially ploughmen, who, in many parts of the country, keep a cow and pig, and have a garden of from one eighth to one sixth of an acre; the other calculated for working mechanics, living in outskirts of towns or in villages, who are supposed seldom to keep a cow, though sometimes a pig, but who, generally, in addition to a cottage, occupy a piece of garden ground of from an eighth to a sixth of an acre, or more.

2235. *The Cow-house and Pigsty.* Many persons object to having these appendages near a dwelling, as tending to render it unhealthy, from damp, smells, &c.; but practically, where the construction and management, and especially the drainage, are good, we consider the objections as unimportant. On the Continent, where the summers are much warmer than in England, the smell of a stable or a pigsty, when under the same roof as the cottager's dwelling, is often a nuisance: but this is chiefly when they are entered by the same door as the living-rooms; for, when they are entered at different doors at some distance apart, the case is totally different, more especially in our comparatively cool climate. As a proof of this, we may refer to those agricultural districts where the cottages, cow-houses, pigsties, &c., are properly constructed, and placed; as, for example, the Earl of Leicester's estates in Norfolk. The agricultural labourers, in many parts of Scotland and the North of England, are allowed the keep of a cow as a part of their wages. In the summer season the cow is generally grazed in the fields along with those of the master, and sometimes (and this we consider the best mode) the winter keep is given along with that of the master's cows. In this last case no cow-house is required as an appendage to the agriculturist's cottage. There are, however, many cases in which the master allows the ploughman so much food for the winter's keep of his cow; and there are, besides, a numerous class in agricultural districts who look upon a cow as essential to the comfort of their families. Under these various circumstances, therefore, we have considered it advisable to provide a cow-house to this class of our model cottages.

2236. *Pigs, Rabbits, and Poultry.* Wherever there is a garden there is always a quantity of refuse, and though this, with the waste of the family, will not fatten a pig, yet it will keep it in a growing state; and, when full-grown, corn, beans, or meal, may be purchased for fattening it. At all events, if it will not keep a pig it will keep rabbits. (§ 769. and 1394.) Poultry may almost always be kept by the cottager; and, to derive the greatest advantage from it by having eggs in the winter season, the poultry-house should always be in a warm situation. (See § 1329.)

2237. *General Arrangement.* In the models we have supposed the cottages to be placed on platforms, raised eighteen inches above the natural surface, to insure dryness; and the floors of the yards behind we have supposed to be raised one foot, for the same purpose. The terrace or platform may, however, be dispensed with, provided the floor of the house be raised sufficiently high by any other means; in which case three or four steps must be placed as an ascent to the door of the porch. When there is a platform, the door in the porch of the house is ascended by a half step of three inches, and the back door by a full step of six inches. The aspect of the porch is supposed to be south or south-east, as the best aspects, or, as the next best, south-west; the object being that a north and south line should form a diagonal to the square or parallelogram formed by the general mass of building; in consequence of which (as observed § 124.) the sun will shine on every side of the house during a portion of every day on which he appears. Three aspects are mentioned, in order that the one may be adopted which may be most suitable to the direction of the road near which the cottage is placed; the preference, however, should always be given to the south-east when practicable, as the wind, in most parts of Great Britain, blows seldomer from that quarter than from any other, and when it does blow it is always warm. The south-west is a boisterous quarter, and should only be had recourse to when it is necessary in order to obtain a diagonal to the plan which shall be a south and north line. We wish it to be distinctly understood, that it forms no part of our plan to have either the front or the back of the cottage next to, and parallel with, the road; on the contrary, we prefer, in almost every case of single cottages, to have next the road an angle of the building, by which the views across the road will be oblique instead of being direct; as the former, in every case, exhibits a longer perspective, which must consequently contain a greater number of objects. The grand point to be attended to in putting down every cottage, single or double, ought to be to have the diagonal to the main building a south and north line. This rule ought to be considered as absolute.

The floors of the models have all a gentle inclination, from the front door to the back door, of about three inches, so that no water can stand on any part of them; and the yards all slope to the tank for liquid manure, which is so low as to receive all the water of the yard. An underground drain surrounds the house and yard, three or four feet from the walls, as well for the purpose of cutting off the overflowings of the well or rain-water tank, as for keeping the floor of the house quite dry. To avert damp from the surface of the platform on which the house stands, and also of the back yard, gutters are fixed all round the eaves of the roof of the house; by which the water falling on it is collected and filtered, by some of the simple modes shown in the Encyclopædia (§ 30. and 305.), or by a still more simple mode which will be described hereafter, into a tank or well, from which it is drawn up by a pump placed in the back-kitchen, close to the sink. From the sink, which has a bell-trap to prevent the rising of smells, there may be a small drain or earthenware pipe to the liquid-manure tank; but a simpler and better mode is to have a tub or pail beneath the sink-stone, for collecting the water, which renders it obligatory to carry it from time to time direct to the privy, where it is necessarily poured through the pan into the liquid-manure tank, thereby making certain of keeping the pan constantly clean and not losing any of the liquid. The liquid is to be drawn from the tank by means of a well close to it, eighteen inches square, and of the same depth as the tank, and covered with a stone in which is a bell-trap to admit the water from the yard. When the liquid is to be taken up, this stone or lid must be taken off, and the liquid lifted by dipping a vessel into it; but the best mode is to have a pump in one angle of the well. Between the tank and the well there is an iron grating to prevent the escape from the tank of grosser impurities. It may be built of brick or stone, and either arched over, leaving a man-hole to be covered with a stone, or it may be covered with flag-stone; in either case covering the whole with a layer of earth, to prevent the possibility of the escape of smells. This tank will be described in detail in a future chapter.

The pit for solid manure may be four feet deep, and, if it be thought necessary, it may be covered with a boarded shutter, hinged at half its width, which can be kept closely shut at all times, except when manure is being put in or taken out.

The principal difficulty which we feel we shall have with the cottager will be in convincing him of the importance of the liquid manure tank. We consider the liquid manure of a cottage as decidedly of more value to the garden than all the solid manure which the cottager is likely to be able to collect; and, therefore, in our opinion, wherever there is a garden to a cottage, there ought to be a liquid manure tank.

2238. *The Accommodation* in the model designs varies from three to six rooms; one or more of these rooms in the latter case being intended as a working-place for village mechanics, such as a tailor, shoemaker, weaver, &c. Besides these living and working rooms, there are, in each cottage, a small back-kitchen or wash-house, a pantry, a place for fuel, &c.; and in the agricultural cottages, except the lowest in the scale, a dairy and a pigsty. We have so arranged that the living-rooms in all the cottages may be heated by flues under the floor, proceeding from an oven or furnace in an outbuilding. We are aware that we shall have great difficulty in getting this arrangement adopted, but we introduce it because we consider it by far the most economical mode of applying fuel when that material is scarce, and, in particular, the only mode in which faggot-wood, slender branches, or spray, can be made the most of. This we have shown in the Encyclopædia, in § 34. and 35., p. 17. At the same time there are open fireplaces in the usual manner, to be used in conjunction with this mode of heating, or exclusive of it, for those by whom it is not approved of. Such persons, therefore, will merely consider the furnace to the flue as an oven for occasional use for baking; or, if the place is used as a poultry-house, for which it is well adapted, for communicating warmth to it.

2239. *Construction.* The materials with which these cottages may be constructed are not limited to any particular kind or kinds. Whatever is most abundant or cheapest in the locality where the cottage is to be built will be most suitable. In Britain, the most general material for walls is stone, and for covering roofs thatch. We have, therefore, shown the walls of sufficient thickness for being built of rubble stone; but if, in any part of the country, brick should be found cheaper, hollow walls of that material (see p. 25. 336. and 374.) may be adopted; or, in those parts of the country where the construction of cob walls, or walls of clay lumps, is properly understood and practised, no material can be better for cottages of this description. The roofs of most of the models we have supposed to be covered with thatch; because that material is found every where, and because in the common mode of putting it on by the use of layers of turves, instead of sewing, and by using turves also for the ridges and hips, it is both cheap and durable. We have known many roofs of this kind in Scotland which have lasted the length of a farmer's lease (nineteen or twenty-one years) without any repairs: the surface of the thatch becoming covered with growing moss excludes air and moisture, and prevents decomposition. In many parts of England, particularly in Sussex, instead of thatch, the chips made in working up coppice-wood, with or without spray, are used; and this makes a warm and durable roof, which might, perhaps, be rendered still more durable by steeping the chips in lime-water, or in Burnett's or some other preservative solution. The great advantage of roofs of thatch, chips, spray, or heath (which forms a common and most durable roof in the Highlands of Scotland), is, that they retain the heat of the rooms in winter, and exclude that of the sun in summer: but one disadvantage is their liability to be consumed by fire, which, however, rarely happens; and another, that, in the case of straw roofs, a quantity of material is lost, which might otherwise have been converted into manure. Those who disapprove of thatch may use tiles or slates, with a ceiling parallel to the sides of the roof about eighteen inches within it, so as to form, as it were, a double roof, which will, to a certain extent, answer the same purpose as a roof of thatch. The floors should slope gradually, that is, at the rate of one inch to seven feet, from the entrance porch, which should be the highest point, to the outer door of the back kitchen, which ought to be the lowest; in order that, when they are washed with a mop, the water may run before the operator, in whatever part of the house she may commence, towards the back door. The floors of the upper rooms may either be laid with boards, or with a composition of lime and clay, or lime and ashes, beaten smooth, in the manner to be hereafter described. This kind of bed-room floor is not uncommon in the East of England, particularly in Norfolk and Huntingdonshire, and also in Staffordshire. The height of the rooms on the ground floor should not be less than nine feet, nor should those in the roof be less in the middle, though at the sides they need not be more than five or six feet. The windows, where economy is the object, may be of cast iron, and either of the form used at Belper, or that recommended by the Highland Society of Scotland, both of which will be described in the chapter (v.) on construction.

2240. *The Elevations* to the models are wholly without ornament, unless facings or architraves to the doors and windows, a plinth to the walls, and a cornice to the chimney tops can be considered as such ; but we have given some ornamental elevations to the same plans, and others to plans having the same amount of accommodation.

2241. *The Gardens* we have shown as surrounding the cottages ; being convinced that a garden does not afford half the enjoyment to the possessor, when it is separated from his dwelling, that it does when attached to and surrounding it ; and that, though those portions of ground called cottage allotments are better than no garden at all, yet they are, and ever will be, very far from answering the end of gardens attached to dwellings. We have shown the garden to each cottage surrounded by a hedge, which ought generally to be seven feet high for the sake of privacy ; and we have shown it cut architecturally, because we think the cottager ought to be encouraged by every means to show his taste in and about his garden, so as to win applause for his exertions. Indeed, we are of opinion that all garden hedges that are cut or clipped into regular forms ought to have piers at the angles and openings, and sometimes even pilasters at regular distances, terminating in balls or other forms : in other cases there may be arcades, open or recessed, and ornamented by verdant vases, or other objects that can be readily formed in living materials, at no other expense than that of a little labour with the hedge-shears. The planting, cropping, and culture of the garden, we think, should in general be left to the cottager, as otherwise he cannot take sufficient interest in it ; assisting him with fruit trees, seeds, and ornamental plants, and with advice, or a suitable gardening book, if he require it. The extent of garden ground, in all ordinary cases, need not exceed one sixth of an acre, including the space occupied by the house and court-yard. A greater space than the sixth of an acre a labourer who has nearly constant employment cannot properly manage ; and even this space, unless he has a large family, will admit of his occasionally producing articles for sale, whether vegetables, fruits, flowers, seedling plants, or seeds. We have shown, in the model designs, the gardens surrounded by hedges, as being cheaper than any other kind of fence ; but we greatly prefer walls, as affording an opportunity of covering them with fruit trees and ornamental plants, and as not exhausting the soil.

2242. *The essential Requisites* for a comfortable labourer's cottage may be thus summed up :—

1. The cottage should be placed alongside a public road, as being more cheerful than a solitary situation ; and in order that the cottager may enjoy the applause of the public when he has his garden in good order and keeping.

2. The cottage should be so placed that the sun may shine on every side of it every day throughout the year, when he is visible. For this reason, the front of the cottage can only be parallel to the public road in the case of roads in the direction of north-east, south-west, north-west, and south-east ; in all other cases the front must be placed obliquely to the road, which, as we have previously shown, is greatly preferable to having the front parallel to the road. (See § 2237.)

3. Every cottage ought to have the floor elevated, that it may be dry ; the walls double or hollow, or battened, or not less than eighteen inches thick, that they may retain heat ; with a course of slate or flagstone, or tiles bedded in cement, six inches above the surface, to prevent the rising of damp ; the roof thick, or double, for the sake of warmth ; and projecting eighteen inches or two feet at the eaves, in order to keep the walls dry, and to check the radiation of heat from their exterior surface.

4. In general, every cottage ought to be two stories high, so that the sleeping-rooms may not be on the ground floor, and the ground-floor ought not to be less than from six inches to one foot above the outer surface.

5. The minimum of accommodation ought to be a kitchen or living-room, a back-kitchen or wash-house, and a pantry, on the ground floor, with three bed-rooms over ; or two rooms and a wash-house on the ground floor, and two bed-rooms over.

6. Every cottage, including its garden, yard, &c., ought to occupy not less than one sixth of an acre ; and the garden ought to surround the cottage, or at all events to extend both before and behind. In general, there ought to be a front garden and a back yard ; the latter being entered from the back-kitchen, and containing a privy, liquid-manure tank, place for dust and ashes, and place for fuel.

7. If practicable, every cottage ought to stand singly and surrounded by its garden ; or, at all events, not more than two cottages ought to be joined together. Among other important arguments in favour of this arrangement, it may be mentioned, that it is the only one by which the sun can shine every day on every side of the cottage. When cottages are joined together in a row, unless that row is in a diagonal direction, with reference to a south and north line, the sun will shine chiefly on one side. By having cottages singly or in pairs, they may always be placed along any road, in such a manner that the sun may shine on every side of them ; provided the point be given up of having the front parallel to the road ; a point which, in our opinion, ought not for a moment to be put in competition with the advantages of an equal diffusion of sunshine.

8. Every cottage ought to have an entrance porch for containing the labourer's tools, and into which, if possible, the stairs ought to open, in order that the bed-rooms may be communicated with without passing through the front or back kitchen. This, in the case of sickness, is very desirable; and also in the case of deaths, as the remains may be carried down stairs while the family are in the front room.

9. The door to the front kitchen or best room should open from the porch and not from the back-kitchen, which, as it contains the cooking utensils and washing-apparatus, can never be fit for being passed through by a stranger, or even the master of the family, where proper regard is had by the mistress to cleanliness and delicacy.

10. When there is not a supply of clear water from a spring adjoining the cottage, or from some other efficient source, then there ought to be a well or tank partly under the floor of the back-kitchen supplied from the roof, with a pump in the back-kitchen for drawing it up for use, as hereafter described in detail. The advantages of having the tank or well under the back-kitchen are, that it will be secure from frost, and that the labour of carrying water will be avoided.

11. The privy should always be separated from the dwelling, unless it is a proper water-closet, with a soil pipe communicating with a distant liquid-manure tank or cesspool. When detached, the privy should be over or adjoining a liquid-manure tank, in which a straight tube from the bottom of the basin ought to terminate; by which means the soil basin may always be kept clean by pouring down the common slops of the house. No surface being left from which smell can arise, except that of the area of the pipe, the double flap, to be hereafter described, will prevent the escape of the evaporation from this small surface, and also insure a dry and clean seat.

12. The situation of the liquid-manure tank should be as far as possible from that of the filtered water tank or clear water well. It should be covered by an air-tight cover of flag-stone, and have a narrow well adjoining, into which the liquid should filter through a grating, so as to be pumped up or taken away without grosser impurities, and in this state applied to the soil about growing crops.

13. In general, proprietors ought not to intrust the erection of labourers' cottages on their estates to the farmers, as it is chiefly owing to this practice that so many wretched hovels exist in the best cultivated districts of Scotland and in Northumberland.

14. No landed proprietor, as we think, ought to charge more for the land on which cottages are built than he would receive for it from a farmer, if let as part of a farm; and no more rent ought to be charged for the cost of building the cottage and enclosing the garden than the same sum would yield if invested in land, or, at all events, not more than can be obtained by government securities.

15. Most of these conditions are laid down on the supposition that the intended builder of the cottage is actuated more by feelings of human sympathy than by a desire to make money; and hence they are addressed to the wealthy, and especially to the proprietors of land and extensive manufactories or mines.

SUBSECT. 1.   *Agriculturist's Model Cottage.*—No. I.

The elevation of this cottage is shown in fig. 2040.

2040

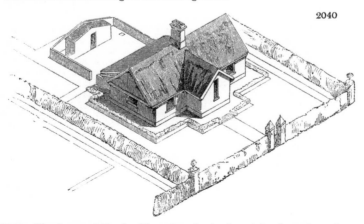

2243. *The Accommodation* in this cottage is the lowest in the scale, and may be considered as offering the first stage of improvement, in departing from those agricultural hovéls in the South of Scotland and North of England which at present consist only of a single room. (§ 2233.) In this model we have two rooms, each seventeen feet square, a back-kitchen or wash-house, and two garrets of the same size as the rooms over them. The access to these garrets is by a step-ladder in the porch. The garrets may be used as sleeping-places, the one for grown-up girls or a female lodger, or both ; and the other for grown-up boys or a male lodger, or for both. The bed for the master and mistress, and the bed or cradle for the infant children, may be in the best room on the ground floor. The details, as shown in fig. 2041., are as follow :—*a* is the kitchen, seven-

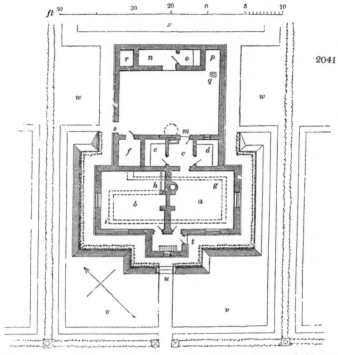

teen feet square, containing a boiler at one side of the fireplace, and, if necessary, an oven may be placed at the other ; *b*, the best room, in which is a closet or press, *h*, and room for two beds ; *c* is the back-kitchen, with a sink and pump ; *d*, the pantry ; *e*, the dairy, or place for beer, &c. ; and *f*, a place for an oven, for occasional baking, and to heat the floors of the two rooms, as indicated by the dotted lines *g*. Should an oven not be wanted, or this mode of heating not be approved of, then this compartment may be used for containing fuel or roots, poultry or rabbits, or for any other purpose that may be wanted. The highest point of the sleeping-room floor is at *g*, and of the kitchen floor at *i* ; the highest point of the pantry floor is at *d*, and of the dairy floor at *e* ; and from these four points the floors gradually slope, at the rate of one inch to seven feet, to the sill of the back-kitchen door at *m*. A place for wood or other fuel, or for a pig or rabbits, according to the taste or circumstances of the occupant, is shown at *n*, a privy at *o*, a tank for liquid manure communicating with the privy at *p*, a place for pumping or lifting out the liquid manure at *q*, and a pit for solid manure at *r*. The surface of the yard slopes from the entrance-door, *s*, to the liquid-manure pump, *q* ; and the door to the back-kitchen, and the door to the porch in front, at *t*, are each entered by a step. The terrace platform is entered by three steps, as at *u*. In the front garden there are two plots, *v v*, which may be planted with low fruit trees or fruit shrubs ; and two other plots, *w w*, which may be planted with standard fruit trees to shade and shelter the back court : *x* shows the commencement of that part of the garden where culinary vegetables are supposed principally to be growing. The narrow borders, walks, the low box hedge to the parapet, and the boundary hedge, require no explanation.

2244. *Construction and Materials.* The walls are supposed to be of rubble stone, or of prepared earth, and the roof of thatch.   The floor of the kitchen is to be paved with stone or brick, or, at all events, the flues are to be covered with these materials, and the rest of the floor of composition of lime and clay, or of lime and smithy ashes, or of whatever may be cheapest and best in the given locality.   The floor of the best room, if heated by a flue beneath, may be of the same material as that of the kitchen; but if not heated by a flue, then it ought to be of boards.

2245.   *The Garden* is only partially shown, the portion omitted being a parallelogram of the breadth indicated, and of sufficient length to make the contents of the whole plot one sixth of an acre.   It is surrounded by a thorn or holly hedge.   The slope of the terrace or platform may be covered with small stones, flints, or any other similar material most abundant in the country, as requiring less labour to keep it in order than turf: or it may be planted with chamomile or lavender, for the sake of the flowers, which may be collected and sold; with low creeping ornamental plants, such as ivy or periwinkle; or with thyme, heath, or some other low flowering plant, for the sake of the bees. The best effect, however, will be produced by covering it with the same kind of stone or brick which is used in the walls of the house.   No shrubs are proposed to be trained against the walls of the house, except a vine, an apricot, or a pear, at each end, according to the climate; but a border six inches wide is shown close to the wall of the house, in which may be planted a few China roses and some early flowers; while currants, morello cherries, or apples, may be trained on the outside of the walls of the court-yard.   The narrow borders next the hedge may also be planted with flowers; and the larger compartments with gooseberries, currants, and dwarf apple trees.   The culinary crops are proposed to be grown in the back compartment, the commencement only of which is shown in the plan.

2246.   *General Estimate.*   The cubic contents are 10,163 feet, which, at 2*d.* per foot, is £84; at 1*d.*, £42; and the actual cost would not, it is believed, amount to much more than the latter sum.   As a proof of this we refer to § 2267.

2042

2247.   *Remarks.*   The idea of this model cottage was suggested to us by the plan of the Closeburn cottage, given in next section.   It may be lowered in its accommodation by omitting the bed-rooms in the roof, and making the porch narrower and without a step-ladder.   If the places for the oven or the dairy are not wanted, they may be added as closets, the one to the kitchen and the other to the bed-room, by opening doors in the back wall.   An oven might be added to the kitchen fireplace on the opposite side to the boiler.   All the divisions in the lean-to behind, which now form the pantry, dairy, back-kitchen, &c., might be enlarged by continuing the lean-to the whole length of the house.   Fig. 2042. is an elevation with a slate roof for this plan, by Mr. Lamb.

SUBSECT. 2.   *Agriculturist's Model Cottage.*—No. II.

The elevation of this design is shown in fig. 2044., and a variation of it in fig. 2045.

2248. *Accommodation.*   Here we have obtained one good room, fig. 2043. *a*, instead of the cow-house and pigsty.   This, with two bed-rooms over the two principal rooms, will form a very commodious cottage, and enable the occupant to let out a room to a lodger.

2043

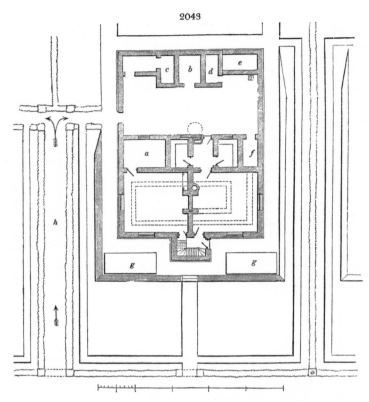

The cow-house, b, and pigsty, c, are separated from the house, and placed along with the other buildings in the yard. There are a privy, d; liquid-manure tank, e; poultry-house for heating the floor, f; two flower-beds, $g g$; and a passage to the back-yard, for the cow, &c., serving for two cottages, h.

2044

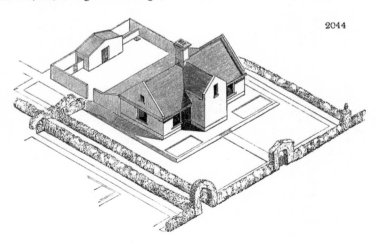

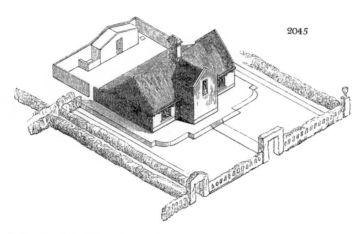

2045

2249. *Remarks.* When the cow-house and pigsty are not wanted, they may be united, and by opening a door in the parlour they may form a bed-room or work-room communicating with it, and lighted by a window either at the end or at the back. This may also be done with the dairy and oven rooms, should they not be wanted ; so that, by this means, two additional rooms may be obtained on the ground floor.

SUBSECT. 3. *Mechanic's Model Cottage.*

2250. *The Mechanic's Model Cottage* may be built singly, but the most economical arrangement is obtained by building them in pairs, as in fig. 2046.   For the idea of this model we are indebted to Thomas Wilson, Esq., of the Banks near Barnsley, who sent us the design, fig. 2048., on which our draftsman, Mr. Marks, made the improvement, with a view to economy in building, shown in fig. 2049., which being sent to Mr.

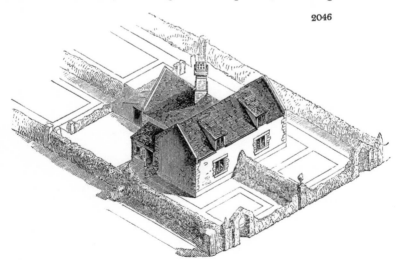

2046

Wilson, he completed the work by changing the entrance to the stair from the back-room to the porch, as in fig. 2050., the advantages of which, to use his own words, " are great : the sitting-room is altogether private ; and, in case of illness, there is an obvious gain in not having to pass through the house from a sick-room.   There is another point not usually considered : when an inmate has to be removed to his last home, the pre-

2047

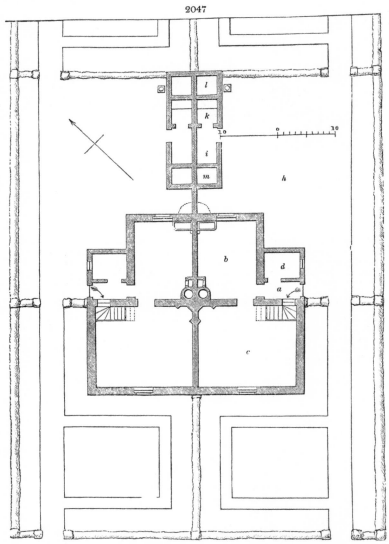

parations, and particularly the carrying down stairs, would by this arrangement of the
stair, all be accomplished while the family were in the sitting-room.   In cottages as they
are at present built, that which is never accomplished without difficulty, is almost
always rendered scarcely practicable by the narrowness and awkwardness of the stairs.
No architect of feeling should overlook this." In fig. 2047. *a* is the porch into which the
staircase opens; *b* is the back-kitchen, with a pump and sink-stone, arranged in connexion with a tank or well, as in the agriculturist's model cottage; *c* is the principal
room; *d*, a pantry; and there is a light closet under the stair, *e*, in fig. 2050. There are
three bed-rooms shown in the plan of the adjoining cottage at *e*, *f*, *g*, in fig. 2048.   In
the back-yard, *h*, there is a place for fuel, *i*; a privy, *k*; a liquid-manure tank, *l*; and
place for ashes, &c., *m*.   The gardens may be arranged as in the figure, or in any other
mode that is considered most convenient.   The isometrical elevation of fig. 2047. is
shown in fig. 2046.

2251. *General Estimate.* The cubic contents of the two cottages are 15,200 feet, at 6*d.* per foot, £380; at 4*d.*, £253; at 3*d.*, £190; and at 2*d.*, £126; or for each cottage, £190, £126, £95, and £63.

2252. *Remarks.* Our readers, we are sure, will agree with us in thanking Mr. Wilson for his most economical and commodious plan, and for his very humane and feeling observations respecting it. We consider the design, finally improved, as uniting more comfort at less expense than any other given in this Supplement. The only drawback to the arrangement that we know is, that it is necessary to pass through the back-kitchen in order to enter the best room;

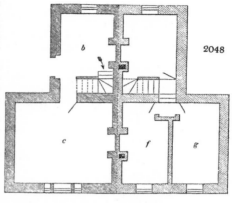

2048

but this might be remedied, either by enlarging the porch, or by adding a porch in front. In either case additional expense would be incurred. Where comfort is more the object than expense, we would recommend the fireplaces not to be placed in the angles, but back to back, as in fig. 2048., by which more room is obtained for persons sitting round the fire, and the heat is more equally radiated through the room. For the sake of economy we have shown dormer windows in the elevation, fig. 2051., and also in the isometrical view; but where economy is not an object, we would prefer having the side walls as high as the tops of the windows. A cottage of this form may be rendered highly ornamental by enlarging the parlour window, and projecting it with a bay; by forming two separate windows to the principal bed-rooms, ornamenting the gables, and forming a group of columnar chimneys. It might even

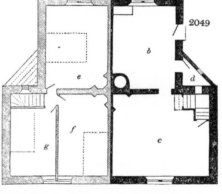

2049

be rendered more artistical by simply splaying the jambs of the doors and windows, slightly rounding their upper angles, and either raising the side walls so as not to have the windows in the roof, or retaining them in the roof and finishing them with pediments and span-roofs.

As this design is not shown placed on a platform, it is peculiarly suitable for having the walls covered with ornamental shrubs, such as climbing roses, honeysuckles, clematises, chimonanthus, and Virginian creeper; or with fruit trees or vines.

All the ornamental climbers which have been mentioned, with the exception of chimonanthus, may be planted about two feet apart, and trained in direct lines from the ground to the eaves; but the chimonanthus, being a woody plant, should be trained

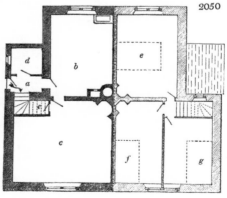

2050

more in the fan manner practised with plums, peaches and
apricots.

The fruit trees should be
trained differently, according
to their kinds : the pear and
the apple horizontally ; the
plum, cherry, apricot, and
peach, in the fan manner; and
the gooseberry and currant
perpendicularly, one shoot
only, or at most two, being
carried up from each plant.

The vine may be trained in
the perpendicular manner,
placing the plants at two feet
apart, retaining only one
shoot to each plant, and obtaining the bearing wood by
spurring in that shoot: but

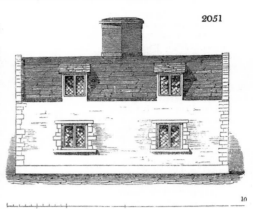

2051

10

the best mode of training the vine against a house is to have the main branches of
every plant in the form of the letter T, and to train the bearing branches upwards
from the two horizontal arms, in the manner practised at Thomery near Fontainebleau,
on the houses in Stockbridge and Broughton in Hampshire, and in the vineyard of
Mr. Hoare at Southampton. These hints on training trees against the walls of cottages
will be sufficient for any one who knows a little of gardening ; for those who do not,
we would recommend the *Suburban Horticulturist*, in which the subject of training trees
is treated in detail, and more especially the training of vines against cottages.

With respect to the propriety of training fruit trees against cottages, much depends
on the climate and aspect. We cannot recommend it as a general practice in a wet
climate, because it would have a tendency to keep the walls damp after rain was driven
against them; nor on cottages that have one side to the south, and another to the north,
except on the south side, because on the north side fruit trees would do little good,
and any other description of deciduous plant would prevent the evaporation of the rain
driven against them from the north. On the walls of all cottages placed with their
diagonal line in the direction of south and north, trees may be trained on every side,
without danger of producing damp, as every side would enjoy sun.

SUBSECT. 4. *Placing the Model Cottages in Rows.*

2253. *The Agriculturist's Model Cottage* may be placed in rows in the manner shown
in fig. 2052. ; in which the entrance to the yards being from a back passage, and the

2052

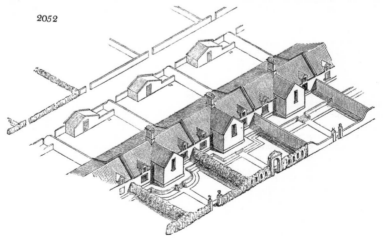

public road being in front, the kitchen-garden to each cottage will be most conveniently placed behind, on account of the manure, and especially the liquid manure; which, if the kitchen-gardens were in front, would either have to be carried through the house, or a good way round.

2254. *The Mechanics' Model Cottages* may be placed in rows, in contact, by the addition of a front porch to each cottage; but much the best mode for this style of cottage is to have them in pairs, as already shown in fig. 2047.

2255. *Remarks.* The objections to placing these cottages in contact in rows are, that it lessens the privacy of each dwelling, and in many cases would prevent the sun from shining on every side of them. It is a great source of independence and comfort for a cottager, to be completely surrounded by his own garden. It is not pleasant, when walking or working in our garden, to be overlooked by our neighbour; or, when sitting quietly in the house, to hear the sounds of his children through the party-walls. It is a great mistake to suppose that this feeling is confined to the educated part of society: it exists among all classes, and certainly much more strongly among persons accustomed to a comparatively solitary life in the country, like agriculturists, than among mechanics accustomed to live in streets. Where cottages of this kind are joined in rows, and indeed in every case of cottages being joined, we would recommend building the party-walls thicker than usual, and having the garden walls or hedges seven feet high, with here and there a standard fruit tree in them, to break the view from the bed-rooms of the adjoining dwellings.

SUBSECT. 5. *Forming Combinations of Dwellings of the humblest Class.*

2256. In the Encyclopædia (§ 493.), we have shown with what economy combinations of dwellings might be built, and how greatly the comforts of the individuals occupying them might, in various ways, be increased by cooperation. It does not appear, however, that mankind is yet in a fit state for entering on this stage in the progress of improvement. To be able to do so men must have been educated from infancy to live in society; and when this shall have been the case, then the increase of comforts and enjoyments that may be obtained by living together in masses will be duly appreciated by themselves. In the meantime, the working classes of society, in common with every other class, appear to us to have a much greater taste for isolation than for cooperation; more particularly in every thing relating to domestic arrange-ments. In short, we are inclined to think that little good will be effected by arrangements of this kind, till those classes for which they are intended, in consequence of superior education, see themselves the benefits which would accrue from them. They will then endeavour to procure their establishment.

2257. *A College for single Working Men.* The only addition that we shall make to what we have already advanced on this subject is a design, fig. 2053., taken from one which we made in 1819, and published in the *Mechanic's Magazine*, vol. xvi., for what may be called a college for single working men. Each floor will contain eight distinct dwellings,

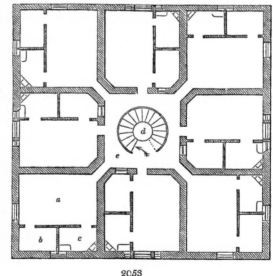

2053

and each dwelling will consist of a living-room twenty-one feet by thirteen feet, *a*; sleeping-room, ten feet by seven *b*; and washing-room, with a sink and water-closet, ten feet by seven *c*; the circular stair is shown at *d*, and the landing to each floor at *e*.

The building is supposed to be of a cubical form, of eight or ten stories high, with a staircase in the centre, and a series of fire-proof rooms on each floor, communicating with a common gallery.

The whole building we propose to be heated from one stove at the bottom of the stairs; and in each separate apartment might be placed two jets of gas for cooking, and one for lighting. As there would be a gas-meter to each apartment, no individual would pay for more gas than what he consumed. The floorings of all the rooms would be of flag-stone, the under side of which would form the ceiling to the room below; and as all the partitions would be of brickwork, or might also be of flag-stone, the first cost of the building would be comparatively low, and the expense of repair very trifling. On the lowest floor a house-keeper might reside, who would have the general charge of the building, and who, if it were thought advisable, might lay in a stock of such articles as were generally wanted by the occupants, and retail them to them at nearly cost price. There might also be a restaurateur and dining-room on the ground floor, arranged so as to supply food on the most economical terms. The building, however, would be chiefly valuable as supplying lodgings of the most comfortable kind at a very moderate expense. As no fires would be wanted in the different rooms, there would be no occasion for fuel, which would be a great saving both of labour and expense; and as water would be laid on to every apartment, to which also there would be a water-closet for waste water, the labour of cleaning would be reduced to a mere trifle. In short, for large towns, there could hardly be a more economical and comfortable mode of lodging single men, such as clerks, shopmen, working mechanics and artisans of every description, and even literary men and artists.

Sect. II.   *A Selection of Plans of Cottages which have been erected in different Parts of the Country.*

2258. *This Selection* of plans is chiefly taken from the *Sanitary Report of the Poor Law Commissioners for* 1842, which contains the best plans which the commissioners could procure from their correspondents in every part of the country. We have only given the plans, because the elevations have no particular merit; and the plans are, in our opinion, defective in not in general showing the relative situation of the back-yard and appendages, and of the garden ground. On the situation of both these depends much of the comfort and beauty of every country dwelling, from the palace to the cottage; and yet, in most cases, when cottages are put down, the situation and arrangement of the garden are commonly left to chance. The garden, whenever it is practicable, ought to surround the cottage, and the boundary ought always to be clearly defined by a hedge or wall. Whatever be the direction of the road before the cottage, the cottage ought always to front the south-east if possible, if not the south-west. There is no comfort in a cottage in our cold moist climate when it fronts either the direct south or the direct north; because, in either case, one side must be in the shade for half the year.

2259. *The Closeburn Cottage.*—Several of these cottages have been erected by Sir Charles Stuart Menteath, one of the most enlightened and benevolent men of his time and country, at Closeburn in Dumfriesshire. Fig. 2054. shows the plan of the Closeburn cottage, in which *a* is the kitchen, sixteen feet square and eight feet high; *b*, the sleeping-room, of the same dimensions; *c*, the back-kitchen, with a sink; *d*, the dairy; *e*, the pantry; *f*, the cow-house; *g*, the privy; and *h*, a porch, in which there may be a step-ladder to the garrets, if

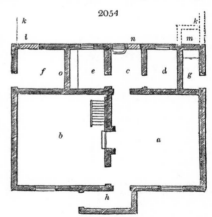

these are used as bed-rooms. In the Closeburn plan, as published in the *Sanitary Report*, the stairs are shown in the bed-room, but the porch is a much better situation for them. The sleeping-room, *b*, may be warmed by having a sheet-iron back to the kitchen fireplace, interposing a flag-stone or some bricks between it and the flue, to prevent the sheet-iron from being too much heated. In the summer season the heat may be kept from entering the room by enclosing the iron plate with a case or box of boards. If there should be bed-rooms over the two lower rooms, these may also be heated by air warmed in the recess at the back of the kitchen fire, by the following arrangement : —

Fig. 2055. is a ground plan of the kitchen fireplace and iron box, in which *a* is the fireplace ; *b*, the orifice by which air is admitted to the iron box by means of the under-ground tube or drain, *c* ; and *d*, a wooden box for enclosing the iron box in the summer season, when heat is not wanted in the room, or when it is desired to enclose articles to keep them warm, or to dry clothes in Mr. Sylvester's manner. (§ 306. and 2053.)

Fig. 2056. is a section through the kitchen fireplace and the iron box, in which *e* is the orifice of the cold-air tube ; *f*, the iron box ; *g*, the wooden box ; *h*, the tube for conveying hot air to the bed-rooms ; and *i*, the kitchen fireplace and flue. When the air is not wanted for the bed-rooms, it might be convenient to be able to let it escape by turning it into another flue, which might be added to the stack of chimneys ; but, if care is taken to open the bed-room windows a little, the escape of the air through them would be advantageous, even in the summer season.

Sir Charles Menteath's son, J. S. Menteath, Esq., in answer to our enquiries as to how this plan was found to work in practice, says : " I consider the introduction of these iron plates into our cottages, whereby two apartments are most economically and most comfortably warmed by one fire, as among my father's most valuable, and most benevolent attempts to make our cottagers happy and healthful." Were we called upon to improve this cottage, we would enclose a small yard behind, the commencement of which is indicated by the dotted lines at *k, k*, in fig. 2054. ; make the door of the cow-house open from the yard, as indicated at *l* ; place a liquid manure tank behind the privy, as indicated at *m* ; open a door from the back-kitchen to the yard, as at *n* ; and place the whole on a platform, and surround it with a garden, as in fig. 2040. in p. 1142. It is probable that some of these improvements may actually exist; but they are not shown in the plan, or in a model which, in 1840, at the request of Sir Charles Menteath, we placed in the Adelaide Gallery.

2260. *The Dalmeny Cottage*, fig. 2057.—This cottage has been erected by Lord Roseberry on his estates in the neighbourhood of Edinburgh, and has been justly considered, by the Highland Society and other competent judges, as a considerable improvement on the habitations for country labourers as they now exist in most parts of Scotland. The custom of having cottages of only one story, and of only two rooms, and of having box beds (see § 658. 1338.) in the kitchen as well as in the other rooms, is general in Scotland ; but it is evident that no great improvement can take place in the habits of the people till they have back-kitchens for their cooking and washing utensils, and till their beds are removed from their living-rooms. The very circumstance, as we have observed (§ 1338.), of having to go up stairs to a bed-room is favourable to delicacy, cleanliness, and health. Nevertheless, Lord Roseberry's cottage is a great improvement on the kind of ploughman's cottage common in the neighbourhood of Edinburgh ; and as such we have considered it desirable to republish here the plan and specification as given in the *Transactions of the Highland Society of Scotland*, vol. xii. p. 527.

2261. *Specification.* The following is published in the work above referred to : — " The walls to be of the best rubble-work, founded with large flat stones, and all well packed and pointed with properly prepared lime mortar. The rebates, soles, and lintels for doors and windows, to be droved on the head and cheek, and broached on the breast. Corners to have broached stone ; and both corners and rebates to be of a proper size, and square-tailed ; the skews to be broached on the top, and droved on the edges, with a proper raglin for the tile ; the chimney tops to be of broached stone, with droved water berge, plinth, and cope ; the jambs, lintels, and hearths of fireplaces to be of droved stone, and the vents made 12 inches by 13 inches, and plastered with haired lime. The partitions to be of stone and standard, the standards to be 4½ inches by 2 inches, placed 2 feet apart upon a sill-plate, laid on a proper stone footing ; all between standards to be filled in with small flat stones, bedded and jointed with lime, and to have warpings 4½ inches by three fourths of an inch, every 2 feet in height, nailed to standards. The floors of porches and privies to be laid with scabbled stone flags ; all the other floors to be laid with a composition of lime and engine ashes, in proper proportions, well riddled, tempered, worked, laid 3 inches thick, smoothed, and well rubbed in ; under the composition, 9 inches in depth of small broken stones to be laid, the earth being first excavated to admit of their being put in. The floors of ash-pits and soil-pit in privies to be kept 18 inches lower than floors of cottages, and an opening made in wall from soil to ash-pit.

"The safe lintels for doors and windows to be of 11-inch by 3-inch red Petersburg plank, with 9 inches wall-hold at each end, the whole space covered and saved by a hammer-dressed stone arch where there is room. Wall-plates to be of single battens, 7 inches by 1 inch and a quarter. The rafters and balks of cottage roofs to be of Memel, the size marked in the section, or of red Dram battens 6½ inches by 2½ inches, placed 20 inches from centres, and the balks half-cheeked to rafters with double-garron nails, three in each joining. The roofs of coal-places and privy to be of the lean-to kind; rafters 4 inches by 2 inches, cheeked to wall-plates at toes, and let 9 inches into wall at top. Tile lath to be 1 inch and a quarter by 1 inch and five eighths each, cut out of red Petersburg batten. The windows to be made of Memel, in the sliding manner, sashes 2⅛ inches thick, well glazed, primed, and bedded in and drawn up with lime; the windows of kitchen and room to have counter-cheek screws and plain deal shutters, barred and beaded on inside; the pantry window to be hinged, and to fasten by an iron button, with ring, &c. The outside doors of cottages, places for coals, and privy, to be of plain deal, 1 inch and one eighth thick, cut out of red Petersburg batten, three bars on the back, hung on crooks and bands; coal-place and cottage doors to have stock-locks of 4s. 6d. value, and strong thumb-latches; privy doors, a thumb-latch and iron bolt on inside. The inside doors to be also of plain deal, barred and beaded, hung with 13-inch T bands upon door standards of red Dram batten 6 inches by 2½ inches, and all to have plain beaded facings and keps, to have neat thumb-latches, and the press and pantry 2s. press-locks. All angles to have ¾-inch beads; and ceilings of cottages lathed with best split lath. The pantries and presses to have three shelves each. A hatchway to be made in ceiling of porch, with hinged cover. The privy to have a properly formed seat of 1⅛-inch timber. The inside doors, window-shutters, and other inside finishing, may be of yellow American pine or white plank; all the other timbers to be of the best red wood, of Baltic growth. The roofs to be covered with grey or red tile, rendered with lime. The walls of cottages to get one coat of plaster, the ceilings two coats, and well finished." (*H. Trans.*, vol. xii. p. 534.)

2057

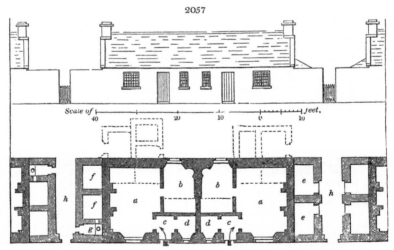

2262. *Accommodation.* The cottages are built in pairs, and each consists of a porch, *c* ; a kitchen, *a*, sixteen feet by twelve feet three inches, in which are two beds; a bed-room, *b*, eleven feet six inches by seven feet, containing one bed; a pantry, *d*, four feet by four feet and a half; and, as appendages, a privy and a place for fuel, *e e*, and an ash-pit. In general, these appendages are placed at one end, but they might be placed behind, as shown by the dotted lines; and sometimes there may be at the end a shed for fuel; a place for potatoes or other roots, or for poultry or a pig, *f f*; with a privy, *g*; and the place for ashes at the back, as indicated by the dotted lines. The gardens to these cottages are placed there; and there is a passage through to them between each pair of cottages, as shown at *h, h.*

2263. *General Estimate.* Cubic contents, 14,100 feet, at 6*d.* per foot, £352; at 4*d.*, £235; at 3*d.*, £176; at 2*d.*, £117; or for each cottage, £176, £117, £88, or £58. The actual cost of these cottages, it is stated in the work referred to, was generally from £75 to £85 a pair. We have given the general estimate in this case and some others, to show that for cottages of the simplest kind 2*d.* per cubic foot is much more likely to be above than under the actual cost.

2264. *Remarks.* The Dalmeny cottages are certainly a step in advance of the common cottages of Scotland, where a taste for comfortable dwellings and for cleanliness is just beginning to be cultivated. The improvements which may be made in them are, the addition of a back-kitchen, which we consider indispensable to comfort, and the detachment of the privies, and their connexion with liquid manure tanks, as shown in our model designs; but, as most farmers in Scotland are not sufficiently aware of the great value of liquid manure, it is not to be expected that their labourers can set a due value upon it. Something ought to be done, however, to introduce these tanks, for the sake of the great additional garden produce that would be obtained by the use of their contents. We have generally found it easier to introduce a taste for ornamental appendages to a cottage, than for improvements or changes which are merely useful; but the former, we also find, seldom fail to pave the way for the latter. We would, therefore, have front gardens added to these cottages, solely for the cultivation of flowers and flowering shrubs; and we would add porches, and either surround the front gardens with low walls, or with hedges cut architecturally, or formed in some way that would call forth the skill and taste of the occupant in managing them.

2265. *The Holkham Cottage,* fig. 2058.— Some of the cottages of the Earl of Leicester, it is stated in the *Sanitary Report,* " are perhaps the most substantial and comfortable that are to be seen in any part of England." They are built in pairs, or in groups of four cottages. The accommodation of a single dwelling consists of a front room, *a,* seventeen feet by twelve feet in width, and from seven feet to seven feet six inches high; a back-kitchen, *b,* thirteen feet by nine feet, and of the same height; a pantry, *c*; and, on the floor above, three bed-rooms. Behind is a wash-house, *d*; a dirt-bin, *e*; a privy, *f,* and a pig-cot, *g.* The drainage is excellent, and the water from a pump-well good, and each cottage has about twenty rods (an eighth of an acre) of garden ground.

2058

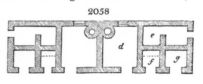

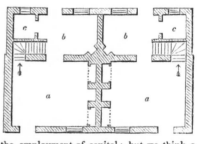

2266. *Estimate.* The actual cost of two such cottages, as stated by Mr. Emerson, the Earl of Leicester's builder, is from £110 to £115 each; which a proprietor, we think, might let for £4 a year, though Mr. Emerson thinks £6 ought to be the minimum rent for such a cottage. We agree that this would be a proper rent to one who had built them with a view to the employment of capital; but we think a landed proprietor, building on his own estate for his own workmen, ought to be content with 3 per cent, or what he would procure from the government funds.

2267. *Remarks.* These cottages, it is observed in the *Sanitary Report,* show what may be done " by a landed proprietor who takes as great a pride in his good cottages and farms as others in fine hunters and race-horses." It is remarkable that with so much lateral accommodation in the rooms of these cottages, they should only be from seven feet to seven feet six inches high; a height which, from the small quantity of air which it allows for breathing in, must be utterly unwholesome in the bed-rooms, and only tolerable in the rooms below in consequence of the frequent opening and shutting of the doors. The improvement that we would make to these cottages would be, raising the rooms to the height of nine feet, forming liquid-manure tanks to all the privies, adding porches, and surrounding them by their garden ground.

2268. *The Culford Cottages.* — These are double and sometimes treble cottages, built with bricks faced with blue flints, and with freestone facings to the doors and windows. At the distance of a few feet behind there is a wooden building roofed with tiles, which comprises a space for fuel, a privy for each cottage, and a common oven. Fig. 2059. shows a double cottage, in which *a* is the principal room,

2059

fourteen feet by twelve feet, and seven feet high, with a small closet, *d*; *b*, a back room, or scullery; *c*, a pantry; and there is a staircase, with a closet under, to two bed-rooms.

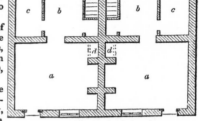

2269. *Estimate.* The average cost of these cottages, of which above fifty have been built within the last twenty years, by the Rev. E. Benyon, at Culford in Suffolk, is stated to have been about £170, or £85 each. Rent, £2 10s. to £3 3s.

2270. *Remarks.* The rooms have the same fault as those of the Holkham cottages, very few builders, until quite lately, being aware of the importance, with a view to health, of breathing in a large volume of air. There is an objection to the door opening at once into the principal room; which might be obviated by porches, which would at the same time take away from the dull uniformity of the exteriors.

2271. *The Harlaxton Cottages.* — These cottages, which have been erected by Gregory Gregory, Esq., at Harlaxton in Lincolnshire, are chiefly remarkable for their picturesque effect, and for the admirable management of the exterior appendages with a view to this result; but at the same time most of them have large rooms, eight feet or nine feet high, and all of them have large gardens. Fig. 2060. shows a plan of a

2060

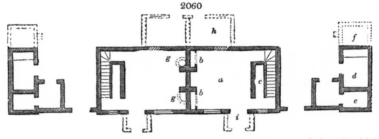

double cottage, in which *a* is the living-room, thirteen feet square, and eight feet high, independently of room for two closets at *b b*, and a large pantry at *c*. The stairs are roomy, and lead to two good bed-rooms, the one opening out of the other. To each cottage there is a building apart, forming a detached wing, containing a privy and hovel, *d*, and a hogsty, with yard, *e*. There is a front garden to each cottage, and a back garden of an eighth of an acre.

2272. *Estimate.* The actual cost of these two cottages is about £130, or £60 each; by which, allowing something for the garden, they might be let at   3 each.

2273. *Remarks.* A liquid-manure tank, with dung-pit or ash-pit over, might easily be added behind the privy, as at *f*; and an oven at one side of the kitchen fire, and a boiler at the other, as indicated by the dotted lines at *g g*, would be an improvement. A great defect is the want of a back-kitchen; but this might easily be obtained for each cottage by lean-tos, as indicated by the dotted lines *h*. No cottage, in our opinion, however humble, ought to be without some description of back-kitchen; for even though it had no fireplace, yet if it have a sink-stone and a window, it is well adapted for washing in, and for keeping tubs and other vessels that ought never to be in sight. A porch, as indicated by the letter *i*, would also be a great improvement. The combination of the privy and the hovel for fuel or pig's food is good. The elevation, like all the others in the village of Harlaxton, is eminently picturesque; the architectural taste of the proprietor being of the very highest order, as will hereafter appear in our section on villages.

2274. *The Turton Cottages* were built by Messrs. Ashworth of Turton, near Bolton in Lancashire, for the accommodation of workmen attached to their manufactories; and they are calculated for being placed in close contact, in rows. In fig. 2061. *a* is the living-room, five feet by thirteen feet; *b*, the kitchen, fifteen feet by nine feet, with an oven, grate, boiler, sink, and a closet under the staircase: above are three bed-rooms, with separate entrances from the landing, as shown in fig. 2062. There is a back-yard, *c*, twenty-five feet by thirteen feet, containing an ash-pit and a privy, with a door to a piece of garden ground or a back lane. If a garden is attached, then assuredly we

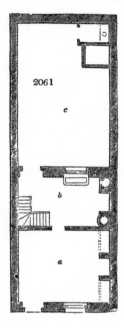

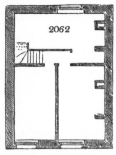

should recommend a liquid-manure tank under the place for ashes, as a certain means of doubling the produce of the garden.

2275. *Street Cottages, or Labourers' Tenements in Towns.* — The plans of these supplied to the *Sanitary Report*, by the committee of physicians and surgeons of Birmingham, as being the best in use in that town, are considered by the authors of the *Sanitary Report* as the best they know of (see

Report, p. 185.); but, as street houses do not come within our plan, we refer to the *Report* itself. We may observe that the Turton street houses are among the best of the kind that we know of in England. In Scotland, those at Deanston are of a very superior description, as are those at New Lanark, and at Crosslee near Paisley. Some at the latter place, built by Archibald Woodhouse, Esq., have two good rooms each, with a pantry and closets; a cellar for fuel and lumber ; a wash-house, privy, and dung-pit, common to six families; and a garden to each. They are let so as to pay 3 per cent on the prime cost. In general, the owners of mills and manufactories in every part of the country build far better cottages for their workmen, than the owners or occupiers of land, and the comfort of families lodged in them is great in proportion.

SECT. III. *Miscellaneous Designs for Cottages, chiefly ornamental.*

Design L.—*A Cottage with ornamental Elevations in the Style of the ancient half-timbered Houses of England.* By T. J. Ricauti, Esq., Architect.

2276. *Accommodation.* In the ground plan, fig. 2063., *a* is a porch, which is for one modification of this design shown in fig. 2064., but which, for the elevations figs. 2067.

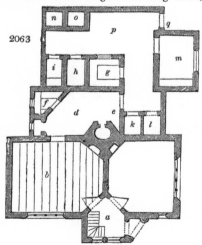

and 2068., contains a stair; *b* is the kitchen shown rather larger, seventeen feet by fourteen feet, than the parlour, *c*, which is fourteen feet by thirteen feet; *d* is the back-kitchen, which contains an oven and sink at *e*, and a pantry, *f*; *g* is a dairy; *h*, a pigsty; *i*, a water-closet, which, however, would be better placed over or adjoining the liquid-manure tank, *n*, because where it is there will be a risk of its contaminating the air of the pantry ; *k*, a place for poultry, most advantageously placed adjoining the sources of heat; *l*, a place for fuel; both these places are low lean-tos. The cow-house, ten feet by seven feet, is shown at *m*, and the liquid-manure tank and dung-pit at *n* and *o*; *p* is an open court, with a door at *q*.

2277. *The Elevations.* Fig. 2064. is a front elevation on the supposition that the cottage contains only one story. Fig. 2065. is a side elevation, showing the cow-house, the entrance to the court-yard, the porch, and the parlour window. Fig. 2066. is a perspective view combining both elevations. Fig. 2067. is a perspective view on the supposition that the cottage is raised higher, so as to contain two small rooms in the roof, and a small loft over the cow-house. Fig. 2068. shows the walls of the cottage carried up higher so as to contain two good bed-rooms, and, if it were thought necessary, a third bed-room over the back-kitchen, dairy, &c. It will be observed, that in this elevation the porch is roofed in a different manner from what it is in any of the others, and that the additional height given to the walls is contained between a horizontal framework, sufficiently high to admit of bringing the roof of the

2064

porch below the line of the general roof.   This, it will be seen, greatly improves the picturesque effect of the group.

2278.   *The Construction and Materials.*   The foundations are of concrete, or of whatever other suitable material the locality affords, and they are carried up eighteen inches above the general surface of the surrounding ground.   The floor within is

2065

raised one foot or two steps above the general surface, so that it is six inches lower than the top of the plinth formed by the foundation.   On this plinth the framework

is placed, which consists of a sill, into which are framed upright stancheons, forming the angles and the sides of the doors and windows, nine inches square ; and they are framed into horizontal pieces of the same dimen-

2066

sions, the interstices being filled in with diagonal pieces, as shown in the elevations and views.   The roof is proposed to be covered with thatch or reeds, in either case steeped

in lime-water, and the chimney shafts to be of brick, to be splashed coarsely so as to imitate weather-stained bricks or stones.   The following details are taken from the descriptive specification of Design I. of Ricauti's *Rustic Architecture :* — " In framing the roof, British fir may be used for the ridge piece, nine inches by two inches, and the

2067

2068

wall-plates, six inches by four inches, which are continued through the walls, as shown in the elevations. The ceiling joists are to be of rough wood, four inches by three inches, also continued through the walls, as shown in side elevation, fig. 2065. The collars of rough wood, five inches by three inches, notched down on the joists, and the openings boarded, or lath and plastered, so as to form ceilings. Forest timber, or the loppings of trees, may be chopped into shape, about six inches by three inches, for the rafters ; these are crossed with light stuff, and covered with thatch. The inside of the walls may be battened and lath and plastered, and coloured with the following preparation, which, when properly mixed, will cover twenty-six square yards :—Quicklime, six ounces, rubbed down with a muller, to free it from all roughness ; linseed oil, six ounces ; Burgundy pitch, two ounces ; skimmed milk, two quarts. The pitch to be melted with the oil over a gentle fire, and gradually incorporated with the mixture. Any kind of colouring ingredient may be added, to bring it to the tint required.
The doors to be hung with T hinges, twelve inches long, ornamented with rough wood ; a Norfolk latch and a 3s. lock to be attached to each door. The ceiling joists, collars, wall-plates, &c., in the interior, should not be concealed ; for it may be observed in the perspective sketch, fig. 2069., that they may be rendered highly ornamental, both as a canted cornice and as a ribbed ceiling. This will be quite in character with the exterior parts of the building, with no additional expense, but only the exercise of a little taste in applying the material."

2069

Where such a cottage is to be considered principally as an ornamental structure in a pleasure-ground, for example, as a place of repose, or to drink tea in occasionally, Mr. Ricauti would recommend the finishing and furniture to be entirely in the rustic manner, the bark being removed, and the wood, as well as the floor, when the latter is of wood, stained with a decoction of walnut husks, to give it a subdued tone.

2279. *Remarks.* Half-timbered cottages are very picturesque objects, and seem particularly appropriate to a woody country ; nevertheless, we cannot recommend them for general adoption, even if the expense were not an object, on account of the thinness of the walls, and the care requisite to keep the roof and other parts of the exterior in nice order. As ornamental objects in parks they are very desirable, both on account of their beauty and their historical interest ; carrying back, as they do, the mind to the time when not only all the better kind of cottages in the central districts of England were built in this manner, but, as Holinshed informs us, most of the houses of the landed proprietors. A cottage built in the half-timbered style, in those parts of England where stone is the building material, or in Scotland where this is also the case, is not appropriate to the scenery of the country ; but it has a strikingly ornamental effect in another point of view, that is, from its rarity and its contrast with the local cottages. No architect, that we are acquainted with, has paid so much attention to timber construction as Mr. Ricauti, of which this design and those in his published works bear ample evidence. In some parts of England half-timbered houses have the roofs covered with tiles, but this material is never so suitable as thatch or reeds ; or, what is still better in point of economy and durability, as well as in appropriateness, the chips made by woodmen in working up coppice wood into wattle-work, hurdles, &c.

2280. *General Estimate.* Cubic contents of figs. 2063. and 2064. are 10,336 feet, at 6d. per foot, £258 8s. ; at 4d., £172 5s. 4d. ; and at 3d., £129 4s.

Design II.—*A Gate-Lodge, combining a Stable, in the Swiss Style.* By R. Varden, Esq., Architect.

2281. *Description.* The elevation is shown in fig. 2070. The situation of the cottage relatively to the house, stables, and other buildings, is shown in fig. 2071., in which *a* is

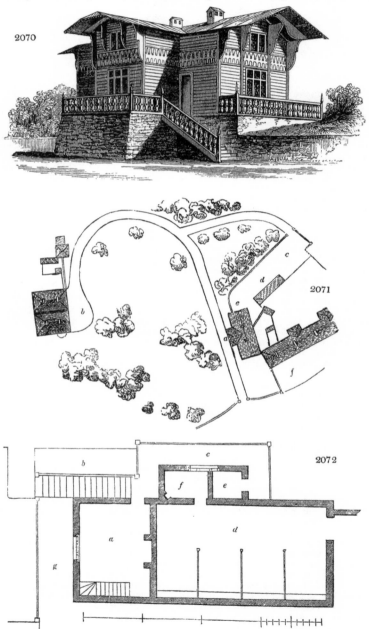

the lodge; *b*, the house; *c*, the stable-yard; *d*, the coach-houses; *e*, the stable end of the lodge; and *f*, cottages, which are screened by the lodge in the view from the house.

The ground plan of the lodge, fig. 2072., shows the cottage, with stairs to bed-room, *a*; outside stair, *b*; upper gallery, *c*; four-stall stable, *d*; seed-room, *e*; harness-room, *f*; and lower-gallery, with balustrade, *g*.

The chamber-floor plan, fig. 2073., shows the cottage bed-chamber, *h*; loft over the

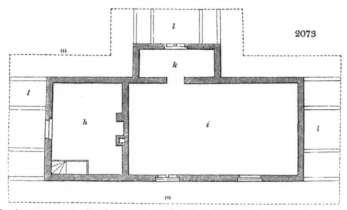

2073

stable, *i*; granary, *k*; brackets, *l,l,l*; and dotted lines, showing the distance which the roof projects from the walls, *m*.

Fig. 2077. is an elevation of the cottage end of the lodge; fig. 2078. is an end view of the stack of chimneys; fig. 2074. is a part of the ornamental weather-boarding on a large scale; fig. 2075. is an enlarged view of one of the brackets for the gables, in which *a* is a section of the inner barge-board; *b*, a section of the outer barge-board; *c c*, rafters, and *d*, the purlin; fig. 2076. is an enlarged view of part of the balustrade.

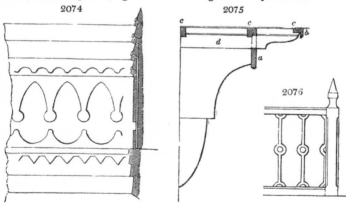

2074   2075   2076

2282. *Description.* This building is just erected at Powick in Gloucestershire, for J. B. Morgan, Esq. It was designed under peculiar circumstances. A new approach road having been formed in a cutting ten or twelve feet deep, almost in front of the dwelling-house, and a screen being required on the farther side of this cutting, to exclude the view of several unsightly cottages, *f*, in fig. 2071., from the dining-room and draw-ingroom windows, it was decided to place there the stables and a small lodge residence, which were to form one building, and be of a somewhat ornamental character. The site being on the abrupt edge of the cutting, a bold and picturesque style of build-ing was required, and the Swiss style was ultimately adopted. The walls under the balustrades are made two feet six inches thick, to support the earth bank on which the building is placed : they are built of unsquared granite, with garreted joints made very rough to enhance the picturesque appearance, and suit the character of the architecture. The walls of the building are formed of nine-inch brickwork, covered with deal weather-

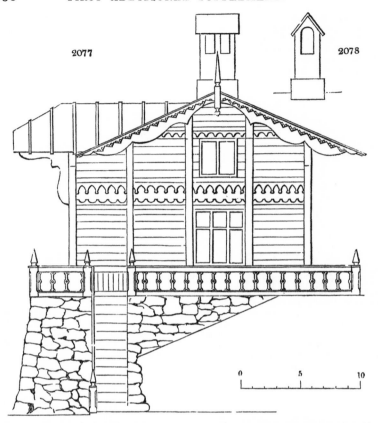

2077   2078

0   5   10

boarding. The boards for this purpose must be chosen free from knots, and are best if cut out of Quebec red pine balk (log or squared trunk) or Riga balk. About one balk out of five of the former, or one out of a hundred of the latter, will be found clean enough for the purpose; and as several must be opened to select from, the same description of wood should be used for the timber framings, that the knotty balks may be converted without loss to the builder; and both these woods are suitable for the purpose.

Wood bricks, two feet three inches apart, should be inserted in every seventh course of the brickwork; and to them upright fir battens, three inches by one inch, should be fixed, and the weather-boards nailed on. The weather-boards should be neatly wrought, seven inches wide, seven eighths of an inch thick on one edge, and five eighths of an inch on the other, nailed on the lower or thick edge only, which will be sufficient to keep them firmly in their places, and allow them sufficient play to expand and contract without splitting.

The brackets are formed of oak, three inches by four inches, fixed with screw-pins to the wall and plate, and are covered with $\frac{1}{2}$-inch boards. The edges of the framework are wrought, and a $\frac{1}{2}$-inch round fillet put on the centre.

The barge-boards are three inches thick, cut out of solid boards.

The roof is covered with patent slating, which is of more suitable character than the common kind, and may be laid much flatter.

2283. *Patent Slating.* "In covering a roof with patent slates, which were first brought into use by Mr. Wyatt, the common rafters must be left loose upon their purlins, as they require to be so arranged that a rafter may lie under all the meeting joists; hence neither boarding nor battens will be needed; and, since the number of rafters depends on the width of the slates, when they are large, very few are necessary. This kind of slating may be laid on a much less elevated rafter than any other, as, the laps being much less than in common slating, it is considerably lighter. It is likewise commenced at the eaves, but is neither crossed nor bonded, the slates lying uniformly, with each end reaching to the middle of the rafter, and butted up to each other through the length of the roof.   The eave slates are screwed down to the rafters by two or three strong 1½-inch screws, at each of their ends.   The joints are secured by filleting, or covering them with fillets of slates, about three inches wide, bedded in putty, and screwed down through the whole into the rafters.   Slating is sometimes laid in a lozenge form, but it is much less durable than the common method." (*Stuart's Dict. of Arch.*)

2284. *Roofs covered with this Description of Slating* do not require lead hips and ridges, for the slates, when properly fastened and puttied, are sufficient to exclude rain and moisture.   The projection of the eaves and gables being very great, it was feared strong winds might raise and damage the roof, therefore a course of bond timber was built into the walls, four feet from the top, to which the plate of the roof was attached by long screw-pins.   By this arrangement the weight of brickwork keeps the roof steady.

Buildings of this character might be formed of timber framing, or of any common material, such as rough stone, concrete, chalk and straw, the consolidated earth or *pisé* walling, that would be cheapest in the particular locality.   For the sake of additional durability, I have sometimes had Roman cement substituted for the weather-boarding, but worked into the same kind of pattern, and, when properly executed, it can scarcely be distinguished from wood ; but, it must be acknowledged, the effect is rather inferior. The boards may be painted or not, according to the taste of the owner.   The building at Powick is grained and varnished to imitate deep-coloured fir-wood ; but a less expensive method I adopted at Cheltenham, by merely giving the boards two or three coats of boiled oil, slightly tinted with burnt umber, which preserves the wood as well as paint, and produces a lighter and more transparent effect, from the natural grain of the wood remaining visible.   If the boards are knotty, the painting is to be preferred.

2285. *Remarks.* It is quite unnecessary for me to offer any remarks on the strong and picturesque character of the Swiss style of architecture, or of its applicability to entrance lodges, park buildings, and small dwellings for gamekeepers, &c.   I reget it is not more frequently adopted, for it offers a pleasing variety from the Tudor and the Italian styles, now so generally, indeed almost universally, adopted for such buildings: it is no more expensive than other descriptions of ornamental building.   With the exception of those I have erected, I do not remember having seen above three or four true Swiss buildings in the kingdom, though my travels, as you are aware, have not been confined to a few counties ; no doubt there are many others, but they have not come under my observation.   A suitable situation is of great importance to a Swiss cottage, but such may generally be found in an undulating, and always in a hilly, country.   The edge of a steep bank, whether natural or artificial, is very appropriate.   The slopes of railway cuttings and embankments are features that point out this style as suitable for small station-houses, if quite in the country ; but there the character of the masses and the detail must receive more attention than railway engineers (who generally reject the architect's aid) are in the habit of devoting to their miscalled Gothic structures, which have become the laughing-stocks of every person conversant with the true principles of Gothic architecture. — *R. V.   February* 3. 1842.

Design III.— *A Gate-Lodge and Gates.*   By F. H.

The elevation of the lodge is shown in fig. 2080., and of the gates in fig. 2081.

2286. *The Accommodation* is shown in the ground plan, fig. 2079., and consists of a living-room, *a* ; sleeping-room, *b* ; back-kitchen, *c* ; two closets, *d, e* ; place for fuel and lumber, *f* ; and privy, *g*.

2287. *Remarks.*   The exterior captivates at the first glance by its air of simplicity and elegance, produced by the general forms and lines, the arches rising from the columns, the arched windows, and the projecting eaves and chimney shafts, which are taller and much more elegant in the original than in our figure.   So far the general design is good ; but the artist has failed in his manner of construction ; in a word, the materials he has used are not homogeneous.   The walls are of plain brickwork, with stone dressings (or which, with respect to effect, is the same thing, and quite unobjectionable, dressings of cement in imitation of stone), and a freestone pronaos or porch, consisting of an arcade of three arches, of a very solid character, without archi-

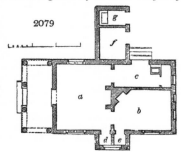

2079

2080

volt (an archivolt is the architrave of an arch) mouldings.   Under this heavy mass of
finished masonry, represented in coloured cement, three columns with the bark on,
which may be taken for shores or props, are placed, provisionally, as it would appear,
till the stone columns are prepared to take their place.   To see a mass of stone or
brickwork supported by props of wood, even though the latter should be hewn, is
unsatisfactory even in the wall of a common shed or cottage; but to see green wood with
the bark on used in a regular architectural design, is contrary to all ideas of fitness and
propriety.   The stone or compo arches over the green wood columns are without

2081

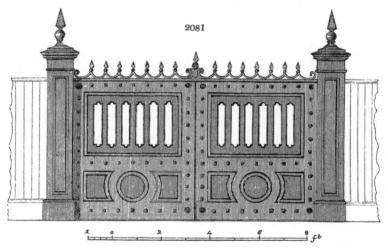

dressings though with keystones; whereas, to be consistent with the windows, they
ought, like them, to have had archivolts as well as keystones.   We think these objections unanswerable, and yet perhaps it is hardly fair to make them, for the artist, in all
probability, intends, or intended originally, to clothe the wooden columns with cement,
and to put cement architraves over the arches.   This may yet be done, and then the
building, as far as seen in the elevation before us, would, in our opinion, be unobjectionable.   The gate is handsome; the piers and their terminations are designed in a
style adapted for being executed in wood, and not in stone, as are the forms which we
sometimes see given to wooden piers.   We have not stated the name of the architect of
this lodge, nor the place where it is erected, lest by any means we should give offence;
more especially as we requested the permission of both parties, whom we highly respect,
to publish the design.

Design IV. — *A Gate-Lodge at Ravensworth Castle.*   By the Hon. Thomas Liddel.

The elevation is shown in figs. 2082. and 2084., and the ground plan in fig. 2083.

2288. *The Accommodation* shown in the latter is a porch, *a*; living-room, *b*; bed-
room, *c*; pantry, *d*; and back lobby, *e*.   The other conveniences are in a detached
building.

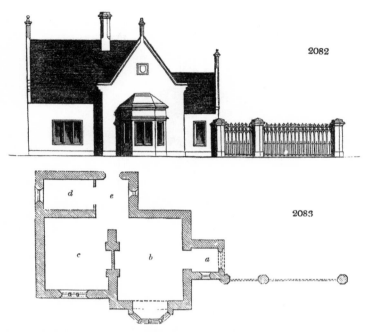

The walls are of stone, and two feet thick; and the pitch of the roof is high, in order to throw off the wet quickly, and it is covered with tiles, which are perfectly weather-tight, and proof against any force of wind. The form of the tile is shown in fig. 2085., and the appearance of a portion of roof covered by them in fig. 2086. It will be seen by fig. 2085., which shows only one tile, that the semi-cylindrical part and the flat part of each tile are moulded and cast together. The material of which the tiles are formed is the Mulgrave cement, mixed with coarse grit, in the proportion of equal parts of each. The composition, after being put in the mould, sets in a quarter of an hour. Each tile is eighteen inches square, and it laps over the adjoining tile about three inches, which renders the roof very little heavier than one of ordinary slate, and perfectly water-tight.

2289. *Remarks.* We were struck with the handsome and substantial appearance of this lodge, when in the neighbourhood of Durham in the autumn of 1841; and having heard that it was designed by the Honourable Thomas Liddel, we applied to him, and he kindly sent us the sketches from which the engravings have been made.

Mr. Liddel is an amateur architect, whose architectural knowledge and taste are such, as to enable him to design and superintend the execution of the additions which have been making for several years past to Ravensworth Cas-

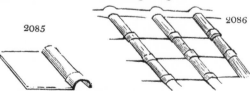

tle, the seat of his noble father. The elevations of the gate-lodge are far from doing justice to the originals, from the roofs not showing the peculiar character given by this description of tile.

Design V.—*A Cottage in the Style of the Wingfield Station-House, on the North Midland Railway.*   By Francis Thompson, Esq., Architect to the North Midland Railway Company.

The elevation, on the supposition that there is a bed-room floor, will be as in fig. 2087.; or should there be no bed-room floor, as in fig. 2089.

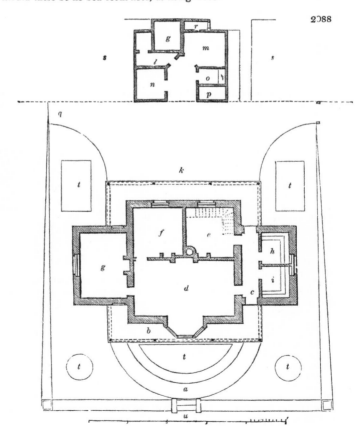

2290. *The Accommodation* is shown in the ground plan, fig. 2088., in which *a* represents a terrace; *b*, a veranda; *c*, the entrance-door; *d*, living-room; *e*, scullery; *f*, bedroom; *g*, bedroom; *h*, dairy;

2089

i, pantry; *k*, yard; *l*, piggery; *m*, cow-house; *n*, coals; *o*, privy; *p*, liquid-manure tank; *q*, dust; *r*, dairy; *s*, garden; *t t t*, flower-beds; *u*, terrace steps.

2291. *Remarks.* This will form a very comfortable cottage, as well as a handsome one. The arrangement is good, particularly that of the detached offices. The two parallelogram flower-beds are not of forms that harmonise very well with the situations, but that is not the fault of Mr. Thompson, as the alterations were made by our draughtsman.

Design VI.—*A Cottage in the Style of the Eckington Railway Station.* By Francis Thompson, Esq., Architect.

2292. *The Accommodation* is shown in fig. 2090., in which *a* is a terrace; *b*, a porch; *c*, a living-room; *d* and *e*, bed-rooms; *f*, scullery; *g*, pantry; *h*, dairy; *i*, coals, &c.; *k*, passage leading to the privy; *l*, privy; *m*, cowhouse; *n*, liquid manure; *o*, dung; *p*, pigs.

2293. *Remarks.* The plan and elevation are both original and handsome, and the arrangement of the offices admirable. This design and the others contributed by Mr. Thompson are very different in character from ornamented cottages generally. They appear to us admirably adapted for the dwellings of persons connected with public or national works, such as railroads, canals, public parks, promenades, gardens, &c.; and they would also be very suitable for country publichouses along main roads. With an additional room or two, any one of them might be rendered fit for the occupation of a gentleman with a small family.

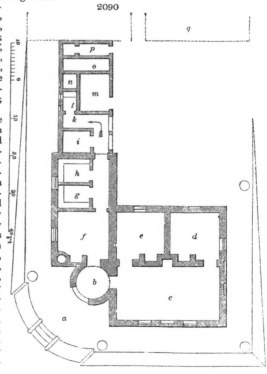

2090

We cannot sufficiently express our admiration of the public spirit of the directors of the North Midland Railway, in causing the erection of such architectural gems along their line of works. They are great ornaments of themselves, and as they will be seen by many thousands of all ranks, and remain, it is to be hoped, for several generations standard models of cultivated design, they can hardly fail greatly to improve the general taste of the country. Even the mechanics who have worked at their construction

2091

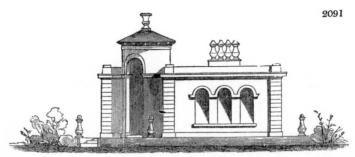

must have had their ideas enlarged, and their taste more or less refined by them.   We wish we could see the same spirit actuating the directors of all railroads, the result of which would be, provided some attention were paid to the verdant scenery on the banks, the most interesting public ways in the world.

Design VII.—*A Cottage in the modern Italian Style.*   By Francis Thompson, Esq., Architect.

The elevation is shown in fig. 2092.

2092

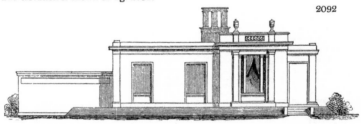

2294.   *The Accommodation* is shown in fig. 2093., in which *a* is a terrace ; *b*, porch ;

2093

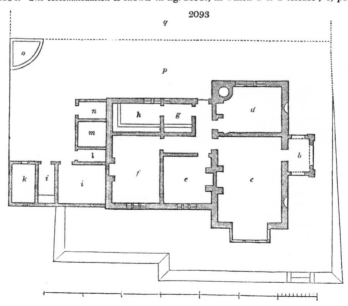

c, living-room ; *d*, scullery ; *e* and *f*, bed-rooms ; *g*, pantry ; *h*, dairy ; *i*, cow ; *k*, pig ; *l*, privy ; *m*, liquid manure ; *n*, coals ; *o*, dung ; *p*, yard ; and *q*, garden.

2295. *Remarks.*   The arrangement is remarkably good, and the elevation elegant.

Design VIII. — *A Cottage in the Style of the Belper Railway Station.*   By Francis Thompson, Esq.

The elevation is shown in fig. 2094.

2094

2296. *Accommodation.*   Fig. 2095., which is to a scale of twenty-five feet to an inch, shows *a*, terrace ; *b*, living-room ; *c*, scullery ; *d* and *e*, bed-rooms ; *f*, dairy ; *g*, pantry ; *h*, piggery ; *i*, cow-house ; *k*, coals ; *l*, yard ; *m*, garden ; *n*, privy ; *o*, liquid manure ; *p*, dust ; *q*, dung ; *r*, back entrance.

2095

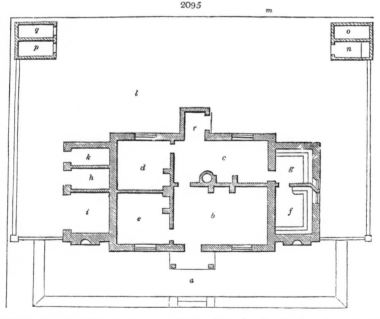

2297. *Remarks.*   The plan is commodious, and the elevation simple and grand.   To render this residence fit for a gentleman, we have only to turn *b* and *c* into living-rooms ; *f* and *g* into bed-rooms ; *d* into a kitchen ; *h* and *k* into a pantry and dairy, or a servant's bed-room and pantry ; *i* into a bed-room ; and *e* into a general dressing-room and cloak and boot room ; a very convenient room in the country, where the master and his friends are much out of doors, and where visitors are received without much ceremony.   The cow-house, *i*, may be placed in the yard, adjoining *p*, and if a cow is not kept it may be used as a stable, and a gig-house may be built adjoining it.   The place for coals, *k*, may be transferred to the space between the porch, *r*, and the window to *d*.   The piggery may be placed in the yard, beside *n*.   We have now a very comfortable small house, with a yard in which any additional offices may be erected that are thought necessary. If the yard is enclosed by walls there should be a broad border for flowers and ornamental climbers; and, if it is enclosed by a hedge, there ought to be ornamental standard trees in it, and flowers and roses in the border. If any plants are trained against the house they ought to be confined to the plain spaces between the quoins and the architraves, so as not to interfere with architectural forms and lines; indeed, as a general rule, all edifices that show much of architectural design should be left free from plants. If a few are introduced in any plain part, that part should first be covered with a wooden trellis painted of a stone colour, on which to train the plants. The subject of training plants, and especially vines and fruit trees, on cottage walls and roofs, will be found treated of at length in our *Suburban Horticulturist*.

Design IX.—*A Cottage in the Style of the Ambergate Railway Station.* By Francis Thompson, Esq., Architect.

The elevation is shown in fig. 2096.

2096

2298. *Accommodation.* Fig. 2097. shows a porch, *a*; passage, *b*; living-room, *c*; staircase, *d*; bed-room, *e*; scullery, *f*; dairy, *g*; pantry, *h*; back-entrance, *i*.

2299. *Remarks.* This design is chiefly remarkable for the elevation, which is surpassingly handsome. Those who wish to see beautiful engravings of the railway stations which form the types for these five designs should have recourse to Mr. Thompson's splendid work entitled *Railway Stations*, folio, 1842, 25s. This work also contains engravings of three other beautiful station houses, on the same line of railroad, besides the splendid terminus at Derby, which is upwards of one thousand feet in length, and replete with every convenience required in such a structure.

2097

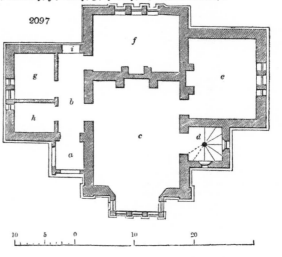

Design X.— *The Edensor Gate-Lodges and Gates at Chatsworth.* By the late Sir Jeffry Wyatville, Architect. The Description by John Robertson, Esq., Architect, Chatsworth.

The elevation of one of the lodges is shown in fig. 2098., and of both, together with the gates, in fig. 2099. The ground plans are shown in figs. 2100. and 2101.

2300. *Description.* Fig. 2100. is the plan of an old English lodge, built of bricks and timber, as shown in fig. 2098. In this plan, *a* is a covered way or open porch ; *b*, porch ; *c*, lobby or inner porch ; *d*, parlour ; *e*, stairs ; *f*, pantry ; *g*, another pantry ; *h*, a recess from the living-room, *i* ; *k*, kitchen ; *l*, privies ; *m*, shed round the piggeries ; *n*,

2098

yard ; *o*, gate to yard. Two families live in this house, which accounts for the two pantries, and the parlour *d* is converted into a living-room.

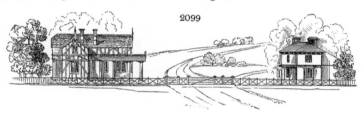

2099

Fig. 2101. is an Italian lodge, shown in the right side of fig. 2099., built of stone : *a* is the entrance-porch, open ; *b*, porch ; *c*, lobby and staircase ; *d*, living-room ; *e*,

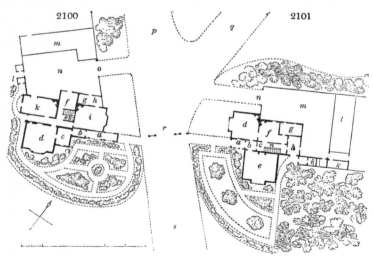

2100   2101

parlour ; *f*, kitchen ; *g*, pantry ; *h*, lobby and back-door ; *i*, covered way to privy, *k* ; *l*, shed including pigsties ; *m*, yard ; *n*, gate to yard ; *p*, road leading to Pilsley and Bakewell ; *q*, road to Edensor Inn ; *r*, gate ; *s*, road to Edensor and Chatsworth. Both houses have chambers over the lower rooms.

2301. *Remarks.* These lodges were both built from designs by the late Sir J. Wyatville : they were finished in October, 1839. They have no merit in an architectural point of view; but the one is historically interesting, as showing the kind of building which was formerly constructed of timber framing filled in with bricks, in no very scientific manner; and the other is a specimen of what, twenty years ago, was reckoned the Italian manner. Such, however, is the grandeur of the scenery where they are placed, and to which the road leads, that these lodges escape critical notice. "There are two handsome lodges at the Baslow entrance to the park, nearly completed. They are also from designs by the late Sir Jeffry. They are built of beautiful rubbed or polished stone in the modern Italian style. Two are likewise to be built at the Beely entrance. These lodges were the last productions of Sir Jeffry for Chatsworth. An entrance-lodge to the village of Edensor is now being built in the castellated style: it is one of mine. — *J. R.*   *Chatsworth, March* 15. 1842."

Designs XI. to XIV.—*Four Ornamental Cottages, with the same Accommodation as in the Model Cottage* No. I., p. 1141. By E. B. Lamb, Esq., F.I.B.A.

2302. Design XI., of which fig. 2102. is the elevation, and fig. 2103. the ground

2102

plan, is in the Scotch style, and characterised by steep roofs, slated, and with the gable walls furnished with what are called crow steps. The ground plan contains a porch *a*, adjoining which is the staircase; a kitchen, *b*; best room, *c*; bed-room, *d*; back-kitchen, *e*; pantry, *f*; dairy, *g*; poultry-house or oven-house, *h*; and cow-house, *i*. The rest is supposed to be as in the agricultural model cottage. This design may be

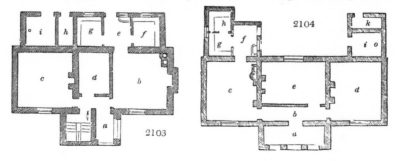

2103

2104

considered as an example of the Scotch style, ennobled by the grandeur of the proportions, and by the projection of the chimney from the gable wall; a feature never seen in
the unimproved Scotch cottage, but one, as we have elsewhere observed, essential to
cultivated architectural expression.

2303. Design XII., of which fig. 2105. is the elevation, and fig. 2104. the plan, is in
the Italian style. The accommodation is much the same as in the model cottage No. I.,

2105

but somewhat differently arranged. The plan shows a porch, *a*; passage, *b*; kitchen,
c; two bed-rooms, *d*, *e*; back-kitchen, *f*; pantry, *g*; dairy, *h*; and cow-house and pigsty, *i*, *k*. The other appendages are as in the model cottage.

2304. Design XIII., the elevation of which is shown in fig. 2106., is adapted for
a plan nearly the same as in the model cottage, but without a porch, or, rather, with
the porch inside of the house. The walls in this design are shown of great thickness,

2106

which renders it suitable for being executed in rough stone, in compressed earth, or in
cob; or, where workmen can be induced to take the trouble, in hollow walls of
brick on edge, two feet in thickness, and filled in with concrete or with a mixture of
clay and lime. Where a cottage is only one story high, we greatly prefer thick walls of
earth, on a solid foundation of brick or stone, to walls nine inches or a foot in thickness, built of brick, or of any other material whatever, on account of their great
warmth. Such walls may always be finished within, in as good a style as brick or
stone walls; as a proof of which we have only to refer to the houses built of compressed earth at Woburn Abbey.

2305. Design XIV., of which fig. 2107. is the elevation, is a cottage of two stories,
containing exactly the same accommodation as the model cottage No. I., but in a
substantial massive style, and with the stack of chimneys carried up in a small
tower.

2107

2306. *Remarks.* These designs are given to show how the humblest dwelling may be ennobled, when it passes through the hands of an architect of genius like Mr. Lamb. It will be observed, that in all of them the ornament is bestowed on the essential parts of the construction, such as the porch, chimney tops, doors, windows, gables, &c., and not tacked on the naked parts of the walls, as frequently practised by architects and amateurs, who do not know the difference between covering an object with ornaments, and enriching it.

Design XV. — *A Cottage in the Style of Heriot's Hospital, Edinburgh.* By John Henderson, Esq., Architect.

The elevation is shown in fig. 2108.

2307. *Accommodation.* The plan, fig. 2109., shows a porch, *a*; a lobby, *b*; a living-room, *c*; a kitchen, *d*; back-kitchen, *e*; a pantry, *f*; dairy, *g*; a bed closet, *h*; store closet, *i*; fuel, *k*; cow-house, *l*; pig, *m*; yard, *n*; privy, *o*; liquid manure, *p*; dust and dung, *q*.

2308. *Remarks.* The inhabitants of Edinburgh are great admirers of this style of architecture, which no

2108

man understands better than Mr. Henderson; as his very beautiful design for a seed-shop, connected with an agricultural museum, erected, the former for Mr. Lawson, and the latter for the Highland Society of Scotland, on the Regent's Bridge, Edinburgh, sufficiently proves. No person of taste can have visited Edinburgh without having been struck by that splendid edifice, Heriot's Hospital, which is the central building of an institution for the gratuitous education of natives of Edinburgh. Fortunately the institution is rich, and the trustees have been enabled to erect branch schools in different parts of the city, and these, with all the farm buildings and cottage dwellings on their extensive landed estates, when rebuilt, are erected in the style of the parent building. This, we think, evinces much propriety and good taste on the part of the trustees, and cannot fail, by the example which it exhibits, to have a favourable influence on the general progress of improvement in agricultural buildings, schools, and labourers' cottages. In Mr. Lawson's seed-shop, every part of the fixtures and fittings-up, and even the furniture, partakes of the style of the exterior; and, in short, it is, we believe, the most complete seed-shop in the world.

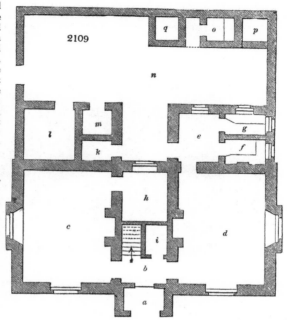

Heriot's Hospital was built in the beginning of the seventeenth century, and the architect is commonly said to be Inigo Jones, and the style that of James VI. or Elizabeth. Many competent judges, however, are of opinion that Inigo Jones was not the architect, the style of that artist partaking much more of the Roman and the Italian, as it existed in his time, than of what we now call Elizabethan. According to Hakewell, in his *Attempt to determine the exact Character of Elizabethan Architecture* (8vo, 1835), the Elizabethan style, or, as its earliest manifestations are called, the style of James VI., is a modification of the *cinque-cento* style of Italy. This style, he says, is wholly unmixed with Gothic forms or Gothic enrichments; it has not the ornamented gable, the bay, or the oriel window, of the domestic Gothic, for these were all in common use long before: but it consists of a number of forms more easily executed than those of either the Grecian or the Gothic styles; and we may add that these forms were chiefly such as could be delineated by the aid of the rule and compasses. A great many Elizabethan houses were erected by John Thorpe, and there is a MS. book of plans and elevations by this architect in the Soanean Library: the plans and elevations are neatly drawn, but, wherever the smallest attempt is made to introduce ornament, or the human figure, it is not above the execution of the most ordinary mechanic. Architects, in those days, were not, as they frequently now are, good artists. Hence, as we have just hinted, all the ornaments and ornamental finishings in the Elizabethan style consist of combinations of geometrical curves and circles with straight lines, angles, and cubes. The Elizabethan style, Mr. Hakewell continues, may be classed under two divisions; the first, or proper, being the *cinque-cento* style of Italy, as introduced at Longleat and part of Hatfield; and the second, or lower order, that in which, as far as possible, the same forms were observed, but the decoration and enrichment confined to such figures as the common mason or joiner could execute, as at Wollaton, Dorton, and many other mansions. It would thus appear that the Elizabethan style, like every other, arose out of a sort of necessity, viz., that of adapting the style of ornament to the means of getting it carried into execution. In the present day the revival of this style pleases by its novelty, and the skill of modern artists has carried it out to such an extent as greatly to increase its beauty, and its distinctive characteristics as a style.

Design XVI.— *The Dairy Lodge erected at Chequers Court, Buckinghamshire, for Sir Robert Frankland Russell, Bart.* By E. B. Lamb, Esq., F. I. B. A.

2309. *The Chequers Dairy Lodge*, of which fig. 2110. is an elevation, and fig. 2111. a plan, is placed near the entrance to the beautiful valley called the Velvet Lawn, at the ancient seat of Chequers, in Buckinghamshire, for the protection of the property in this situation, and also as a dwelling for an upper servant.   It is about a mile from the mansion, and a few yards from a beautiful and plentiful supply of water.

2110

2310. *The Lodge* contains on the ground floor a porch, *a*; sitting-room, *b*; kitchen, *c*; passage, *d*; pantry, *e*; and back entrance, *f*. On the one-pair floor are three bed-rooms. The lodge is surrounded by a garden, *s*; and from the back entrance, by the path *g*, there is a communication to the dairy.   There is a privy, *h*, with a cesspool behind, open at top; *i* is a wood and coal house; *k*, a churning-room; *l*, passage and steps descending to the dairy; *m*, the dairy, the floor of which is three feet below the surface of the ground.

The walls of the ground floor of the cottage are built with brick and flints in chequered courses, flint being one of the common building materials of this part of the country. The sills of the windows, and the arches of the porch and back door, are of Bath stone. The walls of the upper floor are formed of timber framing, covered with ornamental tiles on the outside and plastered within.   The verge-boards and pinnacles, also all the mullions of the windows, are of Memel timber, and painted to imitate oak.   The tiling is coloured to harmonise with the other materials, and the roof is thatched.   The whole of the woodwork is prepared by Kyan's process; and, indeed, all the woodwork for the buildings recently erected and now erecting on this property is prepared in this manner, a tank having been formed for that purpose.

2311. *The Dairy*, fig. 2111., *m*, is fitted up with stone shelves on three sides, and paved with tiles : the window is in the north side; and, when it is necessary to admit air, the casement only is opened, gauze wire being fixed to keep out the flies.   On the south side, externally, every alternate rafter of the roof is continued down, so as to form a lean-to shed, in order to keep the sun off the wall as much as possible; and under this shed, close to the ceiling of the dairy, are openings for ventilation.   The shed is also useful for placing pans, tubs, &c., to dry and season.   It is covered with tiles, as in this situation thatch would be liable to be injured by the cows.   The other part of the roof is thatched.   The walls of the dairy are built hollow.

2312. *The Poultry-houses*, *n n*, with a dove-house over them, adjoin the dairy.   The cow-house and pigsties form a group by themselves.   The cow-house is erected with unbarked timber, and covered with thatch; *o* are the cow-stalls; *p*, calf-pen, which is made large enough to serve as an occasional stall for a horse; *q q*, pigsties and yards; and *r* the yard to the cow-house, poultry, &c.   This building is erected entirely with unbarked timber, principally larch, and some beech.   Young trees, from six inches to nine inches in diameter, are sawn down the middle, and placed in upright, horizontal, and diagonal forms, so as to produce an ornamental appearance.   The whole of the timber was cut down near the spot, and cut to the proper lengths and Kyanised.   The thatching is also Kyanised.   This is a mere experiment.   As the thatch absorbs a considerable quantity of the liquid, the expense is greater than that of Kyanising timber. The lodge is surrounded with a fence of wood in the same character as the building. The posts have ornamental caps.   The fence of the yard is of unbarked larch.

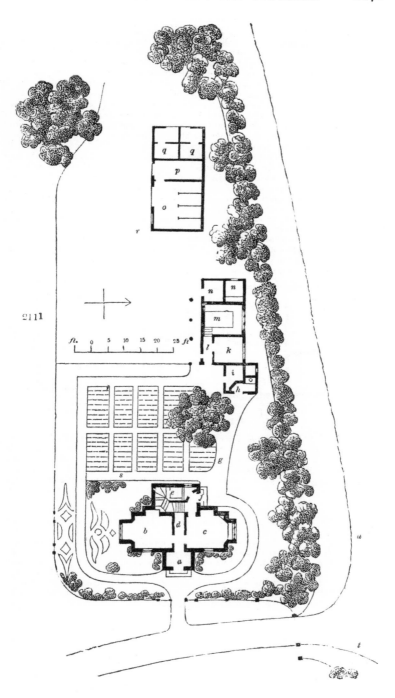

2111

Designs XVII. — XXV. *The Cottages in Cassiobury Park.*

2313. *The late Earl of Essex* took great delight in improving the cottages on his estate at Cassiobury, and many of them were built or improved from his own designs. The following views and plans were published by Mr. Britton, in his very elegant and interesting *History of Cassiobury Park*, published in 1837 ; and to that gentleman we are indebted for the use of the engravings. " In different parts of the park and grounds," Mr. Britton observes, " are various cottages and lodges, which are distinguished at once for their exterior picturesque features, and for the domestic comfort they afford to their humble occupants. Unlike the ragged wretched sheds and hovels which are too often seen by the road side, and even in connexion with some of the large and ancient parks of our island, the buildings here delineated are calculated to shelter, to console, and gratify the labourer after his daily toil, and to make his wife and family cleanly and diligent. The cottages at Cassiobury have been designed with the twofold object of being both useful and ornamental. They are occupied, exempt from rent and taxes, by men and women who are employed by the noble landlord in various offices about the park, the gardens, and the house ; thus, the park-keeper, a game-keeper, a shepherd, a lodge-keeper, a gardener, a carpenter, a miller, a lock-keeper, &c., are accommodated."

In the interior arrangement of these cottages, most of them contain a porch, a sitting-room, one or two bed-rooms, and a wash-house, with an oven and copper.

2314. Design XVII.—*Great Beech Tree Cottage.* Fig. 2112. is a plan of Great Beech Tree Cottage, which, being of larger extent than the others, and highly ornamented exteriorly, may be considered in the light of a cottage ornée. It has five rooms on the ground floor, and others up stairs. The ground plan contains, *a*, sitting-room ; *b*, bed-room ; *c*, porch and passage ; *d*, sitting-room ; *e*, housekeeper's room ; *f*, pantry ; *g*, cellar ; *h*, back entrance ; *i*, kitchen ; *k*, porch.

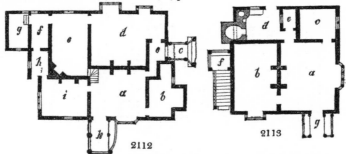

2112   2113

2315. Design XVIII.—*Ridge Lane Cottage.* Fig. 2113. is Ridge Lane Cottage, which is of two stories, each appropriated to a family. In the elevation of this cottage (not given) there is a porch of entrance for the family who occupy the ground floor, and a porch at the top of an outside staircase, for the occupant of the upper floor. The ground plan contains, *a*, kitchen ; *b*, sitting-room ; *c*, bed-room ; *d*, wash-house, oven, &c. ; *e*, pantry ; *f*, staircase to a floor for another family ; *g*, porch.

2316. Design XIX.— *London Entrance Lodge to Cassiobury.* Fig. 2114. is the entrance lodge for two families, in which *a* and *g* are sitting-rooms ; *b*, staircase ; *c*, entrance ; *d*, wood-house ; *e*, passage, with dwarf wall ; *f*, gates ; *h*, octagon staircase to bed-room ; *i*, wash-house. This cottage forms the lodge to the London entrance, and is understood to have been partly the design of Wyatt, and partly of the earl. It certainly forms a very handsome group. The massive gates are hung with Collins's hinges, and move so easily that they may be opened or shut by a child.

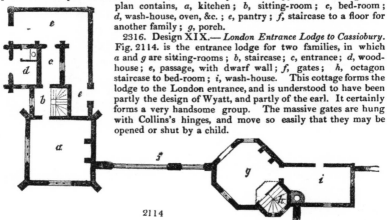

2114

2317. Design XX.— *The Park-Keeper's Cottage.* Fig. 2115. is a ground plan of the park-keeper's cottage, in which *a* is a slaughter-house; *b*, a dairy and larder; *c*, a sitting-room; *d*, kitchen; *e*, entrance; *f*, porch; and *g*, staircase.

2318. Design XXI.— *Thorn Cottage.* Fig. 2117. is a ground plan of Thorn Cottage, in which *a* is the sitting-room; *b*, bakehouse and scullery; *c*, privy; *d*, cellar; *e*, shed over well; *f*, porch and covered way.

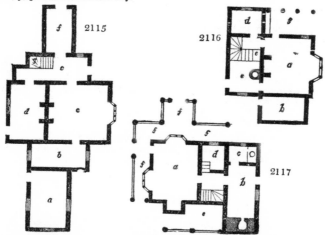

2319. Design XXII.— *The Shepherd's or Keeper's Lodge.* Fig. 2116. is the shepherd's or keeper's lodge, in which *a* is the sitting-room; *b*, wood-house; *c*, wash-house and oven; *d*, pantry; *e*, staircase; *f*, porch.

2320. Design XXIII.— *The Russell Farm Lodge.* Fig. 2118. is called Russell Farm Lodge, and is erected at the entrance to Russell Farm, by the side of the public road between Watford and Berkhampstead. Russell Farm is occupied by General Sir Charles Colville, Bart., who rents it from the Earl of Essex. The ground plan contains, *a*, back porch; *b*, kitchen; *c*, sitting-room; *d*, bed-room; *e*, wash-house, &c.; *f*, front porch, with seat.

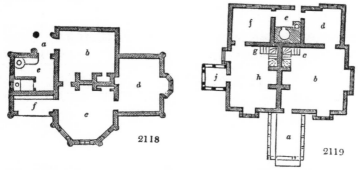

2321. Design XXIV.— *Russell Cottage.* Fig. 2119. is Russell Cottage, for two labourers' families. The ground plan contains, for the one cottage, a porch, *a*; sitting-room, *b*; staircase, *c*; wash-house, *d*; and oven and copper common to both cottages, *e*. The other cottage contains a wash-house, communicating with a room containing the common oven and boiler; a living-room, *h*; stairs to the bed-room, *g*; and porch, *j*.

2322. Design XXV. — *Cassio-bridge Cottage.* Fig. 2120. is Cassio-bridge Cottage, for two labourers' families. The walls of this cottage are covered with split hazel, and other rods, the flat side being applied to the walls, and the bark exhibited externally to the weather and the eye. The pieces are all of the same diameter, but of different lengths, and they are arranged so as to throw the surface into panels, variously composed, in the manner of the Duke of Marlborough's garden structures at White Knights.

The ground plan of each of these cottages shows exactly the same accommodation as in the Russell Cottage; viz. two porches, *a*, *j*; two living-rooms, *b*, *h*; two stairs, *c*, *g*; two wash-houses, *d*, *f*; an oven and boiler room common to both houses, *e*.

2323. *Remarks.* There is much to admire in the arrangement of the plans of these cottages; though there are none of them that might not be improved, if we apply the tests of the model cottages. Nevertheless, they afford excellent hints for composition, and do great credit to the memory of the late Earl of Essex, who was a man of great taste, as well as of active benevolence; his chief enjoyment, for the latter years of his life, consisting in seeing every one about him happy.

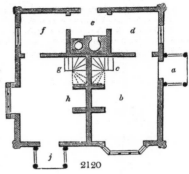

Design XXVI.—*A Gate-Lodge or Cottage.* By G. B. W.

2324. *The front or principal Elevation* is shown in fig. 2121.; the other elevations, being of less importance, are not given. Fig. 2122. is the ground plan, in which

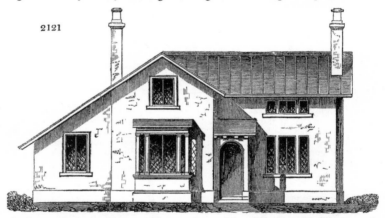

a is the porch; *b*, the living-room, or parlour, sixteen feet by twelve feet; *c*, the kitchen, sixteen feet by thirteen feet; and *d*, a bed-room, fourteen feet by ten feet.

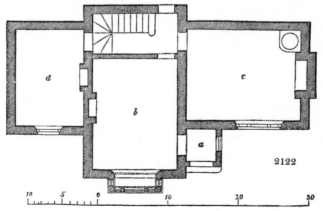

2325. *Remarks.* This plan is deficient in not having a back-kitchen or a pantry, and also in the access to the stairs being through the best room.

Design XXVII.—*A Turnpike Lodge.* By A. C.

The front elevation is shown in fig. 2125., and the side elevation in fig. 2124.

2326. *The Plan* is shown in fig. 2123. The room *a* is fifteen feet six inches by six feet; one side is to be used for depositing the money and keeping the tickets, and on the other side there is room for a chair or two, for the accommodation of any person that might be waiting for the stages. The room *b* is intended, in the daytime, for the collector to eat his meals in, and at night as a bed-room, having a turn-up bedstead; *c* is a closet; *d*, a water-closet.

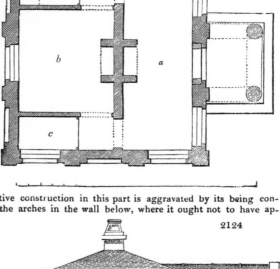

2123

2327. *Remarks.* The marking of the stones in the architrave is deficient in the semblance of truth; half of them appearing to rest on the wall and not on the pilasters; and the defective construction in this part is aggravated by its being conspicuously exhibited in the arches in the wall below, where it ought not to have appeared; since ostensibly these walls have no weight to bear, and might, in fact, according to the principle of Grecian construction, have been of earth. In other respects the design may pass, though the clock in the front elevation ought to have been placed on a raised panel or frame, and there ought to have been a panel for the name of the gate-keeper on the frieze over the door; and another at the end, between the pilasters, for the toll-regulations. What we mean will be, perhaps, better understood from

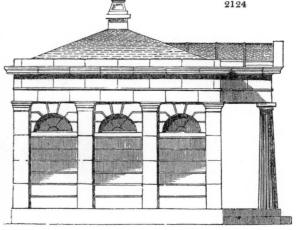

2124

the following remarks on the buildings at the railway stations. We greatly admire the expression of purpose in the bridges and other buildings connected with the railways, but instead of having the name of the station painted sometimes on one part of the structure, and sometimes on another, we would have had it sculptured on a conspicuous part of the front, especially designed and peculiarly characterised for that purpose; and we would have had the name itself in sunk or in raised letters; coloured, if it should have been thought necessary, but, at all events, formed either by sinking or in relief. At most of the railroad stations there are large boards, on which are painted regulations, or other information relative to matters connected with the railroad; and as these regulations may be supposed to be occasionally altered, we would still continue to have them painted on boards; but we would form panels on raised surfaces in which these boards should be fixed, or slipped in, in the same way as a picture is slipped into a frame. The panels should be made sufficiently large to admit of a larger board than might be wanted at the time the station-house was built, in order to provide room for additional regulations that may be supposed to become necessary as the traffic on the railway increases; but the board, whether covered with lines or not, should always be sufficiently large to fill the whole of the panel.

2125

We would carry this principle of rendering writing architectural to turnpike-houses and gates, and to the signs and names of inns, public-houses, and shops; to names on the gates of manufactories; to those on private doors; to the names of gentlemen's seats, which, we think, ought to be sculptured on sunk or raised panels or shields on their entrance-lodges or gates; to the names of cottages and villages; and, in short, to every architectural structure where a name was required or would be useful. Had the art of writing been coeval with that of architecture, there is little doubt that writing would have been introduced on buildings in an architectural manner, as ornaments of leaves and flowers have been, and as writing is on ecclesiastical buildings in the Gothic style. In this style the very character of the letters is architectural, and the words are always placed on scrolls or labels. It is for the modern artist to introduce writing on edifices artistically, and, in doing so, to produce something superior to the mode of putting the hieroglyphics on the Egyptian tombs or obelisks; or the letters on the jambs of the shop-doors in Pompeii, or over the doors and windows of shops in modern towns; something, in short, analogous to what is done in the Gothic style of lettering. (*Gard. Mag.* for 1842, p. 50.)

The design fig. 2126. was made for a gate-lodge to a private road through a demesne, and is very suitable for such a purpose, though by no means so for the gate-lodge of a public road. The latter seems to require a more severe style of architecture, more durable materials, and a more permanent manner of putting these together. There is a curious omission in figure 2126., viz., that of the verge-board, while the hip-knop, or finial and pendant, are inserted both in the gable end and porch, without any meaning whatever. "The

2126

[verge-boards, or] barge-boards, of gables were intended to cover and preserve the ends of the purloins and covering of the roof, which projected over to shelter the front of the building. The hip-knop which terminated the ancient gables was, in reality, a king-post fixed at the junction of the barge-boards, and into which they were tenanted. (*Pugin's Christian Architecture,* p. 39.)

Design XXVIII.—*A Cyclopean Cottage.* By William Wells, Esq.

2328. The term Cyclopean, as here used, applies only to the lower part of the walls

2127

of the cottage, as shown in the elevation, fig. 2127., which are formed of irregular blocks of sandstone, without the slightest indication of horizontal or vertical courses.

The effect, as contrasted with the numerous straight perpendicular lines formed by the studwork in the upper part of the walls, and with the horizontal lines of the roof, is exceedingly good. The studwork is filled in with brickwork plastered over; the smoothness and finished appearance of which, as contrasted with the rudeness of the Cyclopean part, is forcible, and at the same time pleasing. A great beauty in this cottage results from the horizontal division of the main body of the roof; the upper part of which projects slightly over the lower part. The chimney-top is massive, and original. The whole was executed by a local carpenter and mason, from the sketches of Mr. Wells, out of timber and stone produced by the estate. The plan, fig. 2128., contains a porch, *a*; kitchen, *b*; parlour, *c*; light closet, *d*; pantry, *e*; a staircase, *f*, to two good bed-rooms above, and to the cellar under the parlour below; also an open shed, *g*, for fuel; *h* is a place for rabbits or

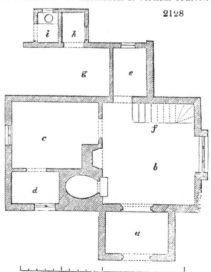

2128

pigs; and *i*, a privy. The oven in the kitchen is shown large, to suit the description of fuel in general use by cottagers, viz. faggot wood. We have shown, in our *Manual of*

Cottage Gardening, how this fuel may be grown by every cottager for himself, provided he has an acre of ground, instead of one sixth of an acre.

Design **XXIX.**— *The Penshurst Gate-Lodge, at Redleaf, the Seat of W. Wells, Esq.*

The elevation is shown in fig. 2129.

2329. *Accommodation.* The plan, fig. 2130., shows an entrance-porch, *a* ; lobby, *b* ;

2129

kitchen, *c* ; parlour, *d* ; family bed-room, *e* ; and back-kitchen, *f.* From the kitchen a staircase leads to three sleeping-rooms in the roof, and down to a cellar, pantry, &c.,

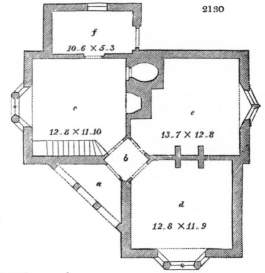

under the parlour and family bed-room floor. A shed for fuel, which in this part of Kent is chiefly wood, a drying ground, small kitchen-garden, and other needful conveniences, are placed adjoining, and appropriately arranged.

2330. *Remarks.* Much of the beauty of this cottage, and of the cyclopean cottage at Redleaf, fig. 2127., results from the break in the roof, by which the vulgarity of so large a plain surface is removed, and a second horizontal shadow obtained, in addition to that produced by the eaves; thus breaking up the plain surfaces and rendering them more picturesque. The connexion of the rooms with the lobby, *b*, is good, and there is no great objection to the stair in this case being in the kitchen, because it leaves the entrance to the room free.

This cottage forms the entrance-lodge to one of the most remarkable country seats in England ; one which combines the romantic with the pastoral, and wild nature with a very high degree of horticultural cultivation and riches. A singular feature in the lawn is a rocky flower-garden, formed in an excavation, two sides of which are masses of native rock, and the other a smooth even surface, blending with the sloping lawn. In consequence of this flower-garden being sunk, no part of it is seen from the house, though it is within two or three hundred yards of it; and hence all the beauties and enjoyments of a flower-garden are obtained without injuring the romantic character of the view from the house or the main walks.

Design XXX.— *The Home Lodge at Chequers Court.* By E. B. Lamb, Esq., F.I.B.A.
The elevation of the north front is shown in fig. 2131, and of the east front in fig. 2132.

2131

2331. *The Accommodation* is shown in figs. 2133. and 2134., in which *a* is the entrance
porch, communicating with a stair up to the bed-rooms and one down to the kitchens;

2132

b, the living-room; *c*, the kitchen; *d*, the back-kitchen or wash-house; *e*, the pantry;
f, a dairy; and *g, g, h*, three bed-rooms. The position of the lodge relatively to the
road is shown in fig. 2135., in which *i* is the situation of the gate, and *k*, the block plan
of the lodge.

2332. *Remarks.* The plan is commodious and convenient, and the elevation
picturesque. The position of the stairs
in the tower, opening into the lobby, is
good, and the descent of a few steps
from the living-room to the kitchens

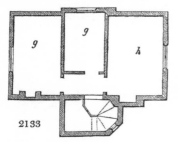

2133

2134

and pantry enables the latter places to be made of a good height in the ceiling, without raising the exterior elevation too high; while, at the same time, it reduces the number of

2135

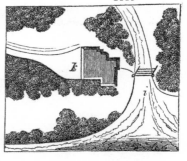

steps necessary for the main stair, the bed-rooms being over that part of the house, and not over the living-room. This way of ar-ranging the stairs is a great comfort both to old people and young children. This lodge was executed some years ago, with some slight variations in the tower and chimney-shafts. Sir Robert Frankland Russell, Bart., the proprietor of Chequers, is a gentleman of high artistical knowledge and taste, and both he and Lady Frankland Russell are devoted to the improvement, not only of their estates here and in Yorkshire, but of the churches and schools in their neighbourhood : both of them are amateur artists.

Design XXXI.— *The Keeper's Lodge at Bluberhouses.* By E. B. Lamb, Esq. F.I.B.A.

2136

This lodge, with some slight variations, was built for Sir R. F. Russell, Bart., on his

2137

estate of Thirkleby Park, in the neighbourhood of Thirsk in Yorkshire, some years ago. The entrance elevation is shown in fig. 2136., and that of the next best front in fig. 2137.

2333. *The Accommodation,* shown in figs. 2138. and 2139., is a porch, *a ;* stair and lobby, *b ;* parlour, *c ;* kitchen, *d ;* back-kitchen, *e ;* pantry and dairy, *f ;* and four bed-rooms, *g, h, i, k.*

2334. *Construction.* The walls are of stone, and the roof is covered with thin flag-stones, or what are called in some parts of the north, slate stones. One of the bedrooms is intended for a lodger.

2335. *Remarks.* The general arrangement of the plan is consistent with the greater part of our data given in p. 1146., though by accident a small window has been omitted in the porch. The spaces between the mullions in the bed-room windows are narrower than the corresponding spaces in the ground-floor windows, which, according to one of Mr. Lamb's principles, ought never to be the case without a sufficient and obvious reason. The fault, doubtless, has been committed by the engraver, in reducing the drawings.

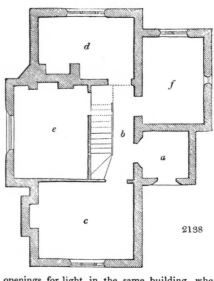

2138

Mr. Lamb's principle is, that all the openings for light in the same building, whether these openings are singly between jambs, or two or more together between jambs and mullions, ought to be of the same width. A certain width is taken as the element or type, and this is repeated, singly or in combination, according to the size of the apartment to be lighted, and quantity of light required, wherever a window is wanted. Another principle might be laid down with respect to the height of windows, viz., that the height of all those on the same floor ought to be the same. To this we may add a third principle, viz., that stair windows should never be on exactly the same horizontal line, and of exactly the same height, as room windows, in order that they may give externally the expression of a stair. Of course, these principles must frequently be modified by others of a higher kind ; as where the window of a chapel forms part of the elevation, or those of a greenhouse or conservatory ; or where the object is the imitation of some old building, in which, to render it faithful as well as characteristic, the accidental deformities must be imitated as well as the accidental beauties.

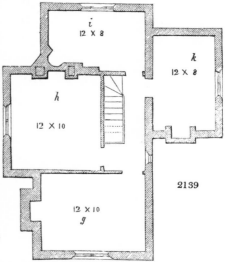

2139

Design XXXII.— *A Cottage in the Gothic Style for an Upper Servant.* By John Dobson, Esq., Architect.

The elevation is shown in fig. 2140., and is in the genuine style of English cottage architecture, purified by the taste of an architect of genius, and of extensive experience, not only as an architect, but as a landscape-gardener. Mr. Dobson's taste in the latter art, it delights us to say, is not inferior to what it is in the former ; and of his practice

in both arts examples may be seen in almost every part of Northumberland and Durham. The ground plan is shown in fig. 2141.

2140

2336. *The Accommodation* (as shown in the plan) consists of a porch, *a*; sitting-room,
fourteen feet by sixteen feet, *b*; kitchen, sixteen feet by fifteen feet, *c*; staircase, *d*;
scullery, thirteen feet six inches by sixteen feet, *e*; pantry, *f*; cow-house, *g*; dairy, *h*;
pigsty, *i*; privy, *k*; dung and ashes, *l*; and coal-house, *m*.

2141

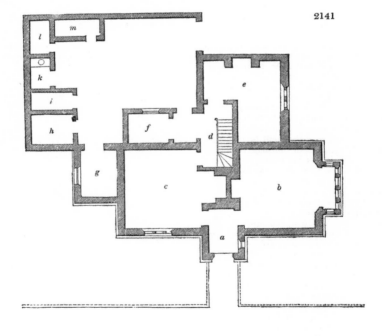

2337. *Remarks.* This cottage was designed for Richard Ellison, Esq., of Ludbrook,
Lincolnshire, and contains accommodation fit either for an upper servant with a family,
or a single gentleman. Of this any one will be convinced by observing the plan; the
upper floor of which may contain a drawingroom over the parlour, and bed-rooms over
the kitchen and scullery, or it may contain only bed-rooms.

Design XXXIII.—*Double Cottage for Two Upper Servants.* By J. Dobson, Esq., Arch.
The elevation is shown in fig. 2142., and the ground plan in fig. 2143.

2142

2338. *Accommodation.* The ground plan of each dwelling exhibits a porch, *a*; sitting-room, fourteen feet by fifteen feet in one house, and ten feet by thirteen feet in the other, with a bed-room over, *b*; staircase, *c*; kitchen, fourteen feet by fifteen feet in one house, and eighteen feet by fifteen feet in the other, with a bed-room over, *d*; scullery, *e*;

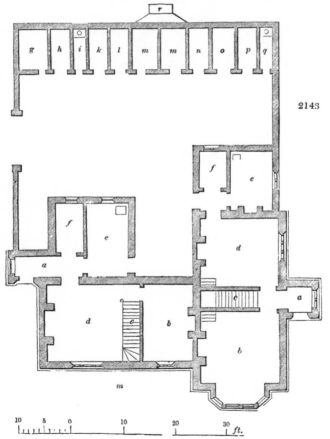

2143

pantry, *f*; dung-pit, *g*; place for ashes, *h*; privy, *i*; coal-house, *k*; pigsty, *l*; cow-houses, *m m*; pigsty, *n*; coals, *o*; dung and ashes, *p*; privy, *q*; liquid-manure tank, *r*.

2339. *Remarks.* The arrangement of the plan is very ingenious, and the elevation is eminently picturesque. With a view to the liquid manure, the two privies ought to have been placed next to the two cow-houses, and next to the privies the pigsties ; because this would have facilitated the conducting of the liquids from these places to the central tank. It is very possible, however, that this oversight may have been made in sketching the plan, which Mr. Dobson most kindly did for us entirely from memory. He also furnished us with a plan for a treble cottage, which we much regret that time has prevented us from having engraved. We shall, however, publish it in the *Gardener's Magazine.* We have shown, in the *Suburban Horticulturist,* how the walls and roofs of fig. 2142. may be covered with grape-vines trained on Mr. Hoare's principle, by which a pound of fruit is produced on every square foot of wall or roof.

Design XXXIV.—*A Cottage in the Old English Style.* By John Dobson, Esq., Architect.

The elevation is shown in fig. 2144., and the ground plan in fig. 2145.

2144

2340. *Accommodation.* The ground plan shows a porch, *a* ; sitting-room, twelve feet

2145

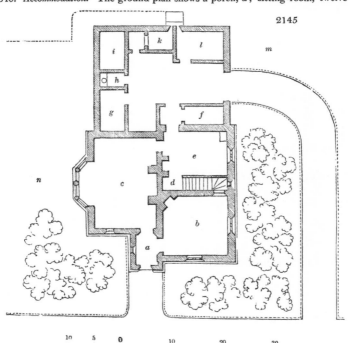

square, *b*; kitchen, twelve feet by eighteen feet, *c*; stair, three feet wide, *d*; scullery, ten feet by twelve feet, *e*; pantry and dairy, *f*; coal-house, *g*; privy, *h*; dung and ashes, *i*; pigsty, *k*; and cow-house, *l*. There is a communication from the cow-house and the pigsty to a liquid manure tank, which is placed behind so as to be centrical to both. There is a wood at *m*, and the garden is at *n*.

2341. *Remarks.* The privy, as we think, ought to have been placed adjoining the cow-house or the pigsty, for the sake of the liquid manure. We should have preferred placing the staircase so as to open into the porch, for Mr. Wilson's reasons, mentioned § 2252.; but this is perhaps being too fastidious. In every other respect we approve of the plan, which is compact, and contains every thing that could be wished; and the elevation we think admirable. This cottage was executed at Lilburn, in Northumberland.

SECT. IV. *Construction and Materials of Cottages.*

2342. We have little to add to what is contained in the Encyclopædia. Some improvements have been made in cottage windows by the Highland Society, and by the Messrs. Strutt of Derby, which will greatly reduce their price and facilitate ventilation. A mode of building brick walls, fourteen inches in thickness, with a very few more bricks than what are required for a solid nine-inch wall, deserves attention for its greater economy and warmth, and also because a wall so constructed can be carried to a greater height without piers than a solid nine-inch wall. The patent brick walls of Mr. Hitch promise to be very durable and economical, though, like other deviations from routine practice, they have not yet become so general as they deserve to be. The mode of building walls of "clay lumps," practised in Suffolk, appears to be both durable and economical, and to make a very dry warm cottage. Cottages that have only walls nine inches in thickness, and roofs covered with slates or tiles, must necessarily be exceedingly cold in winter and too hot in summer; in the former case requiring a great expenditure of fuel, which is almost everywhere scarce and dear. If the walls of a cottage were made two feet in thickness, and the roof covered with one foot in thickness of thatch, heath, spray, or the chips of woodmen, they would be warmer in winter (the floor being perfectly dry) almost without fire, than they are now with it. Whatever heat was generated in the cottage could neither escape through the walls nor the roof; and if the building was placed so that the sun shone on every side of it every day in the year, great part of the heat which was radiated externally from the walls and roof during the night would be replaced during the day. As there is a prejudice against thatch in many parts of the country, there should, where tiles or slates are used, always be a plastered ceiling to the rooms in the roof, made air-tight, and enclosing a vacuity between the plaster and the slates of at least a foot, so as, in fact, to form a double roof: this is the nearest approach that can be made to a thatched roof. If the durability of timber, and especially of young native timber, could be increased by any of the compositions, such as Burnett's, now being experimented with, it would greatly lessen the first cost of cottages, as well as increase their duration. As most of the improvements in the construction of cottages which we have to notice are applicable to farm buildings, and in part to villas as well as to cottages, we have brought the whole together in our fifth chapter, p. 1255., to which we refer the reader. (See Contents in p. 1134.)

SECT. V. *Cottage Fittings-up and Furniture.*

2343. *Little Improvement* has been made in this department. A cheap and economical cottage fire-grate is still a desideratum, and probably will continue to be so till a change takes place in cottage cookery, roasting against open fires is dispensed with, and the value of stews understood. The most economical stove for warming a cottage, and at the same time for cooking food, is, beyond all doubt, in our opinion, the Bruges stove, but unfortunately it cannot at present be procured under £7. If, indeed, there were a general demand for these stoves, they might probably be manufactured at little more than half the price, but the difficulty is to introduce them at all. Next to this stove we would recommend one in very general use, which has a small fireplace in the middle, an oven at one side, and a boiler for water at the other; they cost from £1 to £3 each at the wholesale cast-iron warehouses. If these are carefully set, and the throat of the chimney contracted, so as not to create too great a draught, a good deal of heat will be thrown out into the apartment, though nothing like so much as by the Bruges stove; which, being of iron except the fire-pot, supported on legs, and completely isolated except by the connexion of its small smoke-pipe with the chimney, radiates heat on every side. In various parts of the country a brick oven is used, heated by faggotwood; and if it could be so contrived that this oven could be placed below the kitchen floor, and the smoke conducted from it in a flue under the floor, a large portion of heat now lost would be saved. There is, however, a prejudice against this mode of adding to the heat of a cottage; and, therefore, though we have indicated it in our model designs, we do not expect it will be much followed at the present time. Were some such stove as the Bruges stove employed, such a mode of heating would be in a great measure unnecessary. An improvement has been made in the box bedstead which deserves adoption where that kind of bed is still used; and some minor improvements in furniture and fittings-up, applicable to cottages, will be found in our sections on fittings-up and furniture, in a subsequent page.

SECT. VI. *Villages.*

2344. *The congregating of Cottages in Villages* is attended with many advantages and with very few inconveniences. The advantages are: society; the use of certain articles in common, such as a well or other source of water; a common sewer for drainage; a school; a public wash-house and drying-green; a general play-ground for children; a village library and reading-room; and, if the village is large, a church or chapel, not to mention the proximity of village tradesmen, mechanics, &c. The chief disadvantage that we know is, the distance to which agricultural labourers and out-of-door country mechanics, such as carpenters, masons, &c., have to go to and return from their work. On the Continent, and in this country, cottages and farm-houses were formerly collected together in villages for mutual protection against thieves and wild beasts, and in a more civilised and refined state, they are, or will be, similarly congregated for social comforts and enjoyments. These comforts and enjoyments might be greatly increased, were the art of cooperation for their attainment properly understood; were the village to have a common kitchen, dining-room, wash-house, dairy, &c., as well as a common school and church: but the time has not yet arrived for improvements of this kind, and it would be of little use attempting to introduce them, till every member of society is enlightened and refined by a general system of education, which shall comprehend every kind of useful instruction, communicated alike to all, even the poorest, up to a certain age. Such a national education as we contemplate already exists in some parts of North America and Germany, and will unquestionably, sooner or later, be introduced into this country; but, in the meantime, we must take men as they are, and endeavour to suggest what may be useful for the present generation.

2345. *Rows of Cottages.* Next to congregating cottages together in villages, that of placing them in rows or groups of half a dozen or a dozen is to be recommended; because in this state one cottager may assist another in case of distress, and there is also an opportunity given to the families to mix together occasionally, without which there can be no civilisation. But though such a congregating of cottages as admits of the families associating together at pleasure is desirable, it ought not, in the present state of things, to be carried so far as to compel any two families to come constantly in contact. The selfishness and bad passions are not yet sufficiently under control, nor the benevolent feelings sufficiently developed, for this purpose. For this reason we would as seldom as possible join a row of cottages like the houses of a street, but rather isolate each by surrounding it with its garden. In some cases one family occupies the ground floor of a cottage, and another the floor above, which is in general very disagreeable to both parties. This is also the case when two families enter through the same porch, or through the same front garden, or when cottages joined together have only thin party-walls. Complete isolation, therefore, ought, if possible, to be joined to congregation.

2346. *Solitary Cottages,* such as gate-lodges, cottages for game-keepers, gardeners, &c., are generally not merely isolated, but solitary; but common humanity requires that this solitariness should be mitigated by building some dwellings for persons of similar condition near them. For example, the habitations of the gardener and bailiff might frequently be placed at no great distance from each other, and the dwellings of the carpenter, mason, hedger, and woodman, of a large estate, might form a group. It is unnecessary, however, to go into details; it is sufficient to direct attention to the general principle, founded as it is on the fact, that man is a social animal, and only to be improved in manners and increased in happiness by social intercourse.

2347. *Laying out Villages.* The most beautiful villages in Britain are, for the most part, the result of accident, heightened by the taste of the proprietor of the estate; as, for example, in the case of Dirleton, one of the handsomest villages in Scotland, or of Harlaxton, one of the most picturesque in England. There are many very formal and disagreeable villages, designed purposely to be ornamental, or to give consequence to the entrance-lodge of a mansion; and if we compare these with an agreeable village that has sprung up by accident, we shall soon find what we should imitate and what we should avoid. In villages the houses ought never to be put down in rows, even though detached, unless the ground and other circumstances are favourable for a strictly regular or symmetrical congregation of dwellings. There is not a greater error in forming artificial villages, or in placing houses by road-sides, either singly or in rows, than always having one side of the building parallel with the road. Instead of making this a leading principle in the country, it ought to be a subordinate one; since it is unfavourable both to the comfort and enjoyment of the cottager, and the beauty of the cottage and the scenery. It is unfavourable to the comfort of the cottager, because it often requires his cottage to be set down with one side to the south and another to the north; whereas, as we have shown in a hundred places, one of the fundamental principles of setting down a house, whether a cottage or a palace, ought to be to place it so that the diagonal to its square shall be a south and north line. It is unfavourable to the cottager's enjoyment, because, as the principal room is generally placed next the road, the occupant is forced to look directly across the road, which is the dullest and stupidest view that the situation admits, and not for a moment to be compared with looking obliquely across or along the road; while, if the front is to the south, it is impossible for the occupant to look out at the windows during the finest part of a sunny day. These arrangements are unfavourable to the picturesque beauty of the cottages composing the village, because it necessarily produces a great degree of sameness in the manner in which they group with the scenery. On the other hand, when the principle of the diagonal line is constantly kept in view, the cottages on both sides of a road, even if they were built all of the same form, can never be placed in the same manner; and the moment the idea of the usual dull repetition of the same forms in the same relative positions is got rid of, that moment the idea of picturesque beauty begins: the cottages will be put down in all manner of positions; some will be nearer the road than others, some will look across it at one angle, and some at another; if the general surface of the ground is uneven, some will stand on a higher level than others; and if the direction of the road should be any other than straight, the general effect will be every thing that could be wished. It cannot be too strongly impressed on the mind of the reader, that the idea of putting down all cottages that are built along a road with their sides or ends parallel to that road is destructive of all picturesque beauty. The idea of doing so can only have arisen from the practice of building streets in towns, where the great value of the land obliges the builder to place the houses as close together as possible, and where, in consequence of this, the only part seen by the public is the front; but even in towns, where this continuity of frontage is interrupted by projecting buildings and retiring ones, the beauty and variety of the elevations is greatly increased.

2348. *Every Character of Surface is adapted for a particular Character of Village*, but on all surfaces it is necessary to the full enjoyment of the advantages of congregation, that there should be a certain degree of concentration. Every cottage in a village should be surrounded with its own garden ground, and nothing more. If fields are allowed to intervene, the too great separation of the cottages will interfere with the advantages of concentration. Nevertheless, we are far from asserting that all the cottage gardens ought to be of the same size; on the contrary, variety will be produced by a difference in this respect, as well as by a difference in the accommodation and style of the cottages. The dwelling of the clergyman and of the schoolmaster will not only be larger than the others, but will have more ground attached; and there may be a row of almshouses with very little ground, and, in the outskirts of the village, a union workhouse with a great deal. The most favourable surface for a regular or symmetrical arrangement of roads and dwellings is one that is perfectly even. In a village on such a surface all the water will generally be obtained from wells. A village on a knoll, with the church or school in the centre, will not be so favourably supplied with water; but one on the side of a hill will generally have water in abundance, which, as it descends from the upper to the lower part of the declivity, may form a succession of fountains of different kinds, which is beautifully effected in the village of Great Tew in Oxfordshire; and will generally prove highly ornamental as well as useful, because, without abundance of water, there can be no efficient cleanliness. In all villages there ought to be a system of drainage for carrying off the superfluous rain and subsoil water, and the overflowings of the liquid-manure tanks; though, if these tanks are properly attended to, they will never be suffered to run their precious contents to waste. Villages along rivers or streams ought always to have an intercepting drain close to the river, and parallel with it, to keep its waters pure, and at the same time to remove from the village what is superfluous. It is almost needless, to observe that the main drain of a village, like that of a field, ought to commence at a lower level than that of the surface to be drained, and that this may frequently be at some distance. It is no part of our business here to speak of the sewerage of large towns, otherwise we would recommend to notice the improvements suggested for the London sewers by Mr. Roe in the *Sanitary Report;* nor does it form part of our plan to speak of the formation of towns, otherwise we should refer to Fleetwood in Lancashire, one of the best arranged artificial towns, and at the same time one of the most prosperous in the empire. We shall conclude this section by an account of the village of Harlaxton in Lincolnshire, the property of Gregory Gregory, Esq., of Harlaxton Manor, a gentleman of the most refined taste in architecture and gardening, and who devotes his time and his income to the display of these arts on his estate in a manner which we cannot sufficiently admire.

2349. *The Village of Harlaxton* is situated about nine miles from Grantham, in Lincolnshire, and occupies a portion of the bottom of a broad fertile valley, through which runs a stream of pure water, that expands into a broad pond near the ancient Manor House of Harlaxton, one of the oldest manorial dwellings in England.   We have seen many ornamented villages, both at home and abroad, but none so original, and so much to our taste, as this of Mr. Gregory's.   Some of old date are too like rows of street houses, such as those of Newnham Courtenay near Oxford, and Harewood near Leeds ; others are too affectedly varied and picturesque, such as that at Blaize Castle near Bristol ; and some have the houses bedaubed with ornaments that have not sufficient relation to use, as when rosettes and sculptures are stuck on the walls, instead of facings being applied to the windows, porches to the doors, and characteristic shafts to the chimney-tops.   We recollect one near Warsaw, which is a repetition of the Grecian temple, with a portico at each end ; and one at Peckra, near Moscow, every opening in which has a pediment over it, with highly enriched barge-boards.   In some villages, the attempt is made to ornament every house by trelliswork round the doors and windows, which produces great sameness of appearance, and, if ornamental, is so at the expense of comfort ; the creepers, by which the trelliswork is covered, darkening the rooms, and encouraging insects ; while, in other villages, the cottages are so low and so small, that it is obvious to a passing spectator that they cannot contain a single wholesome room.   However, though we find fault with villages ornamented in these ways, we are still glad to see them ; because any kind of alteration in the dwellings and gardens of country labourers can hardly fail to be an improvement on their present state, both with reference to the occupiers and to the country at large.

The great value of Mr. Gregory's improvements in the village of Harlaxton is, that all the leading features have some kind of relation to use, and are, in fact, to be considered more as parts added to the very plainest cottages, in order to render them complete, than as ornaments put on to render them beautiful.   All the cottages were built by Mr. Gregory's predecessor in the plainest possible style, but fortunately substantial and comfortable, and two stories high ; some of them single, and some of them double ; and almost all of them of stone, some yards back from the street, and surrounded by ample gardens.   In improving them, Mr. Gregory would appear to have been guided by the following considerations : —

1. *To bestow the principal expense on the main features, such as the porch, the chimney-tops, and the gardens.*   Almost all the cottages have porches, some projecting from the walls, and others forming recesses: the latter have sometimes open places like loggias over them ; and the former, sometimes roofs in the usual manner, sometimes balconies, and occasionally small rooms with gable-ends, or pavilion roofs, according to the style.   The greatest attention has been paid to the chimney-tops, which are in some cases of brick, and in others of stone ; sometimes of English domestic Gothic, at other times local English, such as those common in the neighbourhood of the Lakes or in Derbyshire, &c. ; Italian, French, or Swiss, chimney-tops, of different kinds, also occur.   The gable-ends are finished with crow-steps in the Belgian and Scotch style in some cases, with Gothic parapets in others ; and various descriptions of barge-boards are used, wherever the roof projects over the end walls.   Porches, cornices of brick or stone, ornamental cornice boards, and stone or wooden brackets, are also introduced in front, as supports or ornaments to the roof.   Every garden has been laid out and planted by Mr. Gregory's head gardener ; creepers and climbers being introduced in proper places, in such a manner as that no two gardens are planted with the same climbers.

2. *Always to have some architectural feature in or about the garden, as well as on the cottage.*   For example, almost every garden here has its draw-well, and each of these wells is rendered architectural, and ornamented in a different way.   All the wells are surrounded by parapets, either circular or square, of openwork or solid.   Some are covered with roofs supported by carpentry, others with roofs supported by stones, round or square ; some are in the form of stone cupolas: in some, the water is raised by buckets suspended from a picturesque architectural appendage ; in others, it is raised by pumps attached to wooden framework of most original construction, massive and architectural ; and so on.   All the gardens are of course separated from the street by a fence, and there are not two of these fences in the village exactly alike.   Some are hedges rising from the inside of dwarf walls ; some are walls like those of sunk fences, the garden in the inside being of the height of the top of the wall, which is covered in some cases with a plain stone coping, in others with a brick coping ; in some with a stone coping in the Gothic manner, in others with an Elizabethan coping ; in some with a parapet of open-

work, in others with stone or brick piers for supporting horizontal bars of wood for creepers, as in Italy, or without being connected by bars of wood, but terminating in rough earthenware jars for flowers. Each front wall must, of course, have a gateway to enter to the garden and the cottage, and no two of these gateways throughout the village are alike. Some are wickets between wooden posts, others Gothic or Elizabethan gates between stone piers, square or round ; some are close gates, in the manner of many in Switzerland, in others the gates are under arches, some of which are pointed, and others round-headed ; some have pediments over the arches, others horizontal high-raised copings, as in the neighbourhood of Naples ; and some have small wooden roofs or canopies after the manner of the gateways to the country houses in the neighbourhood of Dantzic. The gateways, in short, afford great variety of character. Besides the front boundaries of the gardens, there are the side boundaries, which are also varied, partly in a similar manner, and partly differently. In some cases, the boundary, though sufficiently well known to the occupants, does not appear at all to the stranger ; in others it is of holly, of box, of laurel, of thorn, of flowering shrubs, of fruit trees, or of a mixture of several or all of these, with or without architectural piers, bee-houses, arbours, covered seats, tool-sheds, or other appendages. The gardens, it may be observed, are all laid out differently. In some, the main walk from the street gate to the porch is of flagstone, in others it is paved with small stones ; in some with wood, in others with brick ; in some with gravel, and in others with broken stone It is edged with box, with thyme, with ivy, with a broad belt of turf, with a raised edging of stone, or with a flat belt of brick, and sometimes even with wood. The gardens are variously planted, and in some there are very properly trees and shrubs clipped into artificial shapes ; two spruce firs form very handsome balls.

3. *Never to employ two styles or manners of architecture in the same cottage, or at all events not to do this so frequently as to lead a stranger to suppose that it has been done through ignorance.* We omit what may be said on the necessity of keeping the recognised eras of the Gothic distinct, as well as the Elizabethan, Swiss, Italian, &c., as sufficiently obvious. In every cottage and its accompaniments, the appearance of one system of construction should prevail, as well as one prevailing direction in the lines of the masses. For example, in a Swiss cottage, with its far projecting eaves and its surrounding balcony, horizontal masses, lines, and shadows are decidedly prevalent ; and, beyond a certain point required for contrast, it is not desirable to introduce any vertical masses, lines, or shadows. The windows, therefore, in such a house, should be broad rather than high ; and, as those of the ground floor are protected from the weather by the balcony, and those of the upper floor by the projecting eaves, the very simplest form of dressings to the doors and windows is all that is required. To surround them with rich dressings, or protect them by cornices or pediments, such as indicate the purpose of throwing off the rain, or casting a shade on the glass, would be in bad taste, because it would be superfluous, or working for an end that could not be attained ; it would, in fact, be counteracting nature, and setting at nought the principles of art ; not to speak of weakening the associations connected with style independently of the use of parts of walls and roofs.

4. *Not altogether to omit objects purely ornamental, where they can be introduced with propriety.* There is no reason why a cottage garden should not have its sculptural ornaments as well as the garden of a palace ; and it is quite reasonable that in both cases the occupant should endeavour to get the best ornaments he can afford. Formerly, the doctrine used to be, that the dwelling of the cottager ought to be low, in order to be expressive of humility ; and void of exterior ornaments except creepers and flowers, to express the condition of life, or, in other words, the poverty of the inhabitant. But the cottager is now becoming a reading and thinking being ; and having a taste for health, comfort, and ornament, in common with other classes of society, he requires higher and better lighted and ventilated rooms ; and these, as well as his garden, he will ornament as far as his circumstances will permit. The time has gone by for one class of society to endeavour to mark another with any badge whatever ; and therefore we would wish all architects, when designing cottages, to abandon their long received ideas. " In the construction of cottages, as well as of all other kinds of buildings, great care should be taken that every part should be in its proper character ; for nothing can appear more absurd or out of place, than to see mouldings or ornaments which belong to the regular styles of architecture introduced in a cottage." This was published in 1805, in a work on Labourers' Cottages, by an architect of eminence ; but in 1840, in the recently improved cottages throughout the country, we see the "mouldings and ornaments which belong to the regular styles of architecture " as carefully applied as in larger dwellings ; and, fortunately, vases of the most elegant forms are so cheap, that no cottage parapet, seat, or bee-house, need be without them. What is most offensive to taste, both in the gardens of the wealthy and of the poor, is the misplacing of sculptural ornaments. In

Harlaxton village there are sundials and vases, of different forms and kinds, most judiciously placed; for example, as terminations to piers to gates, or along parapets on piers or other preparations, on the piers at the ends of stone seats, &c.   In how many instances, not only in cottage gardens and on cottages, but in the gardens and on the buildings of the wealthy classes, do we not see vases set down where they have no legitimate right to be placed whatever; in places from which they might be removed without ever being missed, or without any derangement to the scene in which they were put, but of which, in an artistical sense, they formed no part.   Some of the situations proper for vases are : where the vase forms a termination to an object, as to a pillar of a gate, a pier or pilaster in a wall, or a detached column, &c. ; where lines of walks or of walls join, meet, or intersect, as in the centre of a system of beds for flowers, or at the angles made by the junction of walks in a pleasure-ground ; where niches in buildings, or gravelled or other recesses along walks, are prepared for them, &c.   In all cases where a vase is put down in a garden, it ought not only to have a base formed of one or more plinths, but a pedestal to raise the vase nearer the eye, and above the surrounding vegetation, as well as to give it dignity of character.   No ornament whatever, whether in a garden or on a building, ought ever to be placed in an inconspicuous situation, or in the less noble parts of the grounds or edifice ; and no ornament ought to be made use of which is formed of a material of less value or durability than the material or object on or against which it is to be placed.   Hence the bad effect of rootwork and rusticwork in many situations in gardens, and in verandas and other additions or accompaniments to brick or stone houses.

5. *To indicate the occupation of the inhabitant, where it can be done.*   For example, the smithy, or blacksmith's forge, when properly introduced, can never be mistaken, nor the carpenter's shop.   These two village tradesmen require houses, yards, and gardens, peculiarly arranged, and afford fine sources of variety.   The shoemaker may have his stall as a projecting appendage, and the tailor his workshop.   Some of the cottagers will possess cows, others pigs or rabbits ; some pigeons, and all more or less poultry.   The provision required to be made for these kinds of live stock affords interesting sources of architectural and picturesque effect; though in small villages a common cow-shed, as well as a common bakehouse, wash-house, and drying-ground, is frequently found preferable.   The house of the schoolmaster adjoining the village-school, and the house of the clergyman near the church, will always be principal objects ; and shops for the sale of different articles speak by their windows.   Every large village ought to have an open shed, or other public building, in a central situation, to serve as a kind of market or gossiping place, and also as a playground, or place of amusement, for the boys in rainy weather.

Whoever intends to ornament and improve a village, we would strongly recommend to study Harlaxton.   It is impossible to reflect on that village without imagining what a continued scene of ornament and appearance of comfort all England, and even all Europe, would present, if proprietors would follow the example of Mr. Gregory.   Happily, in this country, many have been engaged in this work for a number of years, and considerable progress has certainly been made.   Though the best mode to succeed is to have the very best advice at the commencement, and submit every elevation that is to be carried into effect to an architect of taste, yet let those who do not value advice of this kind make the attempt with what knowledge they have, or can derive from books, or from observing what has been done by others, and they cannot fail to do good to a considerable extent.   The way to insure artistical buildings throughout the country is, not so much here and there to employ a first-rate architect, who may erect a splendid mansion with a handsome cottage as an entrance-lodge, as to create a demand for architectural taste and knowledge among country builders, carpenters, masons, and bricklayers, generally, since it is by these persons that the great majority of country buildings are both designed and executed.   For the general improvement of cottages, therefore, we must educate the eye of the country carpenter and mason, and give the cottager himself a taste for architectural and gardenesque beauty.

The Village of Edensor at Chatsworth, which was beginning to be improved when we last saw it in 1839, is said by a writer in the *Gardener's Chronicle* to be a dell gradually opening as it descends gently towards the park, profusely studded with architectural gems.   " The buildings embrace houses of almost every calibre, from the spacious farmhouse to the humble cottage, and they are distributed with admirable skill ; some on the level ground at the mouth of the dell, and others on gentle declivities, while not a few overhang the brow of a precipice, or occupy a snug position that has been excavated out of the solid rock.   The buildings are entirely of stone, except where enriched wooden gables or other ornamental carvings have been introduced ; and they present a perfect compendium of all the prettiest styles of cottage architecture, from the sturdy Norman to the sprightly Italian."   (*Gard. Chron.* for 1842, p. 187.)

CHAP. II.

Cottage Villas and Villas.

Design I.—*A Villa in the Swiss Style.* By E. B. Lamb, Esq., F. I. B. A.
The elevation is shown in fig. 2146., and the ground plan in fig. 2147.

2146

2350. *Accommodation.* The plan shows a covered doorway, with the house-bell over, *a*; entrance-court, *b*; porch to the house, *c*; hall, and staircase to drawingroom and bedrooms, *d*; study, sixteen feet by twelve feet six inches, *e*; dining-room, twenty feet by

2147

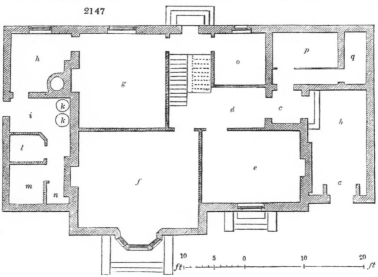

sixteen feet six inches, with drawingroom over, *f*; kitchen, sixteen feet by fifteen feet, *g*; back-kitchen, with boiler, *h*; kitchen-court, *i*; two buts for holding the water from the roof, *k k*; place for dust and ashes, *l*; for coals, *m*; and servants' water-closet, *n*.

2351. *Remarks.* This design was made by Mr. Lamb for John Murray, Esq., the author of many esteemed works on natural and experimental science, who intends it for a very interesting situation on his property in the neighbourhood of Stranraer. Here it will be backed by a steep wooded bank on which Mr. Murray has created various interesting scenes and walks, and will have a rich garden immediately before it, bordered by the magnificent bay of Stranraer, and in the distance a range of mountains. It will be executed at a very moderate expense, from there being abundance of stone on the spot, and from the great simplicity of the roof, which does not contain a single gutter, and on which there are neither hips nor valleys. The estimated cost is about £650. In the neighbourhood of London it would cost considerably more.

Design II.—*A Villa adapted for a Situation in the Neighbourhood of Ayr.* By E. B. Lamb, Esq., F. I. B. A.

The elevation is shown in fig. 2148., and the ground plan in fig. 2149.

2148

2352. *Accommodation.* The plan shows a porch, *a*; hall, *b*; dining-room, eighteen feet six inches by fifteen feet, *c*; parlour, fifteen feet six inches by thirteen feet six inches, *d*; staircase, with closet under, *e*; kitchen, *f*; scullery, *g*; pantry, *h*; and back entrance, *i*. In the floor of the dining-room, *e*, there is a bath, the lid to which opens like a trap-door, and the descent is by steps, as in the design for a parsonage-house, by Mr. Barry, in p. 841. The bath is supplied with hot water from the boiler in the scullery, *g*, and with cold water from a cistern also in the back kitchen.

2353. *Remarks.* This design was made for a situation in the neighbourhood of Ayr, nearly flat, with a command of the sea. The walls are of freestone, and of considerable thickness to insure warmth. The design is massive and original. The estimated expense is about £500.

2149

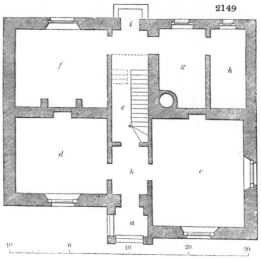

Design III. — *A small Villa in the Modern Style.* By E. B. Lamb, F. I. B. A.
The elevation is shown in fig. 2150., and the plan in fig. 2151.

2150

2354. *Accommodation.* The plan shows an entrance-porch, *a*; hall, *b*; dining-room, twelve feet by ten feet, *c*; parlour, ten feet by nine feet, *d*; staircase, with closet under, *e*; kitchen, ten feet by nine feet, *f*; water-closet, *g*; back entrance, *h*; pantry, *i*; scullery, *k*; and place for coals and lumber, *l*.

2355. *Remarks.* The staircase is lighted from the tower, and there may be a borrowed light either from the staircase or the passage to the water-closet, which, being completely within the house, is less likely to be injured during severe frosts. As the situation is on a level with the sea, and quite near it, a saltwater bath might easily be contrived in a cellar, or under the floor of one of the parlours. Estimated expense about £500.

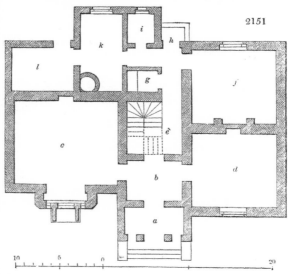

2151

Design IV. — *A small Villa for a Gentleman much attached to Gardening.*

2356. *Covering the Walls with Vines or Fruit Trees.* Fig. 2152. is the front elevation of this design, in which is shown the manner of covering the walls of a house with vines and fruit trees. There are seven vines, *a* to *g*; and four fruit trees, *h* to *l*. The vines *d* and *e* are trained in the Thomery manner, each with two arms, which produce short bearing shoots, to fill that part of the wall which is under the sill of the parlour window, and between the bed-room windows and the roof. The other vines are all trained in Mr. Hoare's manner, each with two arms, and each arm producing only two shoots, viz., one for bearing, shown by wavy lines in the figure, and the other for producing wood, which is indicated by dotted lines. The length of the wavy lines may vary from five feet to ten feet; and there is no limit to the length of the main stems, but the height

2152

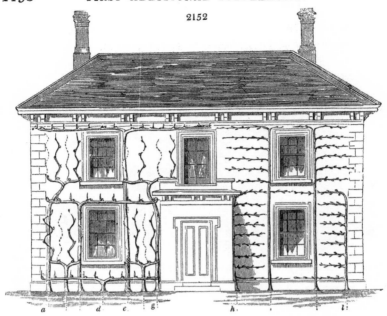

of the wall or house.   The fruit trees, *h, l,* on the lower part of the wall may be apples, cherries, or plums, and those on the upper part pears.

2153

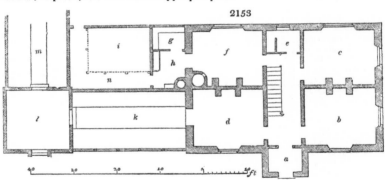

2357. *Accommodation.*   The ground plan, fig. 2153., shows a porch, *a*; dining-room, sixteen feet by fourteen feet, *b*; library, fifteen feet by fifteen feet, *c*; drawingroom, of the same dimensions as the dining-room, *d*; water-closet, *e*; kitchen, *f*; pantry, *g*; back-kitchen, *h*; open court, *i*; conservatory, opening into the drawingroom, *k*; tea-room, three steps higher than the floor of the conservatory, *l*; propagating-house, *m*; and covered way to the garden and to the stoke-hole to the propagating-house *n*.   The bed-room floor, fig. 2154., shows four good bed-rooms, each with two closets, and a water-closet, *o*.

2154

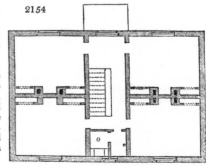

2358. *Remarks.* This design was made for a retired mercantile man, who has given himself up to the culture of his garden, in the open air during summer, and in his propagating-house during winter and early spring.

Design V.—*Annat Cottage, near Errol, Perthshire.* By Archibald Gorrie, Esq., F.H.S., &c.

The elevation is shown in the isometrical view, fig. 2157. ; the plan in fig. 2155., and the section on the line A B in fig. 2156.

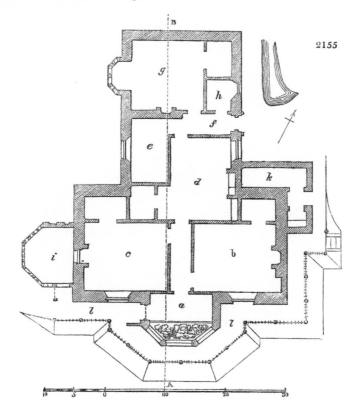

2359. *Accommodation.* The plan, fig. 2155., contains a lobby with flower-stage, *a* ; sitting-room, *b* ; stranger's bed-room, *c* ; kitchen, *d* ; writing-closet, *e* ; lobby or passage,*f* ; bed-room, *g* ; pantry, *h* ; greenhouse, *i* ; place for fuel, *k* ; raised terrace, with open veranda, on which roses may be trained as seen in the isometrical view, *l.*

2360. *Description.* Lofty trees surround the cottage on three sides, and I feared that this might cause the chimneys to smoke, to prevent which, on the plan of Dr. Dicks of Broughtyferry, I caused the masons to contract the chimney flues about eighteen inches above the lower part of the lintel to about seven inches square, widening gradually to ten inches. This had the effect of promoting a draught, and keeping the rooms clear from smoke. The place for plants in the lobby is two feet and a half above the floor ; it contains a small space in the centre for silver or gold fish. The pots are plunged in fine sand, removable at pleasure. Under this floor is ample room for cellarage. The terrace, suggested by several plans in your excellent work, is generally admired. I preferred reeds to slates, as more in character with the cottage and grounds. The veranda pillars are covered with Noisette and other roses, reaching over the terrace walk on cross rafters, three or four feet separate, to admit light. The cottage is happily

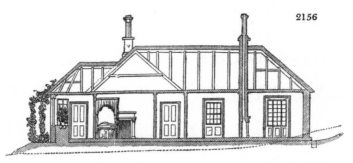

2156

situated, having a finely wooded background, with an extensive view of the rich vale of the Carse of Gowrie in front, and is generally reckoned a good thing of its kind. The artificial stone chimney-tops seem to stand the weather well, and, at a very cheap rate, add to the safety from fire by conveying the sparks to a considerable height above the reeds. They also, it is thought, improve the appearance of the roof. — *A. G.*

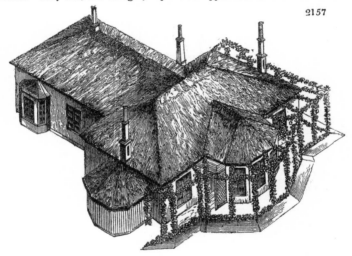

2157

2361. *Remarks.* We admire this design exceedingly, and we are informed by our friend, Robert Chambers, Esq., the editor of the most useful journal of the age, who occasionally spends a day or two with Mr. Gorrie, that the house is as comfortable within, as its exterior is picturesque. The terrace, the veranda, the plant-stage on the entrance-lobby, and the greenhouse, heated from the room *c*, and doubtless looked into through a window over the fireplace, have a fine effect in elevating the character of the cottage, and bringing it within the regions of elegance and taste.

Design VI.—*A Cottage in the Old English Style.*   By John Robertson, Esq., Architect.

The elevation is shown in fig 2160.; the ground plan in fig. 2158., and the bed-room floor in fig. 2159.

2362. *Description.* This cottage is about to be built in Berkshire, for a gentleman with a small family. The ground to be attached to it is chiefly level throughout, with the exception of a raised bank near the adjoining property, which would have been the best site for the intended building; but the proprietor objected to this situation, lest at a future period his neighbour should erect any thing near the cottage that might 'give annoyance, or appear disagreeable. It was not likely that this would be the case ; but its bare possibility led the proprietor and architect to adopt a situation at the opposite extremity of the ground, near the public road. The first object in choosing this latter site was to select the highest and driest spot, and that whence the most extensive and best view could be obtained from the windows, as well as to secure the greatest seeming extent of pleasure-gardens when the ground should be properly laid out.

The entrance-porch was originally in the garden front, in the situation of the ante-room, fig. 2159., and the approach swept round the east end of the building from the public road behind; but here again the proprietor suggested that, while the chief front was to the south, and consequently facing the pleasure-grounds, he should like the entrance-porch to be behind, or to the north; as it would, he thought, give the family, in his absence, a feeling of greater security in so lonely a spot, by having the entrance to the public road. The plan was, therefore, altered to suit these views, and is here presented in its amended form.

The building is to stand about fifteen or sixteen yards from the road, and is to be approached by a covered way to the entrance, from which no view will be had on either side. This arrangement is intended to carry out the idea, that however ill chosen or unsatisfactory the situation may appear to a visitor on his first entrance, yet, when taken to the sitting-room windows, or to the lawn in front, he would be rather surprised, and ready to give up his first impressions as to the inapropriateness of the site.

The family at present being small, the two servants kept are to occupy one of the up-stairs bed-rooms; but should the family become larger, it is intended to raise the wing containing the wash-house, &c., and make two bed-rooms over for the servants.

2363. *Accommodation.* Fig. 2158. is the ground plan, in which *a* is the entrance-porch, which is to be finished with a coved roof, and to have Gothic niches in the angles for statues, &c. From this we pass to the hall and staircase, *b*, by a Venetian door, the upper part of which is glazed with stained glass; thence to a small ante-room, *c*, from

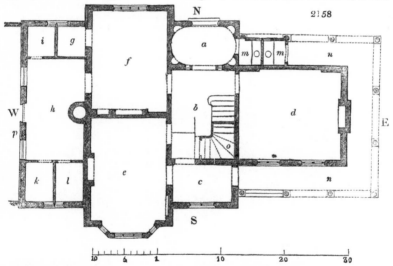

which there is a door to the covered terrace, *n*. From the hall we enter the dining-room, *d*, the two windows of which are to be brought down to the floor, and to open like French casements, so as to admit of easy access to the terrace when the ante-room is occupied. From the hall we likewise enter the drawingroom, *e*, which has a door to the ante-room; also the kitchen, *f*. The kitchen-door from the hall is finished on the staircase side in the same manner as the doors of the principal rooms. This door will only be occasionally used as an entrance from the porch to the kitchen, as there is a back entrance through the yard and wash-house for servants, &c. From the kitchen there is a coal-closet, *g*; back-kitchen or wash-house, with copper, *h*; place for cleaning knives, &c., *i*; larder, *k*; store-closet or pantry, *l*. There are two water-closets, *m m*, both under cover, one entering from the porch, and the other from the terrace. Under the principal stairs is a flight of steps, *o*, shut in by a door, descending to the wine and beer cellars, &c., which are underneath the dining-room and terrace, and are lighted from grated openings in the paved flooring of the latter. Behind the wash-house, at *p*, there is a kitchen-yard hid by shrubbery in front, which contains the undressed meat larder, coal-shed, wood-house, privy, well, drying-ground, &c.

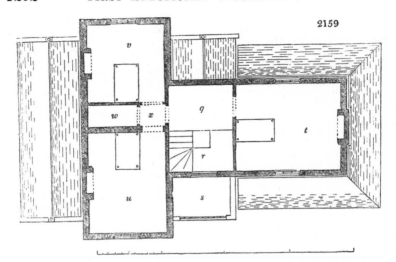

2159

Fig. 2159. is the plan of the chamber floor, in which *q* and *r* show the landing and stairs; *s*, balcony over ante-room, entered from the staircase window; *t*, principal bedroom; *u*, second bed-room; *v*, third bed-room; *w*, linen closet; *x*, lobby.

Fig. 2160. is a perspective view of the south and east fronts.

2160

A few other apartments and conveniences might have been introduced in this design, did the amount to be expended and the size of the family warrant it, but this not being the case, the architect's endeavour was to make the most of the means allowed him, and to produce a comfortable little habitation for a gentleman of limited income.   His instructions were, to design "a neat cottage in a Gothic style, with a covered terrace, that should contain two sitting-rooms and three bed-rooms, with other conveniences, and the estimate not to exceed from £650 to £700."   How far he has succeeded he leaves the reader to judge.

2364. *Specification.*   The foundations are to be eighteen inches thick, with proper footings, and the walls carried up of fourteen-inch brickwork ; the best grey stocks to be used externally, and to be picked of a uniform colour for the fronts, and finished with a neat straight joint.   The openings all round, and chimneys, to be faced with cement in imitation of stone. The roof of the terrace to be supported by rustic limbs of trees, having the bark left on, and placed on stone plinths, with wooden caps, frieze, and cornice. The pendants and finials to gables to be of oak, and the verges to be finished with moulded boards, and ornamental hangings, of 1½-inch well seasoned deal, painted in imitation of oak. The bow window to be finished above the level of the sills with wood painted in imitation of oak, and covered with lead. The roofs to be covered with countess slates laid on ⅝-inch deal boarding, with proper lead flashings to chimney-shafts. The ridges and valleys to be covered with lead. The windows to be splayed and finished with mullions and transoms, as shown by the drawings. The balcony to have an ornamental iron railing in front. The flues to be ten inches by twelve inches, except that of the kitchen, which is to be twelve inches by fourteen inches. The terrace wall, above the surface, to be bounded by a stone plinth, and the door steps and steps from the terrace to the garden to be of York stone. The bearing timbers to be of the best Dantzic or Memel fir, with oak sleepers for the ground floor, and oak lintels over the openings, &c. The windows to be glazed with the best second crown glass.

The interior to be finished with the best well seasoned yellow deal, in a plain but substantial manner, and all the door panels, mouldings, room cornices, chimney-pieces, and other finishing, characteristic of style, to be of a Gothic description. The stairs to have an ornamental Gothic railing or balustrade, and boarded in from the string to the floor. The upper part of the door from the hall to the ante-room to be glazed with stained glass. The whole of the woodwork, externally, to be painted in imitation of oak.

2365. *Estimate*, including the out-offices, &c., about £670.

Design VII.—*A small Roman Villa.* By E. B. Lamb, Esq., F.I.B.A.

An elevation of the garden front is shown in fig. 2161., and fig. 2162. shows the ground plan.

2161

2366. *The Accommodation* which the latter contains is, an entrance hall, *a*; drawing-room, *b*; library, *c*; dining-room, *d*; passage to the kitchen and stairs to the bed-rooms and cellars, *e*; kitchen, *f*; back-kitchen, *g*; pantry, *h*; conservatory, *i*; and terrace and stairs on the lawn front, *k*. On the floor above are three good bed-rooms and a servant's bed-room; and on the cellar floor there are a dairy, larder, and other conveniences required for servants' use.

2367. *Remarks.* This casino was designed for a citizen, chiefly for the purpose of occasional re-tirement. During the greater part of the week, the only occupants will be the gardener and his wife. There is a stable, coach-house, and other offices, at a short dis-tance; and the whole is surrounded by a lawn, enclosed by a shrubbery,

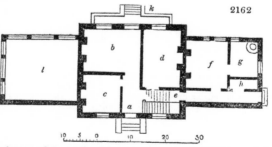

2162

in which the height of the plants, and especially of the evergreens, is calculated to exclude other houses or buildings, and admit, as much as possible, such verdant scenery as is characteristic of the country. Over the fireplaces in *b* and *c* there are windows into the conservatory, each of which consists of one plate of glass, without bars. There is no communication between the rooms and the conservatory by doors, a prejudice existing in the family against the moist air essential to healthy and vigorous vegetation.

Design VIII.—*A Roman Villa, designed for a particular Situation.*   By E. B. Lamb,
Esq., F.I.B.A.

The front elevation is shown in fig. 2163.   This villa was designed by Mr. Lamb
for one of those beautiful knolls which occur on the Dover road, between Dartford and
Canterbury.   Like the preceding design, it was made at the desire of a wealthy
citizen, chiefly for the purpose of enabling him to display his wealth and taste to his

2163

friends on holidays.   Hence, as it will be observed in the plan, fig. 2164., all the rooms
are arranged for the purpose of display, and the whole building is surrounded by an
elevated paved terrace, which commands, on every side, the scenery of one of the richest
and best of England's counties, and her noblest river.

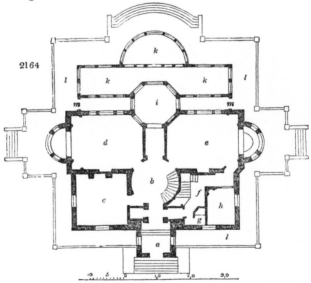

2164

2368. *The Accommodation* contained in the principal floor consists of an entrance-porch,
a; lobby, hall, and staircase, *b*; library, *c*; drawingroom, *d*; dining-room, *e*; back-stairs,
f; water-closet, *g*; dressing-room for day visitors, *h*; statuary room, *i*; conservatory,
k k k; and terrace, *l*.   There is a passage between the conservatory and the house,
which is shut up at the ends so as to form an aviary, and the birds can be admitted to
the conservatory, the drawingroom, the dining-room, and the sculpture room at pleasure.
2369. *Remarks.*   The windows to the offices have each small sunk areas, taken from
the terrace, and covered with iron grating.   These windows, though not seen in the
elevation, being concealed by the terrace parapet, yet reach nearly three feet above the
level of the terrace, so that there is abundance of light to all the lower apartments.   By
closing the doors at the ends of the covered passage *m m*, and taking out the conservatory windows on that side, the width of the conservatory may be increased at pleasure;
and by taking out the windows of the dining-room and drawingroom, the conservatory

may be united to them, so as to have the appearance of the whole being only one apartment, or, rather, one Oriental garden. In the centre of the aviary there may be a fountain; and in the sculpture saloon there ought only to be one group of statues in the centre, and one statue against each of the eight piers between the windows, in order not to interrupt the view of the conservatory and the fountain from the saloon and the two principal rooms. The conservatory is heated by hot water, from the sunk story.

Designs IX. to XII.— *Small Villas in the Gothic Style.* By E. B. Lamb, Esq.

These villas are some out of a number that were designed by Mr. Lamb for a gentleman who had taken an extensive tract of land in Kent, not far from Gravesend, on a building speculation. As it ultimately failed, none of them were erected, except one, which, with some variations, was built by a gentleman in the neighbourhood.

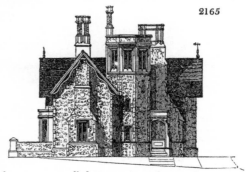

2165

2370. Design IX. is shown in elevation in fig. 2165.; and the plan, fig. 2166., contains on the principal floor an entrance-porch, *a*; staircase, *b*; lobby, *c*; drawingroom, *d*; dining-room, communicating with the drawingroom by folding doors, *e*; kitchen, *f*; back-kitchen, *g*; a gravelled terrace, *h*; and a paved terrace, *i*.

2371. *Remarks.* The arrangement is good. The passage between the kitchen and the dining-room affords a convenient way out to the kitchen-garden, and there is a door in the back-kitchen which communicates with a small kitchen court not shown in the plan. The elevation is picturesque, and though the situation of the barge-board may be objected to by the rigid followers of Pugin, yet what is to be done in a case like this, where the roof projects as much as the chimney?

2372. Design X. is shown in elevation in fig. 2167.; and

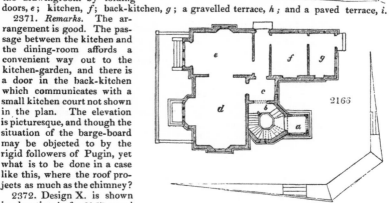

2166

2167

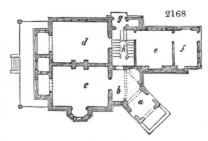

2168

the plan, fig. 2168., contains an entrance-porch, *a*; lobby, *b*; dining-room, *c*; drawing-room, *d*; kitchen, *e*; back-kitchen, *f*; water-closet, with door to the kitchen-garden, *g*; stair to bed-rooms, *h*; plant cabinets, *i i i*; and paved terrace, with steps to the lawn, *k*.

2373. *Remarks.* The recesses, *i i i*, are intended as plant cabinets, with glass roofs, the windows of the room forming ornamental Gothic screens glazed with long strips of glass. If these cabinets are separated from the rooms by sliding sashes, they may be taken away in summer, and the space added to the room.

2169

2374. Design XI. is shown in elevation in fig. 2169.; and the plan, fig. 2170., contains an entrance-porch, *a*; dining-room, *b*; drawingroom, *c*; stair down to kitchens and up to bed-rooms, *d*; and glazed verandas, open in front in summer, and closed by glass in winter, *e, e*.

2170

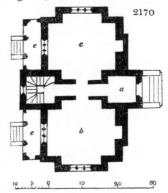

2375. *Remarks.* There is something grand in this elevation, from the prevalence of vertical masses, and the small proportion of wall pierced with doors or windows, as compared with the solid part. Add also, that both in the plan and elevation the walls appear thicker than usual. The design might crown the summit of one of those low hills which often advance into the plain from the lower part of ranges of mountains; such hills, sometimes rocky, sometimes smooth, are frequently met with in the north of Scotland. The unusual thickness of the walls is required in consequence of their being of rubble. The quoins are of scappled stone, and the mouldings and other dressings worked smooth or finely tooled. The whole of the woodwork throughout the house might be of larch, and, where it is used for doors, &c., it should be either oiled or varnished; painting would be quite unnecessary. The approach will be obtained of a very gradual ascent, so as to display the house in connexion with the scenery, in a variety of combinations.

2376. Design XII. is shown in elevation in fig. 2171.; and the plan, fig. 2172., con-

2171

2172

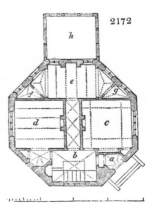

tains an entrance-porch, *a*; hall and staircase, *b*; dining-room, *c*; drawingroom, *d*; library, *e*; reading-closets, *f, g*; and conservatory, *h*. The dotted lines show the manner in which the ceilings of these rooms are to be finished.

2377. *Remarks.* This design is chiefly to be valued for the ingenious manner in which the space is disposed of. Like the last design, it seems peculiarly adapted for crowning an eminence.

Design XIII.—*Sir John Robison's House, Randolph Crescent, Edinburgh.* By John Milne, Esq., Architect.

2378. *Sir John Robison's House, Randolph Crescent, Edinburgh.* This house is given as an example of the most perfect application of the system of heating with hot air that we have any where met with, except in the houses of the inventor, W. Strutt, Esq., and his friends in the neighbourhood of Derby. This house is also equally perfect in every other respect; and, in short, it is allowed to be the most complete street dwelling in Edinburgh. It is a first class house, forming one of a crescent built on a very steep bank on the river Leith, presenting three stories to the street, and six stories to the river, on the sloping side behind. There are small gardens on the slope, and a sunk area of two stories next the street. The following account was drawn up by John Milne, Esq., architect, Edinburgh, in November, 1839; and we had ourselves an opportunity of examining every part of the house in September, 1841, and found it exactly as described by our correspondent. " Pursuant to your instructions, I applied to Sir John Robison for the loan of the working-plans of his dwelling-house here, and for leave to view and examine the house itself. Having obtained free access, and every information I required, I have been enabled to make out the accompanying sections and relative details, figs. 2173. to 2184. In describing these, I shall confine myself to such points in the construction or arrangement as appear to be improvements on the usual routine followed in the laying out and fitting up of street houses of this class. The distribution of the space is so managed, that, with the exception of two partitions in the first chamber floor, which cross the floors without resting on them, all the internal walls reach from the foundation to the roof. The two par-

titions above mentioned are likewise of stone, and are supported in a manner which insures their permanent stability. The walls forming these partitions stand on cast-iron beams, isolated from the floors, the joists of which are supported by wooden beams placed alongside, but not connected with the iron beams, as shown in fig. 2173., in which *m* is the cast-iron beam. The movements of the flooring, therefore, are not communicated to the partitions, which, not being subject to vibration, remain secure. By this construction, also, the spreading of fire must be impeded and danger lessened, as it affords the means of continuing a stone staircase to the attic chambers; see section, fig. 2174., and section, fig. 2177., at the chamber floor.

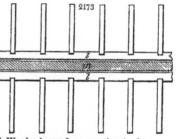

l l, Wooden beams for supporting the floor. *m*, Isolated cast-iron beam for supporting the brick partition.

2379. *The System of Ventilation* employed in this house appears to be as perfect as can be desired; as, while the mass of air in the rooms and passages is constantly undergoing renewal by the escape of the vitiated air above, and the admission of large supplies of fresh air from below, no currents are perceived in the apartments, which, even when crowded with company and amply lighted, preserve a remarkable freshness of atmosphere. The sectional area of the cold-air passages is equal to nearly fourteen square feet; in calm weather, however cold the season, both passages are quite open. This is effected by means of cylindrical flues of earthenware, nine inches in diameter, built into the gables, in close proximity to the smoke flues of each room. The lower ends of these ventilating flues open into the spaces between the ceilings of the respective rooms and the floors of those above them; and there is one or more of these exit air-flues in each room, according to its size and use. The heated and vitiated vapours pass upwards through the ceilings by a continuous opening of about one inch and a half wide (behind one of the fillets of the cornice) all round the rooms, and having thus passed into the space between the ceiling and the floor immediately above, they ascend by the flues in the wall, and are discharged by them into the vacant space between the ceilings of the attics and the roof; from whence they find their way through the slates to the open air. The passage for the air through the cornice is not visible from the floor of any of the rooms, as you will see in section, figs. 2174. and 2177., and on a larger scale in fig. 2178. The air-flues are made to terminate above the ceilings of

2174

Section through the Building on the Line A B in fig. 2175.

a, The cold-air passage or tunnel from the garden opening into the stove place *m,* fig. 2175.
b, Situation of the stove.
c, Opening to the bottom of smoke-flue for the removal of deposited soot.
d, Opening, with sliding damper, which, by admitting air to the flue, checks the draught when the fire is too strong.
e, Pipe which conveys the smoke from the furnace into the flue.
f, Warm air chamber.
ff, exit passage for the warm air from th stove into the well of the staircase.
g, Opening in the ceiling of the dining-room all round it, by which the vitiated air escapes into
h, The ventilating flue for the dining-room.
i, The ventilating flue for back drawing-room; both terminating as at *xx* in fig. 2177.

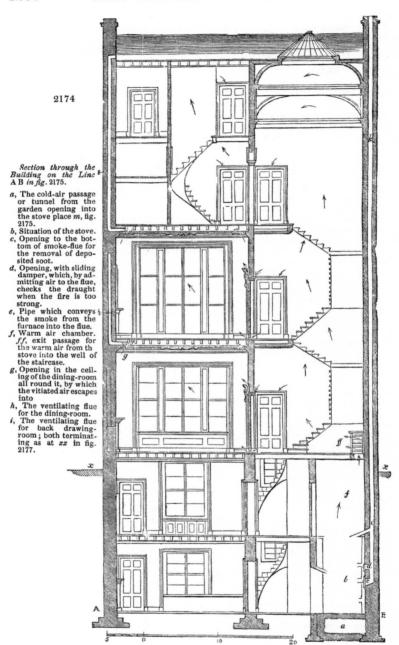

the attics, and below the roof of the house, rather than at the chimney heads, in order to prevent the possibility of smoke being ever brought down by reverse currents; and an advantage is likewise gained in protecting the attic story from the cold which would otherwise be communicated from the roof during winter.   The

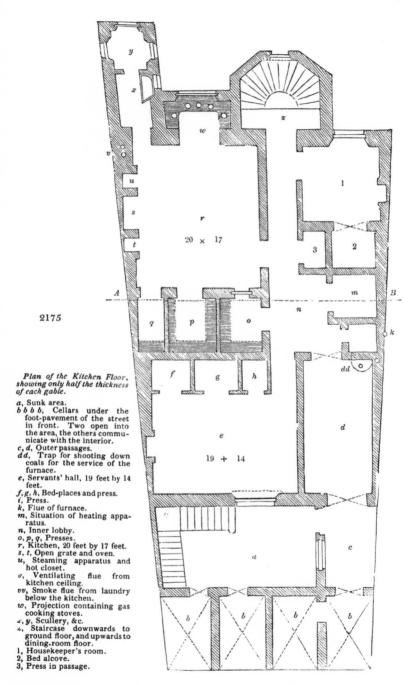

2175

Plan of the Kitchen Floor,
showing only half the thickness
of each gable.

a, Sunk area.
b b b b, Cellars under the
  foot-pavement of the street
  in front. Two open into
  the area, the others communicate with the interior.
c, d, Outer passages.
dd, Trap for shooting down
  coals for the service of the
  furnace.
e, Servants' hall, 19 feet by 14
  feet.
f, g, h, Bed-places and press.
i, Press.
k, Flue of furnace.
m, Situation of heating apparatus.
n, Inner lobby.
o, p, q, Presses.
r, Kitchen, 20 feet by 17 feet.
s, t, Open grate and oven.
u, Steaming apparatus and
  hot closet.
v, Ventilating flue from
  kitchen ceiling.
vv, Smoke flue from laundry
  below the kitchen.
w, Projection containing gas
  cooking stoves.
x, y, Scullery, &c.
z, Staircase downwards to
  ground floor, and upwards to
  dining-room floor.
1, Housekeeper's room.
2, Bed alcove.
3, Press in passage.

continued supply of fresh air to the lower part of the house, to replace that which
goes off by the ventilators and by the chimneys, is brought in from the garden behind

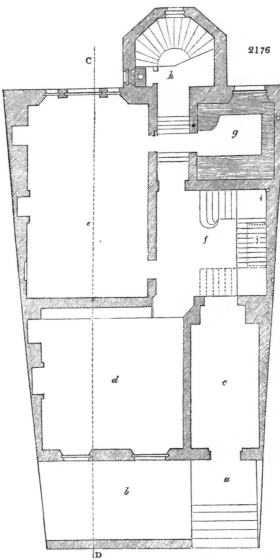

2176

Plan of the Dining-room Floor and Entresol.

a, Street door.   *b*, Sunk area.
c, Hall, 19 feet by 10 feet.
d, Parlour, 19 feet 6 inches by 19 feet.
e, Dining-room, 27 feet by 18 feet.
f, Well of main staircase, 16 feet by 15 feet.
g, Butler's pantry in entresol.
h, Stair to kitchen, from the landing in which is seen a water-closet.
i, Covered raglet (groove) in wall of staircase, in which the water service-pipe is situated.
j, Dotted lines showing the opening by which the warmed air enters the staircase under the stair.

the house by a passage, the sectional area of which is eight superficial feet.   The cold
air admitted by this passage (or by another similar one from the front of the house)
is made to pass over a stove in the chamber *b*, in fig. 2174., on the principle of the late
William Strutt, Esq., of Derby, which has a surface of nearly ninety feet, by which means

2177

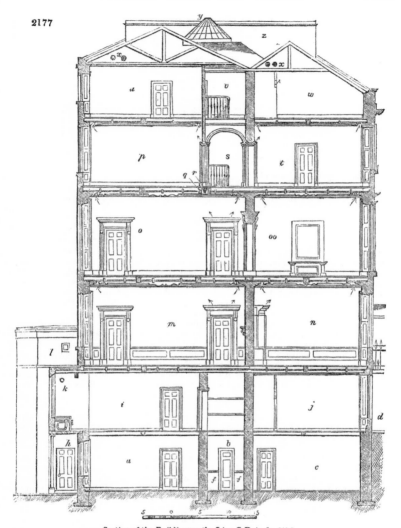

Section of the Building on the Line C D *in fig.* 2176.

a, Laundry. *b*, Wine-cellar. *c*, Stove-room. *d*, Entrance from area to kitchen floor.
h, Door to garden. *e*, Steps to garden. *ff*, Bins of wine-cellar. *i*, Kitchen. *k*, Ventilating flue
from cooking-stoves.
l, Exterior of staircase to the lower floors. *m*, Dining-room. *n*, Parlour.
o, Back drawingroom. *oo*, Front drawingroom. *p*, Chamber. *q*, Beam carrying the joisting
r, Iron beam carrying brick partition and attic stairs. *s*, Attic staircase. *t*, Chamber.
v, Passage to rooms on attic floor. *w*, Attic chamber. *x x*, Openings of ventilating flues over the
ceilings of attics. *y*, Cupola lighting the principal staircase. *z*, Chimney-heads.

a temperature varying from 64° to 70° of Fahrenheit is communicated to it. In very
cold weather 70° is occasionally given to compensate the cooling effect of the walls and
glass windows, so as to keep up the temperature at 60° throughout the house; but
the usual temperature of the air issuing from the stove is as low as 64°. The whole of
this air is discharged into the well of the staircase, which forms a reservoir from which
the rooms draw the quantity required to maintain the upward currents in the chimneys
and in the ventilating flues. The air in the staircase finds its way into the apartments
by masked passages, of four or five inches wide and four feet long, over the doors, and by
openings left under each door of about one inch wide. The sectional areas of these
passages are more than equal to the areas of the chimney and ventilating flues; there is,

2178

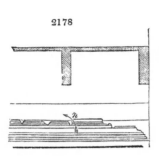

Section of Part of the Ceiling and Floor over.

The object of this section is to show the manner in which the air passes into the vacuity between them by means of concealed openings at *n*, which are also shown at *g* in fig. 2174.

2179

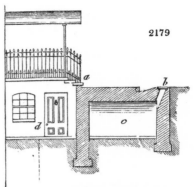

Continuation of the Section in the Direction of C D in fig. 2176.

a, Main entrance under an open porch. *b*, Opening in the side of the street for shooting down coals, with a cast-iron cover. *c*, Coal-cellar. *d*, Door and window to the passage marked *c* in fig. 2175.

therefore, no rarefaction of the air within the rooms, nor any tendency of the external air to enter at chinks of windows, or other irregular apertures. The course of the air, from the great aperture over the stove, through the staircase, over and under the doors, into the rooms, and thence through the ceilings and upwards by the escape-flues, is shown throughout both sections by the direction of the arrows; and the quantity of escape is regulated by hand by means of throttle-valves at the mouth of each escape-flue: hence, by opening or shutting these throttle-valves, the rate of the ventilating current is augmented or diminished. In consequence of the peculiar situation of this house, on the steep slope of the bank of the river Leith, there are two complete stories below the level of the entrance from the street. This gives great advantage in the employment of Mr. Strutt's stove, for producing the temperature required to be given to the air so freely distributed in the upper parts of the building. Circumstances might render this less easy in a house differently situated, and in some cases it may be necessary to have recourse to hot-water pipes or other known methods of communicating heat; but, whatever means of heating may be employed, a proper system of ventilation requires that the supply of fresh air should be large, and that the temperature of it at its issue from the stove be not higher than 70° of Fahr. In houses where the supply of external air is more limited, and where a higher temperature is communicated to it by the heating apparatus, its salubrity is always more or less impaired, as, even at a temperature far below that of boiling water or of steam pipes, the air of towns begins to give out unpleasant effluvia from the animal and organic matters held in suspension in it; and when a high temperature has been attained, air becomes so absorbent of moisture, that it acts unfavourably on the lungs of those by whom it is breathed. Again, when a heating apparatus of small extent of surface is used, and a small supply of external air is admitted, this air is usually raised to a high temperature; and, as a sufficient supply of air must necessarily get in somewhere else, to enable the chimneys of the house to draw, the hot air coming from the stove is speedily diluted by the cold air entering furtively. The same temperature may be partially produced as in the arrangement above described; but the unequal distribution of the hot and cold currents causes discomfort in some parts, while the over-heating of the portion which passes the stove renders it less salubrious, and sometimes offensive. It is imagined by many that air is not vitiated by artificial heat when under 100° of Fahr.; but this is a mistake, as, besides the ill effects arising from its too great avidity for moisture, a heat considerably less than this is sufficient to extricate effluvia from it, as has been already observed: hence, a copious supply of air at a moderate temperature is more agreeable and more conducive to health than an atmosphere of the same temperature formed by a mixture of cold and over-heated air. [On the occasion of our visit to Edinburgh, in September last, we took the opportunity of enquiring whether experience had suggested any alterations or improvements in these arrangements. Sir John Robison's reply was, that, if the house were to be built again, the only difference he should make would be to form the air-passages still wider.]

2380. *The Kitchen* is ventilated on the same principle as the rooms above stairs. One flue proceeds from the ceiling over the fireplace, and another from over the gas cooking stoves, seen in section fig. 2177., and also in fig. 2180. The first flue is built in the gable, close to the smoke-flue; and the second passes upwards by the back of the cistern and pipes of a water-closet, defending them from the action of frost in winter. The gas cooking stoves are of the form which you have already described (p. 690.). They are eight in number, the mouth of each being four inches in diameter, a size which experience has shown to be the most useful. An improvement has lately been introduced in these stoves, which consists in spreading a layer of fine gravel, or coarse sand, of half an inch thick on the wire gauze tops. This completely protects them from oxidation and over-heating, yet does not interfere with the free passage of the current of mixed gas and air. The kitchen fireplace is no larger than is requisite for roasting ; all the other processes being performed either in the oven, the steam vessels, or on the gas stoves. These stoves are placed in the bay of a large window, giving the cook the advantage of a good light above the level of the pans. A close boiler at the back of the grate affords steam for the cooking vessels, and for a hot closet. This boiler also contains a coil of iron tubing, through which the water of a bath, placed in a dressing-room in the chamber floor, is made to circulate when a hot bath is wanted.

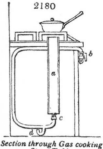

2180

Section through Gas cooking Stove Table.

a, Tube of sheet iron, thirty inches long by four inches' diameter, open at the bottom and covered at top by wire gauze, through which the gas, mixed with common air, passes before it is inflamed.
b, Gas-pipe and regulating stop-cock.
d, Siphon, forming a water-joint to allow of the escape of condensed water.
c, Nozzle of gas-pipe, admitting gas to mix and rise with the air in *a.*

2381. *The House is lighted by Gas* in every part ; but no offensive vapour nor inconvenience of any kind appears ever to be felt from it. The distribution pipes are of greater diameter than are generally employed, and the pressure or current thereby so equalised, that no sinkings or flutterings of the flame are caused by the opening and shutting of doors. The forms and proportions of the Argand burners and glass chimneys are also so arranged as to effect nearly a maximum development of light (of an agreeable hue) from the gas, and to prevent any disengagement of sooty vapour ; that this last object has been obtained, the perfect purity of tint of the white and gold ceilings in the drawingrooms is a satisfactory proof. The mirrors over the chimneys have statuary marble frames, as shown in fig. 2181., and each chimney-piece has two gas-lights. The convenience and economy of gas light being undeniable, it is important to know that in certain circumstances, of easy attainment, it may be rendered as elegant and agreeable a light as any that can be produced from more expensive materials. A paper on the subject of the best mode of employing gas for illumination, by Sir J. Robison, appeared in *Jameson's Journal*, and in the *Mechanic's Magazine*, in 1839 and 1840.

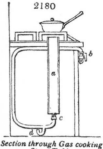

2181

2382. *In the Distribution of Water* through the house, the pipes and cisterns are, as far as possible, placed out of the reach of frost. Instead of the ball-cocks usually placed in cisterns, an apparatus represented on an enlarged scale in figs. 2183. and 2184. is used. It has the advantage of not being subject to wear or to leak, and is not liable to cease to act from becoming stiff.

Drawingroom Fireplace.

a, Flat marble frame, similar in quality to the marble jambs, with a narrow border moulding.
b, Mirror.

2383. *Chimney-flues.* As before mentioned (§ 2379.), the chimney-flues for carrying off heated vapours from the ceilings are made of cylinders of red earthenware, of eight or nine inches' diameter ; those by which the smoke of the fires is carried away are cylinders of fire-brick clay from two to three inches thick, according to their diameters, which vary from ten to seven inches according to the size of the fireplace they belong to. In each fireplace, where the throat of the chimney is gathered together over the grate, there is a valve made of rolled iron plate, which fits into a cast-iron seat fixed in the brickwork : when this valve is in its seat neither soot nor back smoke can pass ; and when it is thrown back the passage to the flue is unobstructed. (See fig. 2182.)

2384. *Escape of melted Snow.* There is a provision for the free escape of melted snow from the roof, which, I am informed, has been copied from the Derby Infirmary. It

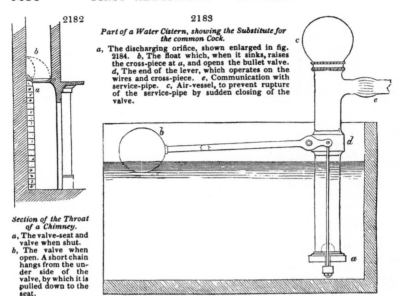

2182

2183

Part of a Water Cistern, showing the Substitute for the common Cock.

a, The discharging orifice, shown enlarged in fig. 2184. *b,* The float which, when it sinks, raises the cross-piece at *a,* and opens the bullet valve. *d,* The end of the lever, which operates on the wires and cross-piece. *e,* Communication with service-pipe. *c,* Air-vessel, to prevent rupture of the service-pipe by sudden closing of the valve.

Section of the Throat of a Chimney.

a, The valve-seat and valve when shut.
b, The valve when open. A short chain hangs from the under side of the valve, by which it is pulled down to the seat.

seems so simple and obvious that it may be wondered why it is not universally adopted. It consists in covering all the gutters and the openings of the vertical pipes with thin boards laid on cross bearers. When snow falls, it lies on these boards and leaves a clear passage underneath, by which, when a sudden thaw takes place, the water runs freely away, instead of being impeded by a mass of half-melted snow, which would otherwise choke up the passages, and might cause an overflow to penetrate the boards on which the slates are laid, and to do damage to the ceilings and walls below.

2385. *The Ironmongery.* Among the excellent articles of ironmongery used in fitting up this house, I may notice the mortise-locks on the doors of all the rooms, as they have the advantage of being let into the doors without weakening them, the latch being contained in a brass tube seven eighths

2184

Enlarged View of the Termination of the Discharge Pipe at a, in fig. 2183.

of an inch in diameter and eight inches long, and requiring only a hole of an inch diameter for its reception. The latch is pressed out by a helical wire spring lodged within the tube; the action of the knob against this spring is particularly agreeable to the hand, as there is no sensible friction. The doors are locked or bolted by a small bolt which fixes the latch bolt. The two-way door-springs on the doors in the lobby and passages are also remarkably good (made by Beattie, Canal Street, Edinburgh); they retain the doors in their middle position with sufficient firmness to prevent them from yielding to the ordinary pressure of the wind, on an external door being opened; yet they do not oppose an increasing resistance when pushed either way towards the wall, and there-fore offer no difficulty to servants when passing through them with both hands occupied in carrying any thing. The locks were furnished by W. and P. Steele, George Street, Edinburgh, and the door-springs by J. Beattie, Canal Street, Edinburgh.

2386. *The Joiners' Work.* As provision is made in the construction of the house for an abundant supply of external air to maintain the necessary upward currents in all the chimneys and ventilating flues, care has been taken to prevent the access of air by irre-gular entrances. The window frames are very carefully fitted; and of the French sashes on the drawingroom floor, one leaf only in each room is made to open. In the usual way in which French sashes are constructed, it is nearly impossible to make them weather-tight, as, when pressed by the wind they yield sufficiently at the joints to allow of rain being blown in. To prevent this here the leaf opens outward; and its frame being beveled, the joint becomes the closer the more pressure it sustains from the wind.

2387. I shall conclude these details by mentioning the way in which the drawing-room suite of rooms has been painted, as it appears to me to be new, to produce a good effect, and to be very durable. The walls have been prepared with several coats of white lead grained to imitate Morocco leather; on this a pattern of gilded rosettes has been laid, and the whole varnished with copal (including the gilding). Another pattern has then been superadded in flat white. The result gives the appearance of a lace dress over satin and spangles, which harmonises with the doors, cornices, &c., which are painted in flat white, with gilt mouldings.—*J. M. Princes Street, Edinburgh.*"

2388. *The Painting and Papering* were executed under the direction of that eminent decorator Mr. Hay, whose scientific work on the subject of his profession, *The Laws of harmonious Colouring*, we have frequently referred to in the body of this work. On applying to Mr. Hay, he sent us the following particulars: — "There was nothing very much out of my usual practice in the painting done in Sir John Robison's house in Randolph Crescent, except the walls of the drawingrooms and staircase. The bed-rooms were done in the usual way; namely, ceilings sized on two coats of oil paint; walls papered with a white, embossed, satined ground paper, with small brown sprigs, and the woodwork painted white, and finished with copal varnish. The dining-room and Sir John's own room were both done in imitation of wainscot, with white ceilings varnished. The staircase ceilings and cornices, painted white and flatted; and the walls and woodwork painted also white, and varnished with copal. The drawingrooms and ante-room were all painted white; the ceilings and cornices, as well as the woodwork, being finished flat, and heightened with gilding. The walls are, as I have already said, rather peculiar in their style of painting. The groundwork is rendered regularly uneven by being granulated, by working it over with the point of a dry brush, immediately after applying the two last coats of paint. This is partly varnished and partly flat, the flat parts forming large rosettes. Between these rosettes, are smaller ones gilded; not in the base metal used upon paper hangings, but in sterling gold leaf. This style of decorative painting, from the great body of paint employed in producing the granulated surface, the copal varnish, and the gold leaf, must be of the most durable description. I may here mention, that, during the last two or three years, I have painted a very great number of drawingrooms in various styles, some with rich borders, others in my patent imitation of damask, and a few in styles similar to that employed upon Sir J. Robison's; and have papered very few. I feel very sure that as the advantages of painting over papering, especially in the public rooms of a mansion, become generally known, the latter style of decoration will be entirely given up. As to the colouring of ceilings, that must be left in a great measure to the taste of the proprietor; as some like pure white, others delicate tints, and a few go the length of the most intense colours, or polychrome. With this last class I myself agree; but I am at the same time aware, that if this be not done with the strictest attention to the laws of harmonious colouring, the effect must be bad. It would be like a person unacquainted with the science of music, running his fingers at random over the keys of a powerful organ. In the one case, white or a light tint is better than colours; and in the other, silence better than such an attempt at music. — *D. R. Hay. Edinburgh, January* 13. 1840."

Design XIV.—*A Land-Steward's House in the Neighbourhood of Inverness.*

The main features of this design were given by the gentleman by whom the house is to be occupied, and the arrangement and details were improved under our direction. The elevation, which is by Mr. Lamb, is shown in fig. 2185. The simplicity of the general outline, and the compact rectangular form of the building, are favourable for economical execution, and for interior warmth; and we think the mode of heating the air of the hall and staircase by an air-stove in the sunk story, and by the same means preserving the water in the cisterns from freezing, is simple and likely to be effective. The serving-room, and the butler's pantry, are placed conveniently for the dining-room. Three sides of the building will appear rising from a terrace, on which, near the conservatory, there will be some flower-beds. In order that this house may be in some degree fire-proof, the floors of the office, the nursery, the kitchens, and all the bed-rooms, are proposed to be laid with stucco. (§ 2457.) On the drawingroom front there will be a terrace garden, connected with an orchard and kitchen-garden by an arcade of trelliswork covered with creepers, and the whole will be sheltered by a plantation, in which will be introduced all the trees and shrubs which will endure the open air in the climate of Inverness, and are procurable in British nurseries.

2389. *Accommodation.* In the basement floor, fig. 2186., there is a scullery with a sink and plate-rack (and it may also contain a baking-oven and boiler), *a*; back-stair, *b*; wash-house, with fixed washing-troughs supplied with pipes of hot and cold water, *c*; servants' hall, *d*; and White's warm-air stove, *e*. The flue from this stove

2185

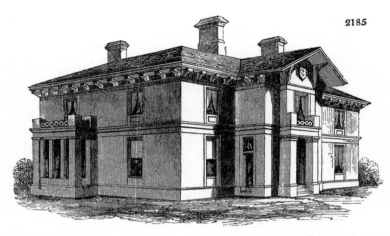

is to be conducted up the adjoining pier, and close to the cisterns of the three water-closets; while the heated air is to ascend to the hall above, *v*, in fig. 2187. This floor also contains a small door to the coal-cellar, for procuring coals for the hot-air stove, *f*; and a coal-shoot, *g*. The cover to this shoot or opening, by which the coals are to be introduced, is a plate of cast iron, made to lift up when the coals are to be thrown down ; it may form the lower step to the side entrance, or it may serve as part of the floor or path before the steps : by means of an iron rod, staple, and padlock, it can easily be secured inside. A closet is shown at *h* ; a servants' water-closet at *i* ; the coal-cellar at *k* ; wine-cellar at *l* ; beer-cellar at *m* ; stoke-hole to the conservatory at *n* ; conservatory

2186

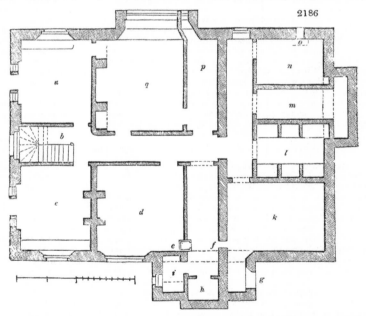

furnace at *o* ; cook's pantry at *p* ; and kitchen at *q* ; the kitchen grate being supposed to contain a boiler behind, and a roasting-oven on one side. There are two back en-trances ; one through the back-kitchen, *a*, and the other through the wash-house, *c* ; both these doors open into a small kitchen-court, round which are ranged a place for ashes, a cleaning-room, bottle-rack, &c., peat-house, wood-house, &c.

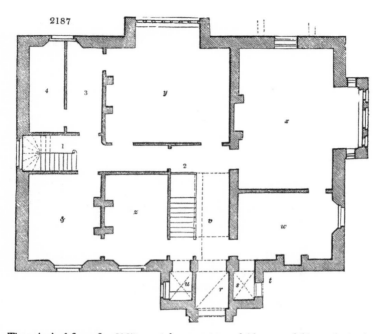

2187

The principal floor, fig. 2187., contains an entrance-lobby, r; a lobby to the business room, s; a separate entrance to the business room, t; water-closet, u; beneath which is one for the servants, and over which is one for the bed-rooms; the cisterns and pipes being kept from frost by the heat of the stove, e, in fig. 2186.; hall and staircase, v; business-room, w; drawingroom, x; and dining-room, y. By introducing a temporary screen of glass, or sliding-doors of glass, so as to separate the bay in this room, a green-house may be obtained in the winter season, and the same thing might be effected in the drawingroom. The object in separating the plants from the general atmosphere of the rooms is, to preserve them from the dust and dry air which they contain, which is so unsuitable for plants, and partly also to make sure of their being kept near the light. There is a school-room at z, and a bed-room connected with it at $\&$; a staircase to the bed-rooms at 1; a swing-door, 2, to exclude draughts of air and smells from the kitchen or wash-house; a serving-room to the dining-room, 3, which may have a hot closet and shelf, heated by the circulation of hot water from the cistern at the back of the kitchen fireplace below; and a butler's pantry, 4. Above this floor are three good bed-rooms, with dressing-rooms, a nursery, and three small bed-rooms.

2390. *Remarks.* The accommodation and its arrangement being adapted to a parti-cular case, have been studied with the greatest care, and we consider that the result is satisfactory.

Design XV.—*A Villa in the Italian Style.* By E. B. Lamb, Esq., F.I.B.A.

2391. *The Object* of this design is to show the marked distinction of the Italian style of architecture, as applicable to a moderate-sized English villa, where utility is more attended to than expensive decoration. Fig. 2190. is the elevation of the garden front.

The style of architecture intended to be conveyed by the elevation is decidedly of Italian origin, and the general form perfectly simple, the variety in the external eleva-tions being produced by the terraces and projecting steps. The small balconies of the chamber floor also tend to enliven the design, and are always an agreeable addition to a bed-room. If it were desirable to make the building fire-proof, or nearly so, the staircases should be of stone, the walls of solid brickwork or stone, and the joists, girders, rafters, &c., of cast and wrought iron. If the ceilings are well plastered, they will be sufficient to cut off any communication of fire. Unless very considerable expense is incurred, there must be a certain quantity of combustible material in the construction of a house, such as floor boards, window frames and shutters, doors, &c., but by some little contrivances, if fire should happen, it might be confined to one spot, and would thus soon be extinguished.

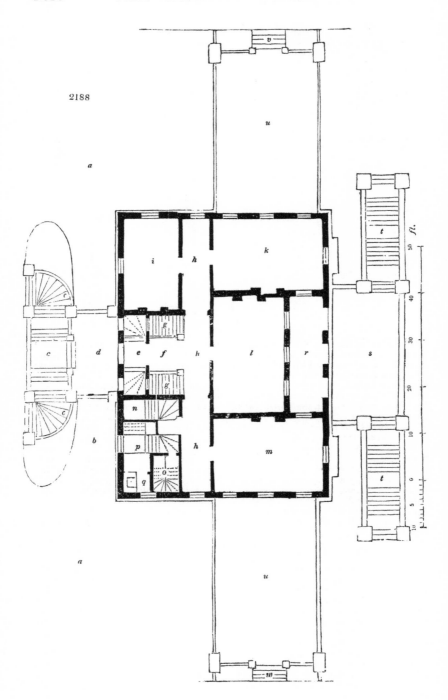

Except in bed-rooms, the furniture of private houses is not usually very combustible, unless some pains are taken to ignite it.

2392. *Accommodation.* On the plan of the principal floor, fig. 2188., are shown: *a*, the approach road; *b*, the road to the under hall; *c c c*, steps and landings to the hall; *d*, great landing; *e*, porch; *f*, hall; *g g*, stairs from the under hall; *h h h*, corridor; *i*, breakfast-room; *k*, drawingroom; *l*, library; *m*, dining-room; *n*, principal stairs; *o*, back-stairs; *p*, dressing-room; *q*, water-closet; *r*, arcade; *s*, landing; *t t*, steps to the lawn, &c.; *u u*, terraces; *v*, steps to conservatories; *w*, steps to billiard-room.

In the basement plan, fig. 2189., *a* is the approach road; *b*, the road to the carriage porch; *c*, the carriage porch; *d*, the under hall, with the staircases leading to the upper hall; *e*, alcoves with seats; this forms part of the foundation of the upper steps, and, for the sake of giving some pictorial effect, has been opened in this manner: *f*, kitchen; *g*, scullery; *h*, pantry; *i*, larder; *k*, servants' hall; *l*, housekeeper's room; *m*, bed-room; *n*, passage; *o*, stairs to the wine and beer cellars; *p*, china closet; *q*, stores; *r*, stairs; *s*, water-closet, and coat and boot room; *t t t*, coal and wood cellars; *u u*, archways shown in the elevation, fig. 2190.; *v*, *w*, *x*, *z*, *a'*, men-servants' bed-rooms; *y*, stairs from the terrace; over *z* and *a'* is the billiard-room; *b'*, yard; *c'*, *d'*, *e'*, under-gardener's rooms; *f'*, conservatory vestibule, with the stairs to the terrace; this vestibule should have an entire glass roof, but the walls, stairs, and other parts, should be decorated with sculpture and architecture, interspersed with flowers in ornamental pots or beds; *g'*, conservatories. The principal chamber floor contains six bed-rooms and three dressing-rooms; and the attics contain four maid-servants' bed-rooms.

2393. *Description.* The house is adapted to a situation near a high road, within a short distance of a large town,

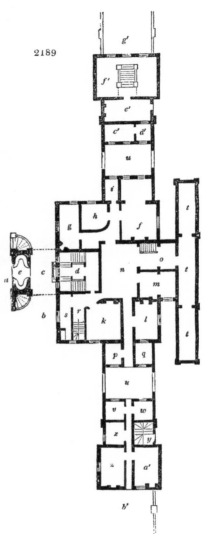

2189

but placed sufficiently far from the road to prevent any annoyance from the dust, or from idle gazers. The terrace walls divide the pleasure-grounds from the entrance drive, giving as much seclusion to the grounds as possible. The principal floor is raised upon terraces, as the views from the windows range a considerable distance beyond the private grounds, and can be seen properly only from an elevated situation, such as the terraces afford. The terraces, being extensive, afford an opportunity of obtaining considerable variety in the prospects, and, by descending to the lawn and pleasure-grounds, the scene becomes immediately changed, and we have numerous beautiful views of another description. The main entrance is placed on the north-east, and is ascended to from the double approach road by a double flight of broad steps to the principal hall, landing, and porch. The porch is entered through the centre arch, which is five feet wide, the side arches being smaller, and enclosed at the bottom, about three feet from the ground, by open paneling and pedestals bearing vases for flowers. The hall is entered through folding sash-doors, and is otherwise lighted by the side windows, which

2190

correspond in size with the small arches of the porch. These windows are filled in with stained glass. The double lines on the plan mark the situation of stone paneling, or balus-trading, terminating at the ends in pedestals bearing appropriate sculpture, or candelabra. This balustrade is the protection from the stone stairs to the lower hall, of which more hereafter. It will be seen from the plan, that the hall forms part of the corridor, extending the length of this floor, and lighted at each end by rich stained glass windows. The hall ceiling is flat, divided into nine panels, by four beams intersecting each other: these beams should be of wood, or in imitation of wood; and in the centre is a panel with a circular shield within a wreath, the shield bearing the family arms painted of the proper colours. The ceiling should be supported by a deep bold block cornice, in imitation of stone. The walls are of stone, or in imitation of stone, and jointed. The corridor should be finished to harmonise, both in construction and decoration, with the hall; and at each end might be placed a vase for flowers or a statue; the vase, perhaps, would be most suitable, as in this situation any object must be almost always presented to the eye in shadow; but where the outline is of particular beauty, and the whole subject does not depend so much upon minute detail as pictorial effect, in no situation can it be better viewed; and, in fact, figures have frequently a more imposing effect when so placed than when in full light. A vase situated here might be properly and agreeably used for containing flowers; or a pedestal, with a glass globe, containing gold fish, would look well. The paving of the hall and corridors should be in patterns, resembling in their general form the panels of the ceiling: this may be effected with Portland stone, and any other stone which would contrast with it; or, if covered with oil-cloth, simple patterns are best. All the doors from the corridor should be framed in three panels, and moulded; they should be of oak, and should be circular-headed to correspond with the windows, so that all the openings should be of the same form on this floor. The handles should be of wood; ebony outside, and cut glass within the rooms. The inside panels of the doors may be ornamented with gilt ornaments, or painted upon the oak ground. If painted, the sort of ornament most suited for this purpose is a flat pattern without projecting shadows, but merely depending upon contrast of colour for effect, it being part of the architectural decoration: imitations of real shadows, or a desire to give relief to flat objects, which, if embossed, would project various shadows, is mean and unarchitectural, and can never produce the effect desired. As a general practice, the imitation, by painting, of wood, stone, or other material, is not satisfactory to the mind, and conveys mean impressions; but increasing the beauty of wood by varnish or polish, and of stone by delicate work, is far more suitable, as presenting the actual material without any attempt to deceive. All deceptions in architecture fail in producing the desired effect. Painting would also become infinitely more beautiful, if applied in a legitimate manner as a decoration, and not merely as a disguise to other materials, and more frequently to bad work.

The library should be furnished with book-cases all round the room; but great attention should be paid to their composition and arrangement, so that each side of the room should be of an equally consistent architectural character. As the peculiar con-struction of the room will not allow of recesses in the walls for book-shelves, without considerable expense, we must endeavour to produce as much effect as we can by detached book-cases, projecting from the walls, yet sufficiently connected so as to pre-serve the unity of the design. The skirting of the room must necessarily form the most important connexion; by the breaking of which round all the cases, and then again round the chimney-piece, though in this place of a different material, the line of connexion is immediately preserved in a satisfactory manner to the eye. Another connexion may be made in the cornice; the impost of the arches may very properly form the cornice of all the cases, and this would be quite high enough for book-cases in a private library. Over the chimney-piece might be a large mirror, or a piece of sculpture, and on the book-cases might be arranged, in a pleasing manner, the busts of some of the most eminent authors. The ceiling should be paneled, and coloured in imitation of wood; the principal beams might be oak, and the panels of a lighter wood. Some few raised ornaments might be placed upon the ceiling, and painted in various colours, and some gilt. Painted ceilings in allegorical subjects, or skies, clouds, moons, stars, and other things of the like nature, have happily gone out of fashion. Nothing can be so ill adapted to a ceiling as a painting with figures and architectural subjects; the situation being such, that when you do strain your neck to obtain a glimpse of them, and endeavour to unravel their mysteries, you are generally puzzled to fix a point where the design can be viewed without distortion. The painted ceilings of the British Museum are sufficient evidence of the absurdity of this practice. The custom is now completely altered, and from the dark gloomy coloured and painted ceilings of the seventeenth century, the opposite extreme is frequently taken, and flat unmeaning plaster, with wiry ornaments which it requires the keenest vision to decipher occupy the place of learned allegorical mysteries.

In the dining-room many sculptural subjects may decorate the walls, and the ceiling may be well and appropriately adorned with heraldic devices. The entrance to the room is in the centre, and on each side should be placed pedestals, or side tables in lieu of the large sideboard, which could not be so well placed in this room. These little circumstances may frequently be the means of producing something out of the common way in composition; and in this room the door forms such an important feature that its position should not be altered. The space on each side is sufficiently wide to admit of handsome designs for the demi-sideboards, where as much display of plate may be made as any person can possibly wish for. At the back of each might be a large plate of looking-glass, which would greatly add to the splendour of the furnished sideboards. Much may be done in this way with good effect, provided a little thought were given to the subject. The windows, which should all open outside, should be glazed with some stained glass and some plain figured glass; the lower portions of the sashes should be plate glass: and in the construction of the sashes, and also in the glazing of them, care should be taken that no sash-bar should come in the way of the sight of a person of ordinary height, either sitting or standing; and that the stained glass should not be placed in the direction of a person's sight, so as to obstruct his view, except in side borders: of course, there may be exceptions to this rule.

From the dining-room is an entrance to the loggia, the ceiling of which should be paneled, so as to harmonise with the rooms to which it is attached; the decorations should partake of some of those of the other three rooms, but still, as the loggia is a subordinate object, its ornaments should be unobtrusive. The heraldic devices of the dining-room, the sombre yet marked display of the library, and the elegant lightness of the drawingroom, should all be united in this loggia; and at the same time we should bear in mind, that, as it is an entrance porch from the external part of the house, the walls should be of stone, and in the ceiling alone can the connecting links be preserved.

The drawingroom, k, in fig. 2188., may be decorated upon the strictest architectural principles, and still the lightness so necessary for this room may be maintained: beautifully grained wood may be distinctly shown in the ceiling, as the apparent strength might require; this wood may be moulded and decorated with gilt and painted carved work. Satinwood panels, with elegantly designed scroll ornaments upon them, would have a rich and beautiful effect; the centre panel should have a rich flower, from which should hang the chandelier. The skirting of the room might be in imitation of Sienna marble, and the walls might partake of the hues most prominent in the ceiling, and so as to combine with the skirting. The centre panel of the door might be looking-glass, upon which should be placed some decoration, picked out in appropriate colours. The windows should have some ornamental stained glass in the upper parts; and much decoration and taste might be shown, not only in the arrangement of the stained glass, but also in the form of the inside of the window-frames, bearing in mind always, that although the general character of the building may be marked as of a particular style, yet the spirit of that style may be strictly followed up without any of the minor details being copied from known examples. However much we may err in our endeavours to produce something new, this should not deter us from persevering; and, if we do so upon fixed and sound principles, success must ultimately be the result of our endeavours.

The decorations of this room may appear at first rather extravagant; but, when we consider the means that are employed for the purpose, it will be found, that in a house where architectural decoration is required, the means here employed are not too great for the end in view. Looking-glass, judiciously applied, it is scarcely necessary to remark, gives great splendour to a room.

The chimney-piece I would wish to be of Sienna marble, or, at least, the lower portion of it, which should be a continuation of the skirting or plinth of the room: this forms the connecting link between the walls and the chimney-piece, and this, in an architectural point of view, is of the greatest importance. The upper portion of the chimney-piece may be of statuary marble: it then becomes a separate part of the design, or, in fact, a part added for a particular purpose to the plinth, which plinth then holds its proper situation in the architecture of the room. It is the bearing part, the base of the whole, and its office should be distinctly marked. A distinct material can be used for the upper part of the chimney-piece with the greatest propriety; for, as the walls of the room, the plinth, and the ceiling, are of different materials, a variety or contrast in this situation will be quite admissible. Connecting lines in the general composition, masses of colour, variety of material, and a single prominent feature, make up the whole of architectural design. This single prominent feature is the leading object from which all others emanate, and it unites itself in its form and colour with the surrounding objects. Suppose, for instance, the chimney-piece were made the most prominent feature in a room, the lines of the plinth are continued round, and the upper portion is repeated in other objects in form and colour, but in a less decorated manner, as they recede from the main feature : they continue round the room till the least decorative parts, as they radiate from the centre, meet and unite in each other.   The blending of form and colour is much more difficult in architecture than in painting.   In the former, the crude nature of the materials, the limited scale it must be brought to, and the necessity of making numerous and frequent changes, are disadvantages difficult to surmount, and only, perhaps, to be properly surmounted in the actual building; but in painting, the subject is in the hands of the artist at once, and when once finished no change can take place in it.

The breakfast-room, i, in fig. 2188., requires but few words, as what has already been said applies as much to this room as to the others.   In many of the buildings designed in the present day, too much attention and expense have been bestowed on the exterior ; and when you enter the house, after seeing the hall and staircase, few of the rooms present a better appearance than those of the meanest cottage : a cornice, with some enrichments, but very moderately applied, and frequently in doubtful taste, and a centre flower, supplied from the plasterer's stores, are usually the utmost decorations, even in large houses.   The ceiling is flat, and as white as possible ; but the walls are papered with rich papers and gilt mouldings by the professional decorator.   Now, it must have been observed by nearly every person, that the bareness of the ceiling never unites with the rich covering of the walls.   Let us spare a little expense externally (and frequently it may be spared without being missed), and apply it to internal decoration.   Let us be consistent in our designs ; and, if we have the means of giving a princely appearance to the exterior, let us remember that it should only prepare us for equal, if not superior, display within.   The resources should be carefully husbanded, that the whole design may be in proper unison, admitting only just such discords as are sufficient to prevent monotony, and give zest to the general effect of the composition.

The principal stairs, n, in fig. 2188., should be of stone ; the first flight enclosed, as shown in the plan, for the dressing-room, p.   The upper part of the staircase may be open ; and, as these stairs lead to the bed-rooms, only a moderate degree of decoration will be sufficient for them ; but some basso-relievo may be very properly placed here, and some attention should be paid to the ceilings and walls, so as to preserve the strictest unity in the design.   The back stairs, o, will be enclosed by a swing door.   These stairs lead from the basement to the different floors of the house.

The landing, s, in fig. 2188., from the arcade or loggia, r, is made broad and ample, as it will form a delightful situation for flowers, for vases, or pieces of sculpture, or for many other subjects of interest, which could not be placed in the open grounds.   This, with the terraces, $u\ u$, if supplied with seats of an architectural character, would form very agreeable lounges when the grounds were too damp to walk in.   The terrace from the dining-room is properly terminated by the billiard-room, and that from the drawing-room by the conservatory.   The basement plan, fig. 2189., shows the entrance to the conservatory at f', and the conservatory, g'.   All the terraces are approached from the grounds in the manner clearly indicated by the plan. — E. B. L.

Design X /I.—*A small Gothic Villa, suited to the Suburbs of a large Town.*   By E. B. Lamb, Esq., F.I.B.A.

The elevation is shown in fig. 2191.   As a general remark, perhaps you will allow me to say a word or two on the wood-engravings.   Frequently the artist who draws the design on the wood, previously to the cutting, from a want of knowledge of architectural forms, or, perhaps, in many instances it may be carelessness, absolutely puts into the drawing the very things I have been writing against, as in the instance pointed out in the windows of the keeper's lodge, fig. 2335. in p. 1135.   In this design, fig. 2191., the parapet appears like a Grecian guilloch instead of Gothic perforated paneling ; the arches do not present the easy curve of the Gothic four-centred arch, and the scroll label over the projecting bays assumes also a different character.   In other respects, this is a good specimen of the art.   It is rather provoking to see sometimes such mistakes that the character of a design is completely altered : but I will not now bring a list of grievances forward ; the subjects, I have no doubt, are difficult for wood-engravers, and, at any rate, I cannot complain more than others.

The intention of this design is to show an ornamental style of architecture, to be executed in a substantial manner at comparatively small cost, as all the external decorations can be executed in Coade's terra cotta, which is certainly more durable than some real stone : the colour can be made of any tint ; and, as the material is burnt in a kiln, it is harder than most stone, and much less porous.   It is also much better than common cement, as it does not require colouring.

2394. *Accommodation.*   In the ground plan, fig. 2192., a is the porch ; b, the hall ;

2191

c c, corridor ; d, lobby to the staircase ; e, staircase ; f, dining-room ; g, drawingroom ; h, library ; i, conservatory ; k, arcade ; l, landing and steps down to the grounds ; m, landing, or terrace, and steps to the grounds from the conservatory ; n n, areas ; o o, sunk or sloped ground to give light and ventilation to the basement ; and p, approach road.

2395. *Description.* To the entrance of every house a porch is not only a luxury, but is necessary to protect the house from cold, and to form a suitable shelter in inclement weather. The entrance archway of this porch, a, should be the largest opening in this front, and it should be conspicuously decorated, in order that it may at once mark the principal entrance. In the gable there should be a panel, with an enriched shield, motto, crest, or other mark, distinguishing the owner. On the apex of the gable would

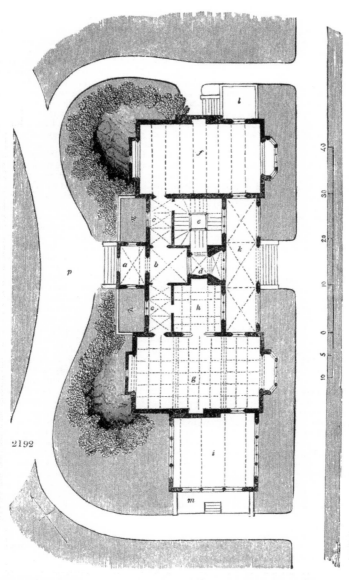

2192

be the best place for the crest. It may be objected to by some that heraldic devices have
the appearance of family pride, when conspicuously displayed in their buildings; but
this is not considered to be the case by architects and antiquarians.   They are forms
and decorations intimately associated with the style of architecture in which they are
employed, and constitute some of the most interesting and picturesque combinations.
In ancient architecture, they are frequently the only means by which we can trace the
founder of a building, or the contributor to its decoration or enlargement: in those days,
brass plates, with huge letters setting forth the names of benefactors, were seldom used,
as in the present time, in which the useful decoration is seldom properly applied, but
the brazen name shines forth in the most glaring manner.   Heraldic forms, monograms,
rebuses, and other devices, in addition to rich sculptures and appropriate foliage, form

the most interesting subjects for Gothic buildings; but none should be used which could not be shown as perfectly consistent, and connected, either with the building as a work of fine art, or with the founder as the badges of his family, his name, or his occupation. This was the custom of the "Masonic Craft:" but mark the difference of the present time. The noble buildings of antiquity are copied, not only in their windows, doors, and gables, but in their heraldic emblems; and frequently we see the arms of monarchs, palaces, and cities, monasteries, abbots, and colleges, jumbled together in one confused mass on a modern domestic building, which, with a little thought, might have been appropriately decorated with the founder's own devices. In this porch I would have the groining executed either in stone or in terra cotta, and not in plaster or papier-mâché (the latter method is now adopted at Ripon Minster for restoring the groining of the transepts); and at the angles, suitable sculpture in corbels, arms, bosses, &c. The ribs of the groining might be executed on the same principle as in ancient buildings, and the interstices built with squared chalk; a common practice with the freemasons, and very suitable from its lightness, and, if not exposed to the weather, durability; and each gusset being perfectly independent of the rib, this method is found to be sufficiently strong. All the heraldry should be properly emblazoned, and not indicated by the modern method, which is poor and insipid, compared with the effect produced by the combination of colours and gilding. A little colour in the groining, and all the proper joints of the masonry, showing the principle of the construction, is highly satisfactory to the mind: again, in the masonry, small forms of stone, in this situation, would be most pleasing, as indicating a lighter method of construction in this manner than could be produced by ponderous masses of material; the latter, presenting a large surface to the eye, conveys an idea of immense thickness, and our sensations are unpleasing, from the apparent insufficiency of the walls, buttresses, or other supports, to bear the burden. At the same time, and probably from the same cause, the large masses do not harmonise with the small general forms so well as small masses. I have mentioned sculpture as appropriate decoration, in foliage, flowers, fruit, and heraldic emblems: the judicious study of ancient examples, for their forms, would be excellent, but then the spirit that dictated the design, and the hand that executed the work, should be clearly understood and impressed upon the artist, that he may do as has been before done, viz. invent new forms, and execute them in the same bold manner, without stooping to the lazy expedient of copying, or rather moulding and reproducing, the ancient works, and placing them in inappropriate situations. With regard to heraldry, the ancient forms must be preserved: they should be considered as mere devices; and when we see animals represented in form and colour as they never did exist in nature, we can only be reminded of the uses which required these incongruities: and, as in all countries, and almost in all ages, these means have been resorted to for distinguishing persons, and are still handed down to us for the same purpose, however incorrectly applied, we should preserve them as symbols of an occasion now no longer required, and records of chivalric ages and historic legends. But not so with regard to distinct grotesque figures, busts, corbel heads, and such things: the artists of the middle ages knew not how to execute their work better; but, at the present time, it would be absurd indeed to copy the faults of the ancients. Figures should have their proper proportions; grotesque corbel heads, if used at all, should be sparingly used, and the execution should not be contrary to nature. Perfect beauty in things of this kind is not so necessary as correct anatomical proportion. Much of the good effect we observe in the application of sculpture (I mean figures) in ancient buildings is owing to the material being of the same description as in the architecture, and to the method of disposing the drapery, so that it harmonises with the architectural forms. In all ancient buildings the figures are fully clothed: there are exceptions, of course, but these are few: they are generally placed in niches (internally more especially), and have canopies over them, the niche is only sufficiently large to admit the figure, and the parallelism of the folds of the drapery, the closeness of the arms to the sides, and the perfectly upright position of the figure, embodies it, as it were, with the architecture.

On each side of the porch is a window, which, to preserve its use and comfort, should be glazed, and some small compartments of stained and painted arms, figures, or mottoes, might very appropriately be used here. The door to the hall should be of oak, with the upper panels glazed, to admit light to the hall. The decorations of the hall, b, and the corridors, c c, and the lobby, d, should be of the same character, and be groined in the ceiling, in the same manner as the porch: the other decorations should be also of similar character, partaking of the same forms, but in a richer degree. The two windows should be glazed with stained glass; and here might be some figures, emblems of the arts of peace, mixed with the heraldry, as appropriate historical mementos. In the hall there might be some ancient armour hung up, with banners and other appropriate implements of war; now merely preserved as matters of history, but all tending to instruct and give interest as well as picturesque beauty. The window in the lobby, *d*, should also have some painted glass. The effect from the porch, looking through the building to the lobby window, and then to the grounds, would, I think, be pleasing ; as there would be a depth of shadow from the hall, with some half lights, forming a varied foreground to the enriched window, with its brilliant hues, in the distance. Although I would wish to have a great deal of stained glass in the lobby window, yet some should be quite plain, that the scenery may be viewed from it with proper effect.

I pass now to the dining-room, *f.* Here a distinct contrast is produced from the groining of stone to the ceiling of wood. Oak is the material usually employed in these situations in ancient buildings, but I should not object to fir ; larch, for instance, would have a beautiful effect, if varnished with boat varnish, or asphalt mixed with varnish. These produce a rich brown tint without disguising the material. I know we are apt to associate meanness with deal, but if the colour be sobered down, the effect will be exceedingly good, and while much more satisfactory than painting in imitation of more rare woods, is also cheaper. The ceiling should have transverse ribs, as indicated by the dotted lines in the plan, fig. 2192., and might be curved at the ends to form an open cusped spandril, the curve terminating with a corbel. The corbels should be of stone or terra cotta : in the cornice might be carved wood ornaments, appropriately interspersed with heraldic devices, monograms, &c. In the recess for the sideboard I would have a window entirely filled with rich stained glass, which would catch the eye as the main object when the plate was displayed here, and would group the whole in the most pleasing manner. The other windows should be sparingly glazed with stained glass, as it would be inconvenient for viewing objects in the grounds, and would tend to give too sombre a character to the room. Where transoms are used in Gothic windows, great care should be taken that they come above the eye when a person is standing in a room, so that no disagreeable obstruction may prevent the view from the window. The fireplace I would take care should form a component part of the architecture of the room, and not be, what it too frequently is, of quite a different and distinct character. This was frequently the case in old buildings. For the walls, if I could not cover them with velvet hangings or tapestry (not subjects full of monstrous figures), I would use flock paper in imitation of velvet hangings ; the effect would be good, and at any rate it would be quite as consistent as painting them stone colour : yet other colours might be used ; and, in general, the fewer imitations there are in a building, the more perfect the effects will be. But there are some things that present difficulties in our way, and therefore paper may with propriety be used as a covering for a wall, where a covering is required in domestic architecture, and more especially where the building is not on a large scale ; but in public buildings, churches, or cathedrals, it would be quite inadmissible. The windows, or rather sash-doors, at the end of the room, are convenient means of descending to the grounds or to the arcade ; and the recess at the end, with the arch corresponding with the sideboard arch, would form an agreeable nook, but more useful as a "retiring place for conference" in the drawingroom.

I will pass through the corridor, which should be similarly decorated to the porch, to the drawingroom, *g.* The same principle which governed the composition of the other parts of the building should be strictly followed here. The ceiling should be of wood, but supported by two large ribs, and divided into panels, as indicated by the dotted lines in the plan. A more lively decoration is necessary for this room, more colour may be used, and gilding should be called in to aid the effect ; but the main supports of the ceiling should be wood, and it should be clearly indicated as such. The panels might be richly ornamented with diaper patterns in gold or coloured grounds, or colour on gold grounds. But even in this kind of decoration in ancient times something of a heraldic system was employed ; that is, metal formed the ground of colour, and colour the ground of metal ; but seldom was colour the ground for colour, or metal the ground for metal ; and to these simple rules we owe the most brilliant effects. In their decorations the ancients were not sparing of their positive colours. As much attention should be paid to the forms of patterns. Large forms, as I have shown before, tend to diminish the apparent size of the room, and small forms to increase the size : warm colours also give the appearance of diminution, but, at the same time, of compactness ; whereas cold colours produce distance or space, but frequently a want of cheerfulness ; therefore, the proportion of warm colours should be greater than that of cold colours. There are many little elegancies fitted for this room which my limits will not allow me to mention ; but the cultivated and delicate tastes of the ladies would, if they built upon such a plan, soon furnish the design, so as to make it perfectly suitable to its purpose.

I have mentioned the fireplace in the dining-room, but not the material of which it should be made. In the present time we generally look upon mantelpieces that are not marble as mean and unsuitable. This occurs in consequence of their mean forms (I speak of moderate-sized buildings) being lost in their costly material. If the marble were worked with suitable decorations and more beautiful forms, the expense would prevent its application; but if the suitable forms and decorations were executed in freestone, the comparative meanness of the material would be doubly compensated by the beauty and appropriateness of the composition. Therefore, however opposite to the present received custom, I would not scruple to use a fine freestone for this building, appropriately carved and decorated, in preference to the mean form in the costly material.

The library, *h*, is divided from the drawingroom by an open screen, behind which, when more privacy was required, a curtain would form an appropriate division. The screen should be carved wood, and of the same colour as the other wood in the room, with rich tracery, which might be partially painted and gilt, so as to produce an exceedingly rich effect, and should otherwise correspond with the decorations of the room. It should be about seven feet high, and surmounted with a rich Tudor parapet. The actual partition of the room should be arched. This library, which, in fact, may be considered only a small book-room, or boudoir, attached to the drawingroom, should be fitted up much in the same manner as the drawingroom, only preserving so much difference as would give variety to the general composition.

Much of the effect of the conservatory (which we now enter), as an architectural composition, will depend upon the walls being pierced with windows as little as possible; and to preserve the character of this portion of the building some sacrifice must be made as regards the plants, but, as the whole roof may be of glass, the sacrifice will be only to a small extent. In a house of decidedly architectural pretensions, if the conservatory is not kept up in the same manner, the pleasure we should otherwise derive from the building, as a work of art, would be destroyed. Many ways are employed to give an architectural character to conservatories; for example, by high decoration with cast-iron or wood ornaments of an expensive nature: but seldom do we see any of the forms of the main building repeated in the conservatory; too often the design is produced by a different person, whose patterns have been used in similar instances, and the consequence is, that the house and conservatory present totally opposite characters. Although we see immediately what is intended by the erection, yet the flimsy wood or iron so called Gothic architecture of the conservatory but ill accords with the massy stone of the building: the horizontal lines of the framing, the thin sash-bars, the low pitch of the roof, and the glaring white paint, offer too great a contrast to the vertical character, the high-pitched gable, and the solid mullion of the building to be pleasing. These things, I am quite aware, are not so much observed when applied to a conservatory, as they would be had the building been erected for another purpose; so much are we reconciled to mean forms when associated with agreeable objects.

I have yet to say a few words on the staircase, which I would have constructed with equal regard to the strict character of the building; but I would not bestow upon it that high decoration which is so frequently done, as if the whole effect of the building depended upon the splendour of the staircase. In this building the stairs might be of stone, the balusters of bronze or iron, and the handrail of oak; the balusters should be ornamental, either in single forms or in connected paneling. There are yet remaining several examples from which, without exactly copying, we might obtain good ideas for these forms; and if we attend to the purpose for which we study them, a little more than to the wish of applying the same design, something consistent will necessarily be the result. The handrail should be in straight pieces, or merely curved upwards next the newels, which at each angle of the stairs should form the abutments; but in no case would I use the distorted, ramped, and twisted slip of mahogany, which modern ingenuity calls a handrail: it is perfectly void of beauty, and the only thing that can be said in its favour is, that the hand in descending the stairs can slip from the top to the bottom without interruption. Can this usefulness make up for its deformity?

The general effect of these rooms, if constructed and decorated in the manner described, would be, I think, satisfactory, as presenting the actual material, and using colour only as a means of giving to that material its best appearance. At once we should observe, upon entering the building, that it was substantial and consistent in construction, appropriate in decoration, and possessing an air of comfort with pictorial effect. I dwell somewhat upon the necessity of applying materials properly, that is, undisguised; as of late years the decorator, instead of the architect, is called in to complete the building, and the architect is dismissed almost immediately after the mere shell is erected. Then come imitations of satinwood, rosewood, oak, or other materials, with plaster ornaments, gilding, gaudy stained glass (if stained glass is used at all), immense plates of looking-glass in frames of all conceivable forms, gold and embossed papers of Alhambra (the fashion now) patterns; wretchedly designed furniture, with Gothic windows and gables for chair-backs; gilt curtain cornices, with inverted crockets, pinnacles, and finials; thickly folded drapery twisted into every variety of grotesque form; Gothic fire-screens, fireplaces, stoves, sideboards, in short, every subject where two segments of a circle can be made to meet in a point: these things, which would have thrown discredit upon Batty Langley, are, after the architect has terminated his labours, thrust into his rooms, to the total destruction of all style, date, and harmony of proportion or colour. I do not wish to quarrel with the decorators; there are many who, I dare say, are capable of carrying out a design with fitness and propriety; but now nearly· every house-painter or paper-hanger, without having studied any thing beyond the compounding and laying on of colour or hanging of paper, calls himself a decorator, and performs his work without knowing one principle of composition, or perhaps scarcely discerning Grecian from Gothic architecture; and the miserable result of his labour is the perversion of all good taste and sound principles.

In the elevation, fig. 2191., I have endeavoured, by appropriate decoration, to give suitable character to a simple general outline, preserving all through the decorations harmony of form: for instance, all the gables are of equal angles; the mullions of the windows of the same form and dimensions, and the openings between the mullions of the same width; and the arches only used where transoms would be liable to break from their inconvenient length. The stones all through should be small, seldom larger than a man can carry on his shoulder, and, if the walls are of brick, the jambs of the windows should show the bond into the brick and never a vertical joint; the former giving the appearance of strength, the latter of weakness. With regard to windows, much of the effect of modern Gothic, ay and of ancient too, is sometimes, destroyed by the variety of dimensions in the mullions and openings. To produce harmony of form throughout a building, very little difference in these dimensions should take place, except where sufficient reason can be assigned for it. Mullions and openings of windows evidently belonging to a series of apartments connected with each other should be of equal dimensions; but a chapel, an institution, or other building, joined to a range of domestic buildings, and requiring windows of larger dimensions or otherwise, to mark its character, should be designed upon the same principle, and the mullions should bear the same proportion to the openings as in the domestic building. A little attention to these rules would produce happy results, but a total disregard of them is mischievous in the extreme; since, if the mullions of a large window, where the openings would necessarily be large, were of the same dimensions as those of the small windows, where the openings are small, it would destroy the effect of the whole building, by presenting, by comparison, on the one hand heaviness, and on the other meagreness. To produce good effects, the balance of parts should be equal. Of external colour I have little to say, except one thing which has struck me in many instances, but more particularly during a late visit to a modern castle in Scotland, viz., that the mullions of windows that are seen from a distance should be of the same material as the jambs of the windows, and not of a dark colour; for if this be the case, the windows, at the distance the building should be seen to advantage with the accompaniment of beautiful scenery, become mere square unmeaning holes, combined with high·gables, battlements, and pinnacles, apparently of a totally different character. This subject requires much consideration, and cannot be too clearly impressed upon those who wish to build. Too frequently the fear of producing heaviness in the windows obliges the architect to reduce the mullions until they become, at a proper distance to view the building, mere clumsy sash-bars; and at the point where the sky line of the building would be seen to the best advantage, namely, when the sun is behind it, the mullions are mere unmeaning lines, lose their distinctness, and produce a poor and insipid effect. It only remains for me to say that the domestic offices are in the basement, and that the chamber plan contains six bed-rooms, all of which I would erect and decorate in suitable character.

Design XVII.—*An Anglo-Grecian Villa.* By E. B. Lamb, Esq., F.I.B.A.

The elevation is shown in fig. 2193.

2396. *Accommodation.* In the ground plan, fig. 2194., *a* is the portico; *b*, the hall; *c*, the saloon; *d d*, ante-rooms; *e*, drawingroom; *f*, dining-room; *g g*, library; *h*, library ante-room; *i*, portico; *k*, breakfast-room, or music-room; *l*, principal staircase; *m*, water-closet; *n*, passage to the offices; *o*, housekeeper's or butler's room; *p*, pantry; *q*, servants' hall; *r, s,* china closets; *t*, kitchen; *u*, scullery; *v*, servants' water-closet; *w*, back-stairs; *x*, servants' entrance. The chamber plan contains seven rooms in the principal body of the house, and six rooms in the wing.

2397. *Description.* The object of this design is, to show the application of decided Grecian forms and character to modern purposes; not as a copy from the works of antiquity, but to be treated in the spirit of the style, as far as that style can be so treated in a modern habitation. The remaining works of the Greeks are taken at the present time as precedents, but seldom are they applied in a manner suited to our climate and customs. Precedent has been the evil genius of the art, the trumpet sound of the employer, and

2193

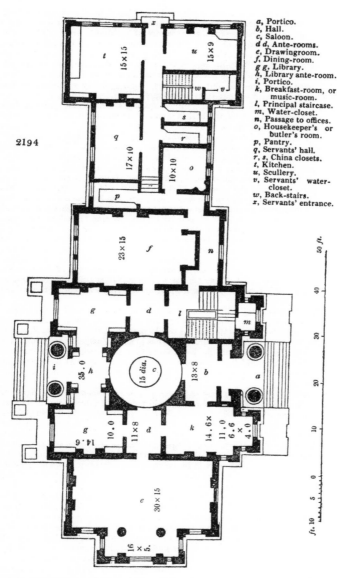

a, Portico.
b, Hall.
c, Saloon.
d d, Ante-rooms.
e, Drawingroom.
f, Dining-room.
g g, Library.
h, Library ante-room.
i, Portico.
k, Breakfast-room, or
　　music-room.
l, Principal staircase.
m, Water-closet.
n, Passage to offices.
o, Housekeeper's or
　　butler's room.
p, Pantry.
q, Servants' hall.
r, s, China closets.
t, Kitchen.
u, Scullery.
v, Servants' water-
　　closet.
w, Back-stairs.
x, Servants' entrance.

2194

the trammel of the genuine architect. Happily, a change is now taking place, and the forms of Greek temples are seldom applied to domestic edifices. The application and arrangement of columns in modern buildings should be quite different from what it was in ancient temples; nor would I scruple to alter the proportions of columns or entablatures, if it suited my purpose. In blindly adhering to precedent, how many have failed in producing the effect they desired! How many temples have been erected with three or four tiers of windows in the height of the columns! How frequently have fitness and propriety been violated by this mistaken predilection for ancient temples! How absurd would it be to copy York Minster, or Westminster Abbey, and put floors into them, for a dwelling-house; and yet the religious edifices of the Greeks have been frequently copied in this way, without the absurdity being noticed. The characteristic features of a particular style of architecture may be employed in a modern building, without its presenting the appearance of a temple, and in this design I have attempted to do so; preserving, in the first instance, a prevalence of horizontal lines.   The application of columns, pilasters, and entablature, the introduction of square-headed openings, and, although the pediment is omitted, the raised centre and lantern, will carry the mind to that form as associated with the buildings of antiquity, and thus mark the proper adherence to precedent.   I speak of the precedent of temples only, as we know so little of the private dwellings of the Greeks; but, if we knew more, probably we should be less able to apply them to our own climate than the temples.

The effect of the portico, *a*, in fig. 2194., will be greatly aided by the entrance-door being placed in the partition wall of the hall at *u*, and thus forming a doorway of solid masonry, and behind a less solidly moulded door-frame for the doors.   In the recesses might be placed figures on pedestals, or candelabra; if the latter, it would be a novel and pleasing way of lighting the hall through the large glass doors.   There is much difficulty in constructing the architrave over the intercolumns consistently in this style, as we are frequently at a loss to obtain so large a piece of stone as will take a solid bearing upon the columns.   For this reason, we are obliged to construct it on the principle of an arch, and thereby destroy the propriety of the application of the architrave.   This is a difficulty only to be surmounted in the way mentioned, and few people consider the impropriety of this construction, unless the architrave settles, and thus forms a curved line between the columns; it then becomes painful in the extreme to look at: this has not unfrequently occurred in some of our new public buildings.   In the choice of an order of architecture, some care should be taken, if we do not use the exact copy of the antique, that it is not one that is most elaborately sculptured, as, in a very short time, the beauty of the ornament is lost by the discolorations and other effects of this climate. In fact, the materials we use being of a coarser nature than the marbles of the Greeks, the elaborate detail, however good it may be, has seldom sufficient brilliancy of light to show it to advantage.   We require more decided forms and bolder execution to produce our effects.

The hall, *b*, should be the height of both stories, and should be stuccoed with a marble cement to receive a polish, if it was not entirely built with stone, which could be the case only in certain situations.   On the walls I would have some basso-relievo, of appropriate subjects, and let into the wall in such manner as to form a perfect connexion with the architecture.   All the doorways in the hall should have their mouldings of stone, or marble cement; the doors might be of mahogany or wainscot, or even of larch or other wood appropriately paneled, but not painted, unless the painting were used as a decoration, not a disguise.

The saloon, *c*, forms the connecting link in the composition between the drawingroom, library, dining-room, and hall, and therefore it should partake of some of the characteristics of each.   It is a small apartment, but I prefer this division from the hall to making that apartment of such large dimensions as it is usually of.   In this arrangement of the rooms, the saloon becomes at any time a private apartment, and can be used as an appendage to either of the other apartments, if required.   Some sculpture, an ornamental coffered ceiling, supported on cantilevers, the centre being figured glass, round which, on the landing of the chamber floor, should be a close screen to protect it.   The lantern-light shown in the elevation is, of course, the means of lighting that landing and the saloon.   The floor might be of mosaic or marble.

From this room we pass to the dining-room.   Here, as in all modern rooms in this style of architecture, there is great difficulty in keeping up a consistent construction. The width of the room will, therefore, oblige us to use wood as the principal material for all the ornamental paneling of the ceiling, but the walls might be scagliola; and in this situation I would place sculpture as the principal decoration.   The sideboard should form part of the architecture of the room, and the effect would be exceedingly good, by having a large mirror covering the whole of the back of the recess, and reflecting the windows, grounds, and sculpture.   In the decorations of the ceiling for this room I would provide two flowers or other ornaments, superior to the rest, from which chandeliers should be suspended.   The chimney-piece should be of sculptured marble, harmonising with the walls of the room.   The windows might have some coloured glass, with characteristic ornaments painted upon them, but not in gaudy colours. A severe style would be most suitable, as uniting better with the decorations of this room.   Generally, plate glass suits Grecian architecture admirably, as it preserves the massy character and distinctness of form so essential to the style.   Broad masses of light and shade, continuous lines, and square openings, are equally necessary.   The general tone of colour should be warm; some ornament might also be painted; but this should be done with great caution, as it would be difficult to make the painted decoration harmonise with the sculpture.

From the ante-room, *d*, we enter the library, *f, e, f*. The numerous breaks, and varied form of these rooms, would produce a good effect, and are capable of high architectural decoration. The bookcases would require to partake of the same character as the rooms; but if placed in recesses terminated with pilasters, and the cases only about eight feet high, the upper parts would form suitable pedestals for sculpture, bronzes, vases, &c., so that a great interest may be given to this room, in addition to its usefulness. The compartments in this room not being so large, stone might be used as a ceiling, but still I think, in this country, wood is most suitable; and by constructing the ceiling in wood, and being directed by the principles of the ancients, we might produce some new arrangement, which, though different from the forms we are accustomed to see, might be in the spirit of their buildings. An interesting question arises out of this difficulty; namely, What is the principle the ancients, when the arts were in the highest perfection, would have adopted in their ceilings had they constructed them of wood instead of stone? or, if any have been constructed in wood, what was the principle? The ante-room, *e*, in the library, would form an agreeable adjunct, and an easy means of passing to the grounds.

I will now speak of the drawingroom, which, to produce those pleasant sensations of cheerfulness associated with rooms of this description in this country, must be light and rather gay, not gaudy, in its decorations; but all the consistency of construction might as well be preserved here as in the other rooms of the house. The ceiling should be a framing of wood in coffers or panels supported upon beams of wood having all the strength necessary for the purpose. Great variety and beauty might be given by wood of various descriptions, gilt mouldings, and painted ornaments. The columns at the window recess should have their proper entablature, which should pass round the room, and should support the wood ceiling. Some appropriate sculpture in the frieze, also some, but sparingly introduced, in the walls, of figures, wreaths of flowers, &c. Within the recess, between the columns and pilasters, might be pedestals for elegant glass vases for flowers; or even small statues of marble or bronze, or other little articles of rarity, might be properly placed in this room; but, unless the furniture was designed in the same spirit, the effect would be destroyed; so that, in fact, the whole arrangement of this room should be under the direction of one person. I would have a fireplace at each end of the room, with a window over it: this should be of one sheet of glass, and should slide back at night, and into its place a shutter should slide in the same manner, but with a looking-glass on the inside. The effect, when the room was lighted in the evening, would be exceedingly striking.

As much attention to style and consistency of construction should be preserved in the breakfast-room, *h*, as in the drawingroom. The stairs, *k*, should be of stone, the balusters of metal, and the handrail of mahogany or oak; and, as I have mentioned in another place, the handrail should stop at the angles of the stairs against the newels, which should be solid and surmounted with some appropriate ornament to give pictorial effect, but not to make the staircase too prominent a feature. The arrangement of the offices is sufficiently marked on the plan; they are conveniently situated for the accommodation required in this design.

There are several effects which would require more notice than I have now time to give them. The vista from the dining-room through the ante-rooms to the drawingroom and grounds, from the variety of lights and shades, would be exceedingly pleasing; and again from the drawingroom to the dining-room, but this would be terminated by the blank wall of the room. The view, again, from the hall to the ante-library, *e*, and to the grounds in this direction, would be striking. Other views will occur upon examining the plan that may be pleasing, and would constantly be changing from the varied light during the day: and when lighted up at night, with all the rooms open, showing the proper distribution of sculpture, gilding, and other decorations, with appropriate furniture, the effect then would be exceedingly interesting and satisfactory.

2398. *Remarks applicable to this and the two preceding Designs.* In a hasty way I have endeavoured to give some account of three distinct styles of architecture, as applied to moderate-sized villas. The elevations in themselves clearly distinguish these styles, but, in addition, I will point out more clearly the marked difference of the styles generally. In the Grecian, of course, the temple forms the type of the style; the horizontal lines predominate, the cornices continue round the buildings in an uninterrupted manner, columns are symmetrically disposed, the openings have all horizontal lintels, the pediments have very obtuse angles, and the stones with which the buildings are erected are of immense size, particularly in the architraves. The ceilings, at least those we have any knowledge of, are flat, and constructed with stone, in coffers, or panels; the sculptured foliage also partakes of the same character, it is severe, but usually beautifully executed. Their statuary, which has served as models for all the schools of Europe, has still, when connected with the architecture, a severity and even formality, which completely unites the two arts. In a general view the buildings are flat masses, with little variety, but possessing much sublimity from their simplicity of form, the magnitude of the materials, and great antiquity.

The distinguishing character of the Italian style I have adopted is great breadth of effect, by masses of blank walls contrasted with richly decorated openings, which latter are frequently curved, combining with the horizontal lines in roofs and terraces; columns of different orders placed over each other, and only used the height of each story; arches used between columns, and constructed with several stones; small stones generally used in the construction : and, internally, coved ceilings coffered, arches rising from imposts, great richness in the sculptured foliage, and generally much variety of form and masterly execution ; a frequent application of colouring and fresco-painting ; and statuary more varied in form, but not blending with the architecture so well as in the Grecian edifices. In a general view, the Italian manner possesses more appearance of comfort and pictorial effect, but less sublimity, than the Grecian, and its forms are more readily applied to modern architecture.

In the Gothic style, the difference is more obvious to every one; the leading features are the openings, and the prevailing character in the lines is vertical, the windows divided by mullions and transoms, the roofs are generally acute angles, the columns seldom single, but formed in clusters; no horizontal cornices upon them, but pointed arches of complex mouldings; the stones seldom larger than can be carried by one man; immense variety and beauty in the foliage ; frequent representations of fruit, flowers, and leaves ; a profusion of heraldic emblems; groined ceilings of the most elaborate tracery ; immense quantities of statues, ill designed and executed, but still connected with the buildings from the admirable disposition of the drapery and their compact forms ; gorgeous display of colours in glass, but figures badly drawn; great variety of colouring and gilding in the ceilings, niches, and canopies; rich tapestry, cloth of gold, and embroidery ; all combining to produce effects of the greatest variety and picturesque character, and forming a style of architecture which it is almost impossible to believe could ever be traced back to the simple grandeur of the Greek temples. Picturesque and interesting, and intimately associated with our earliest history, and furnishing as it does many valuable precedents to study from, there is still much difficulty in applying this style of architecture to modern buildings. Our knowledge has extended, our customs improved, and we wish to combine the useful portions of each style into one that will meet our demands; but this has not yet been done. Perhaps, when a few years more have rolled over, some mightier mind than all who have passed before him may blend in one perfect style all the useful and beautiful now scattered amongst so many.—*E. B. L.*

CHAP. III.

Farm Buildings.

WE are not aware of much improvement having been made in this class of buildings since the publication of the Encyclopædia. Several plans of farmeries have been given in the *London Farmer's Magazine* for 1839 by Mr. Donaldson; and the same gentleman has just published two plans in his *Treatise on Manures and Farming*, of which, as they may be considered as models, we shall here, with his permission, give copies. Mr. Donaldson is a native of Berwickshire, and has practised the most approved modes of farming in that county, in Ayrshire, in Northumberland, in Leicestershire, and in Kent; and he is now engaged as land-steward in Breconshire. In short, we know no person whatever so competent to give plans for farmeries adapted to the most approved systems of agriculture, as Mr. Donaldson.

2399. *An improved Farmery*, Mr. Donaldson observes, will often induce a tenant to pay interest on the cost during a lease of twenty years, besides offering a better rent for the farm. But a new farmery, he says, is not always an improved one. " In many places, where large sums of money have been expended in erecting farm buildings, very glaring blunders have been committed, and much ignorance has been displayed, even of the most simple and evident details of practice, arising from the incompetency and conceit of the persons employed, who have never practised the art they pretend to assist, and therefore do not know the wants they attempt to supply. The landowner generally makes an unprofitable expenditure in unnecessary erections and in useless decorations, or is led away by the plans of architects, who, however well qualified to build dwelling-houses, Gothic windows, pointed arches, and spiral columns, experience has shown to be miserably deficient in contriving and placing the accommodations required on a quantity of land in cultivation. The economy of labour that is derived from the juxtaposition of objects that are required to act or to be used in combination has been wholly disregarded; barns and rick-yards have been placed at opposite sides of a large farmery; stables and cart-sheds in a similar manner, and the granary removed to a distance from the barn, for the apparent purpose of creating useless labour in carrying the grain from one place to the other. Farm horses are often allowed to enter by the fold-yards, and in many cases must travel round the farmery to reach the cart-shed. Many similar blunders might be pointed out, which must be obvious to any experienced person, and which abound in the best publications on the subject. However simple the matter may appear, no person is capable of devising plans of convenient farmeries without the most intimate knowledge, from long and continued personal experience, of the most minute details of practice; and the first requisite is to ascertain the number and size of buildings that may be required for any lands under a certain system of cultivation, without too much curtailment to create inconvenience, and without any useless appendages that require an unnecessary expense, and the second how to connect them so as to afford the greatest possible convenience with the least possible labour."

2400. *In Mr. Donaldson's Model Plans*, the form of a square with an open front to the south, as a warm exposure, has been adopted as the most suitable and convenient for the purpose of combining the necessary accommodations, and at the same time separating the different parts so as not to incommode each other. He has given two designs, each adapted for three hundred acres of arable land, the one with the yard separated from the buildings by a road, which leaves the yard detached in the centre of the square; and the other with the road exterior to the buildings, by which the yard occupies the whole interior of the square.

2401. *Model Plan No.* 1., *fig.* 2195. In this plan of a farmery, "a road of fifteen feet in width divides the covered houses from the open sheds, and admits no disturbance to

2195

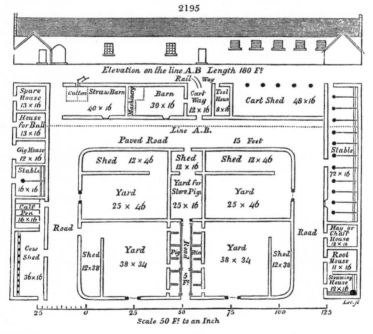

Scale 50 Fᵗ to an Inch

the cattle, except in supplying them with food, which may be much lessened by delivering it through holes in the walls. This separation is of great importance, though the road has met with the objection of occupying space unnecessarily in the interior of the farmery, and hence our second plan, fig. 2196., is given, in which the road is outside the houses, which saves room in the interior, but with the objection of causing a passage through the feeding-yards, and with many persons this objection would have great weight. The admission of any passages through yards, as the drawing of grain threshed or unthreshed, the entry of any thing except the cattle and the carting of the food and dung, is discarded in this first plan, and each department is arranged so as to afford mutual convenience, and at the same time admit carrying forward each separate business without intruding on another.

2402. " *The Dwelling-house, Garden, and Orchard* are supposed to be placed on the west side of the farmery, as being the most sheltered quarter in our climate; but in particular situations either side may be adopted, and probably an eligible situation may occur partly in front of the farm-yard, though that exposure may better be left open. On the end of the west wing of the farmery, adjoining the dwelling-house, the cow-shed is placed, for the sake of convenience, and extends thirty-six feet in length, and will contain ten cows, and the inside width of sixteen feet will afford a feeding-passage, if thought necessary. The calf-pen extends sixteen feet in length, and is divided into five apartments, for one calf in each, either for weaning or when suckling, the bottom being laid with thin laths, or with boards bored with auger-holes, and provided with a drain or open space underneath, that the calves may be on a dry bed. An inside communication to the cow-shed admits the calves to be suckled with as little labour as possible. A stable of two stalls of eight feet each in width, which may be converted into loose boxes, is intended for the riding-horses, and a gig-house is placed next to it; and both houses may be opened to the west, for the convenience of the dwelling-house. A house for a bull or any single animal opens into the yards, and the spare house at the end may open westward, and also communicate with the straw-barn, and serve any purpose that may be required. The exterior length of the wing is 114 feet.

" The back range of the buildings comprehends a straw-barn of forty feet in length, in which machines are fixed for cutting straw, hay, and roots, which are driven by the threshing machine when at work, and by a shaft for horse power when required. Wide doors open on both sides, and all the roots and hay are introduced from the stack-yard, which is placed immediately behind the range of buildings. The length of forty feet may afford ample room for cutting all food for cows, feeding-cattle, and horses, for which purpose deep mangers must be provided on the ground. Straw for litter may be cut by the same machine, by making a change in the power of the feeding rollers. Doubts are yet expressed of the utility of cutting any food for stock, and it certainly wants confirmation if it be not adopted, the barn will contain the straw and trussed hay, and the root which will be in daily request during the winter, and the length of the house could be partitioned for that purpose. The threshing-barn is placed next, and may be used by any kind of machinery; the unthreshed corn is brought into the cartway adjoining, and thrown to the second floor. An inside stair leads to the granary over the cart-shed, which is forty-eight feet in length, and consists of six arches for holding carts and other implements, exclusive of a tool-house; the second floor extends over the end of the stable, and affords an opportunity of conveying into a chest the grains allowed to the horses, without any labour in carriage. When the grain is bruised by machinery, it may be conveyed to the stable by the same method, and given out in measured quantities, cut straw being used at pleasure, which may be lodged in a bin in the hay-house or straw-barn. A range of granary does not appear to be an essential requisite on any farm, but it may be useful in containing grain, cheese, and wool, and the expense of raising side walls is not very great, nor the flooring that is required for the purpose. The grain for market is let down into the carts in the shed by means of a pulley fixed in the cross beams, and through a trap-door in the floor. The external length of the back range of building is 180 feet.

" The east wing of the farmery comprehends a stable of seventy-two feet in length, with a loose box in one end, and the corn chest in the other, and an end door leading to the cart shed, and another in front for a communication with the yards. A hay-house adjoins, and may be useful in containing cut food, and occasionally for a sick animal, or any similar purpose. A root-house is placed next, and may open eastward, for the purpose of receiving roots from the rick-yard; and communicates inside with the steaming-house, in which are prepared in vats and boilers all cooked food for any stock, cows at calving, and particularly for pigs and poultry. The accommodation for the latter kind of stock is shown separately, and will be hereafter described.

" A paved road of fifteen feet in width runs round the inside of the farmery, and gives access to each yard and house, without entering into any one enclosure in order to reach another. The interior space is divided into four yards, with sheds of fourteen feet in width, which may be covered by a common roof, or raised in the front wall and slope backwards, in the manner of an attached building, which will prevent the cattle displacing the tiles or slates with their horns, if a roof of asphaltum be not preferred. The bottom of the yards is sunk about two feet below the surrounding locality, and that of the sheds is raised to throw the water outwards, that the cattle may lie in a dry apartment. In order that the yards may be of a square compact form, a cross wall divides the space equally, and the front yards have sheds placed longitudinally, that the sun may not be excluded from the yards behind by a cross position of the sheds in front. The piggery is placed in the middle of the interior space, and contains a yard and shed for store pigs, which is supplied with litter from the stables, as that article forms an excellent bed for the swine, which must be well supplied with green food during winter and summer; and a few small animals may be allowed to run at large in the yards, to pick any offals that may be dropped, and they are found to move and turn the manure very beneficially. Six or eight sties are built in the remaining space, for brood sows, and for the feeding hogs; and each house is provided with a back-door, by which the dung is at once discharged into the yards; and it is very necessary that all kinds of dung carried into the feeding-yards be spread evenly and thinly over the whole surface, that an equal mixture and quality may be obtained. A road of four feet in width divides the rows of sties, and by it the food is brought forward in a wheeled carriage from the steaming-house.

" A pump may be sunk in a convenient place, or a pond formed, and water may be forced into a cistern placed in the roof of a shed or spare house, from which, by means of pipes and ball-cocks, it may be supplied to the yards in troughs, which may be placed in the division walls, and thus supply two yards by means of one article ; or the water may be supplied to the troughs, as it is required, by pipes leading directly from the pump. The feeding-cribs may be placed in the sheds, and the turnips supplied through openings in the walls, and the cattle may eat under cover. Cribs standing in the open air, and made of wood or built with stones, with close bottoms, are found to retain much filth; and movable hoxes, with latticed bottoms, are now preferred. The bottoms of the yards are intended to be flat; but if moisture be in excess, a declivity may be formed, and the liquid matter carried in a drain to a sunk pit or reservoir, where it will be absorbed by earths, along with similar substances. In most cases, the straw and litter will absorb all the moisture, but if it abound very much, such an application will be more useful than in a liquid state. The wings of the farmery are one story in height, and the range of barns and granary extends to two floors, or sixteen feet: a height of three stories has been proposed, that the grain may pass through two fanners, and be prepared at once for the market. All the walls are supposed to be of stone and lime, or brick; the doors, gates, and all articles to be plain and substantial, and the posts of wood, as they are easier repaired and less susceptible of damage. This farmery will cost about £600."

2403. *Model Plan No. 2., fig.* 2196. "In this plan, the road is outside the farmery. The north range extends in length one hundred and seventy feet, and comprehends barn, straw-barn, and stable, and spare house; the straw-barn being considerably larger than in the former sketch. The straw and roots introduced from the stack-yard are proposed to be cut in the straw-barn, and then conveyed, cut or uncut, by the central road of ten feet, which divides the farmery, and may be given to the cattle in the sheds on both sides, through openings in the walls. The stable contains a walk to communicate with the straw-barn, from which all the provender will be carried to be placed in the mangers. The cart-shed, tool-house, and open shed for cattle in the front yard, occupy the east wing, and on the opposite side of the yards, which are divided by a cross wall, there are a steaming-house on the end of the buildings, and a root-house, which extend the length of the front yard; the remaining space affords a shed for the back yard, and a small shed for the pig-yard, which is placed here to obtain the benefit of the litter from the stable, and divided by an open paling fence to admit the heat of the sun. On the opposite side of the central road, the longitudinal extent of the back yard is occupied by a shelter-shed, and a small feeding-house where five cattle may be tied up to feed if desired; the extent of the front yard is occupied by a shed, and a house for a bull on the end of the range. The cow-shed, calf-pen, riding-stable, and gig-house, all of the same dimensions as in plan No. 1., occupy the west wing of the farmery, and are convenient to the dwelling-house. The granary that may be required can be raised over the spare house, and gig-house, and riding-stable, or over a part of the straw-barn, and not unfrequently over the threshing-barn, but in both cases very inconveniently ; and the first position is most eligible, as it affords an inside communication, which is an object of great convenience. The pigsties are placed inside the front walls, and are convenient to the steaming and root houses, and to the wash of the dairy and kitchen. A separate piggery, in the form of a square, may be placed opposite the central road, with sties ranged round, and enclosing a yard for store-pigs in the centre. This arrangement may be preferable, as it is convenient for the steaming-house, and removes the smell of pigs, which is thought to be very offensive to cattle. A pond of water in the yard would be useful, if it could be got. The moisture from the yards is conveyed, if necessary, to a pit, as in the former plan ; the walls are intended to be plain work, of brick or stone and lime, and the roof to be slates or tiles. If decorations be wished, the eaves may project, and an arch may

2196

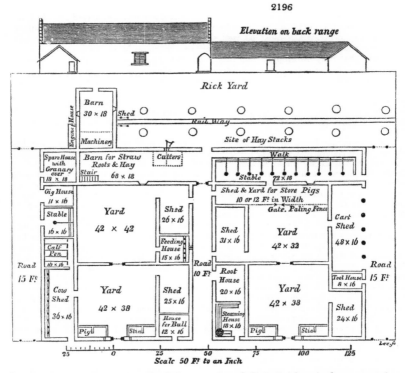

Elevation on back range

Scale 50 F! to an Inch

be thrown over the south end of the central road, in both plans, and may contain a pigeon-house, and be surmounted by a clock. Some small architectural decorations may be added, which would vary the uniformity of plain building, and much improve the appearance.

2404. " *The Poultry-yards* are here made a separate erection, which may be placed on any dry sunny situation that may be convenient to the dwelling-house and farmery. Suitable provision is seldom made for this kind of stock, which is generally huddled into one house in a corner of the farmery, without any regard to distinction or separation. The small square here shown in fig. 2197. may be built of timber in warm latitudes, and may be very cheaply erected in any place. Each kind of animal is provided with a separate apartment, which may be heated as the nature of the species requires. The food is chiefly composed of boiled or steamed potatoes, mixed with the flour of light grain, cooked in the steaming-house, and given to the poultry in troughs under the

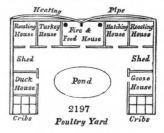

shelter of the open sheds. The small cribs leaning on the ends of the wings of the square are intended for the purpose of confining the young broods of any kind, until they are grown sufficiently strong to go to the roosting-houses. Such separate confinements may be found very convenient.

2405. " *Pasture near the Farmery.* A field of permanent grass, near the homestead, to serve as a pasture for the cows, is a valuable acquisition, where it can be got well sheltered and watered. If it does not exist, and if locality suits, a new formation should be effected, in order to obtain convenience in labour and travel. A paddock is also necessary, and in many places the orchard will suit admirably for the young calves that are weaning, to which they may be brought in succession from the calf-pen, and taught to eat green food, and may then be removed to the pasture-fields. A shelter-shed must be provided; and the same convenience will suit for lambing the ewes in the spring, which process will be finished before the season admits the exposure of calves in the open air. This enclosure and the cows' pasture must be enriched by top-dressing, frequent rolling, harrowing, and duly provided with water and shelter.

2406. " *The Rick-yard.* In both plans, or rather in No. 2., the ricks of grain stand in two rows, with a railway between them, along which a light four-wheeled waggon will convey the unthreshed grain to the barn, and may be moved without horses, as the railroad may have a slight inclination to favour that purpose. The way may be constructed with flat stones, or with cast iron, as may be found most convenient, and runs directly to that part of the barn whence the unthreshed corn is supplied to the feeding-board. But each rick might stand on a four-wheeled platform, in the same position as shown in the plan, and at a sharp angle of divergence, for the purpose of running easily into the railway; and the entire rick would be conveyed to the barn, and placed under a light covering on posts erected outside the barn walls; and the unthreshed grain would be pitched to the second floor, through a door with a lowered platform. A travelling carrier, driven by the machinery, may be devised to convey the sheaves of grain from any quarter, and deposit them on the second floor, which would add to convenience, and save labour. By the plan of moving the entire rick under cover at once, any damage from rain by exposure during the process of threshing would be avoided, which, on large farms, is often attended with much inconvenience; and the expense of the iron railway, and of the wheeled platforms, will not much, if at all, exceed the cost of stone or iron stands for each rick, and the yearly expense will be saved in horse labour by the usual mode of carting, which on a farm of the extent now mentioned will amount to the sum of £3. to £4. If the barn were built on a line with the western wing, the railway would be lengthened, and would afford more room for ricks; and as the straw-barn would be enlarged, a house may be divided by partitions at the end near the open way, for the purpose of containing the cut food of roots and straws. If the spare house form part of the barn, the latter would project only about twelve or fourteen feet; and in that case the railway would run to the end of the barn, and deliver the unthreshed grain to the second floor. A transverse motion of the machinery might be devised to throw the straw longitudinally into the straw-barn. Covers for ricks may be adopted of caoutchouc or waterproof clothing, which, being easily applied and removed, will protect newly made ricks from damage, until time be obtained for threshing. If such coverings be not adopted in the full number of ricks, a few of them on every farm, especially in wet climates, will be found very useful for the above purpose. The rick-yards may be laid with gravel and broken stones, and should be surrounded with a sunk fence, or a wall with a hedge inserted near the top or midway. In a corner of the rick-yard, a shed with a light roof may be placed, for the purpose of keeping dry a few loads of corn over a wet night; and it would be very useful in covering any implements not used constantly during the year.

2407. " *Machinery* is adopted for threshing grain, on the principle that it produces the result at one fourth or less of cost incurred by the usual mode of flails, and the necessary accommodations are erected at one third less expense at the outset; and the saving effected in both ways may be applied to increasing the produce, which will afford profitable labour in the production, additional employment for the machinery, and a more abundant supply of the necessaries of life.

2408. " *Horses are preferred to Oxen* in performing farm labour, and carts to waggons in general, because experience has most amply demonstrated that lands can be cultivated in the most improved modes by the former, without any assistance of the latter, but not in any case by the latter without the aid of the former, and with equal profit and advantages in the despatch and economy of labour.

2409. " *The Dwelling-house* should be constructed to afford ample accommodation. The dairy should be placed near the cow-shed on the west wing of the farmery, and, being half-sunk into the ground, will enjoy the coolness of the eastern exposure, which may be much assisted by a plantation of tall shrubbery. The cheese may be made in the pressing-room, and may be half-dried on latticed racks, and may be afterwards removed to an airy place in the granary, which may be separated and fitted for that purpose. The offals of the dairy and kitchen may be collected in vats, and prepared by cooking with farinaceous matters, and then given to swine; and not unfrequently it is given in an unmixed state. Of all kinds of live stock, pigs are most benefited by cooked food, and it may be justly supposed that the cold mass produced by souring may be advantageously superseded by a cooked application of the different substances.

2410. " *Six Cottages for Labourers* will be required on a farm of this extent, and may be placed not far distant from the farmery, in some situation where suitable spots can be found for gardens, and where an unsightly intrusion shall not be made on a methodical arrangement of the farm." (*Treatise on Manures, &c.*, p. 383.)

2411. *On the Management of the Farm-yard*, and on various other matters connected with it, many excellent practical observations will be found in Mr. Donaldson's work, which we cannot too strongly recommend to the reader who is at all interested in farming. In the *Book of the Farm*, now in the course of publication, by Mr. Stephens, editor of the *Quarterly Journal of Agriculture*, some good designs of farmeries will also be found, adapted for the same style of farming as the model designs of Mr. Donaldson, arranged on the soundest principles, guided by experience; and all the fittings-up and furniture of farmeries are given in that work in great detail, and illustrated with engravings in a very satisfactory manner.

2412. *The Park Farm-yard at Goodwood.* In the London *Farmer's Magazine* for November, 1841, there is a plan of a farm-yard erected by His Grace the Duke of Richmond in the park at Goodwood, Sussex. The editor observes of it, that "it is not calculated for business upon an extensive scale, but taken as a whole is one of the best, if not the best, and most convenient which he has seen." (Vol. iv. p. 326.) The merits of this plan, as compared with those of Mr. Donaldson's models, are not great, but, as compared with Sussex farmeries in general, they appear to consist in keeping the cattle yards distinct from the implement-houses and stable-yards.

Mr. Curtis of West Rudham, near Rougham in Norfolk, who has paid great attention to farm buildings in his part of the country and in Suffolk, says that the great objection to most farm-yards is, that the barn communicates directly with the yards, which consequently become thoroughfares, and the stock in them, whether fattening or otherwise, are disturbed whenever anything is carried to or from the barn. In the plan, fig. 2198., *a a* are dung or cattle yards ; *b*, the rick-yard; *c*, the yard to the stables and

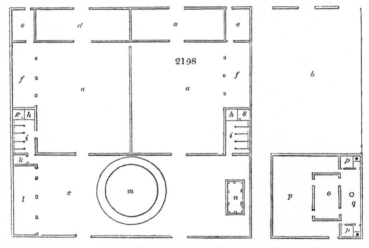

cart-house ; *d d*, barns, each eighty feet long by thirty feet wide ; *e e*, enclosed hovels for implements ; *f f*, open sheds for oxen, each sixty feet long and twenty feet wide ; *g g*, hay-lofts ; *h h*, bed-rooms; *i i*, stables, each forty-two feet long by twenty-three feet wide ; *k*, poultry-house ; *l*, cart-house, sixty-five feet long by twenty-four feet wide ; *m*, pond ; *n*, granary, thirty feet by twenty feet, supported on stone pillars, with projecting caps; *o*, double cottage; *p p*, washing-houses to cottages ; *q*, well; and *r*, garden.

2413. *The Demesne Farm-yard at Putteridgebury*, the seat of Colonel Sowerby, near Luton in Bedfordshire, when finished, will be one of the most comprehensive and best arranged park farmeries in England. Besides feeding-houses for cattle, it contains open sheds and yards for feeding sheep, a complete range of poultry-houses heated by hot water, an elegant dairy, a brewhouse, and a bailiff's house. All the stalls for the cattle are supplied with water delivered into troughs by pipes from an elevated source, and all the liquid manure is drained into one large tank. The buildings have brick walls, and they are thatched with reed, the ridge of the roof being finished with plain tiles, reaching down three feet on each side, to protect the reeds from pigeons. All the subdivisions of the yards are of strong fencing, formed of wrought-iron rods; and the whole is so arranged, that every part may be inspected by the master and his friends from a path, sometimes under cover and sometimes through the open yard, without coming in contact with or disturbing any of the animals, or walking among anything offensive or that can soil the shoes. The effect of the whole group of buildings from the park and the pleasure-ground is excellent, and from the latter scene there is a private entrance. The arrangement is not yet quite completed, otherwise we should have applied for permission to publish the plan.

CHAP. IV.

Schools, Inns, Workhouses, and Almshouses.

A GREAT many schools have been built in different parts of the country within the last ten years, and a great many plans have been published in the *Minutes of the Committee of Council on Education*, printed for the House of Commons in 1840, but we are not aware of any new feature in school arrangements. Some very handsome elevations have been sent us by Mr. Lamb, Mr. Wild, Mr. Elliott, Mr. Henderson, and others; but we have preferred giving a design from Parker's *Villa Rustica*, and the details of a small Sunday-school erected in Warwickshire; because the former design is in a style at present little used for schools, and the expense of the latter is within the reach of a great number of persons. We have given only two public-houses, but they are very handsome ones; and we have added to this chapter a union workhouse, as a specimen of that description of arrangement, and a design for a row of almshouses.

Design I.—*A School in the Italian Style.*

This design, of which figs. 2199. and 2200. are elevations, is taken from the Third Part of Parker's *Villa Rustica*, by the kind permission of the author. The whole of

2199

this part of Mr. Parker's work consists of plans, elevations, and views of school-houses in the Italian style. These are all of great originality and beauty, and we consider their publication at the present time (1842) peculiarly fortunate, since there is a general tendency throughout the country to build schools in the Gothic style, with but few exceptions, even in favour of the Elizabethan manner.

The designs for schools published in the *Minutes of the Committee on Education* being all by the same architect, and that architect also the author of the numerous designs for union workhouses published in the *Reports of the Poor Law Commissioners*, there is a degree of sameness of style in both schools and workhouses, and of meanness in the elevations given for the schools, that in point of taste is to us quite intolerable.

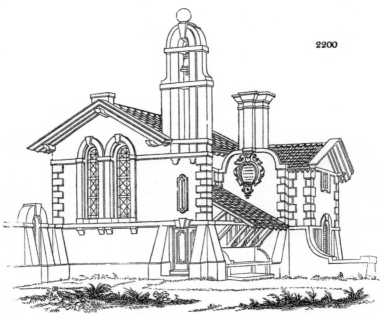

2200

This is a subject which, in our opinion, demands the notice of the legislature, or of public bodies; for why should not the exterior appearance of schools and workhouses be
cared as much for by the nation as the dress of soldiers or sailors, or the architecture of
other public buildings? That only one artist should have been employed by the Poor
Law Commission to design the whole of their published plans, and that the same artist
should also have been employed by the Committee of Education to design the whole of

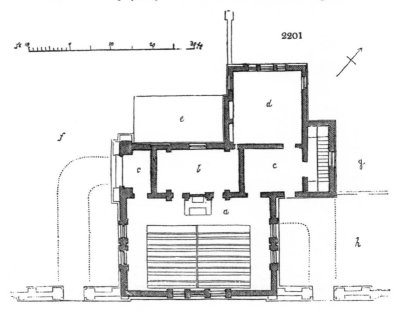

2201

the plans of schools published in their *Report*, amounting to twenty-three, when there are so many able architects in the country, we consider to be disgraceful to these bodies.

2414. *The Accommodation* and the details, as shown in Mr. Parker's ground plan, fig. 2201., consist of a school-room, *a*; class-room, *b*; lobbies, *c c*; master's room, *d*; shed, *e*; play-ground for the senior division, *f*; for the junior division, *g*; and master's garden, *h*.

2415. *Description.* " The building," Mr. Parker states, " has two entrances, with lobbies for the children's hats, and a small class-room. It is intended to instruct the boys and girls together, but, if this be found inconvenient, a movable partition of wood affords the means of separating them. Communicating with the school-room is the residence of the master, containing a sitting-room, two chambers on the upper plan, with convenient offices in the basement. The play-grounds are divided into two compartments, one for the senior and the other for the junior scholars, and both are under the master's supervision. The sketch given in fig. 2199. conveys the front view of the building. At each end there are separate external entrances for the boys and the girls. The light in the interior is obtained on three sides of the school-room, and the windows are raised sufficiently above the floor to allow all the operations of the master to be seen by the scholars without fatigue or distraction. The door-way, bell-turret, and gable ends of the school and master's house, all severally features of Italian architecture, form portions of the view shown in fig. 2200. The principal window is composed of two circular-headed openings, making together a graceful combination, and differing from the apertures on the side of the building. The chimney-shaft of the master's house, perceptible in the distance, is decorated with an enriched shield, on which the arms of the patron are supposed to be carved." (*Parker's Villa Rustica*, explanation of plates lxv., lxvi., and lxvii.)

Design II.—*Description and Specification, with Details, of Dunchurch Sunday-School. By F. Wood, Esq., Architect.*

This school has been recently erected at Dunchurch, adjoining the churchyard and rectory.

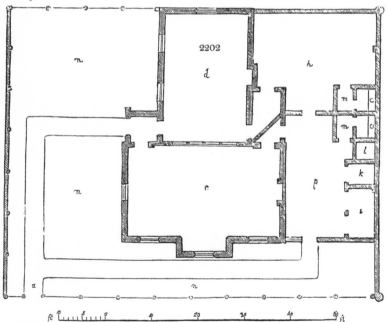

Fig. 2202. is the ground plan, surrounded by walls and railing, in which *a* is the entrance gateway from the churchyard; *b*, entrance porch; *c*, boys' school; *d*, girls' school, separated from the boys' school by folding-doors; *e*, porch to boys' yard; *f*, porch to girls' yard; *g*, boys' yard; *h*, girls' yard; *i*, shed; *k*, coals; *l*, dust; *m m*, privies; *n n*, garden, or play-ground.

Fig. 2203. is a perspective view, showing the effect of the north and east elevations. We have omitted some of the elevations and sections, which, though not necessary for understanding the plan and elevation, are yet essential to the parties contracting to execute the work.

2203

2416. *Description.* The design is in a plain Gothic, or modernised old English style; and by reference to the plan, fig. 2202., it will be seen that every essential accommodation is supplied. The site was of rather a peculiar description, being an old moat, and the foundations otherwise bad; consequently, the footings were carried much below the usual depth, and abutments were formed to carry an arch over the moat under the floor of the school-rooms. The description and quality of the materials is given at length in the subjoined particulars, therefore it is only necessary here to describe the engravings.

2417. *Details.* Fig. 2204. shows a plan and elevation of the doors; they are surrounded on one side by splayed bricks, and are six feet high to the springing of the arch.

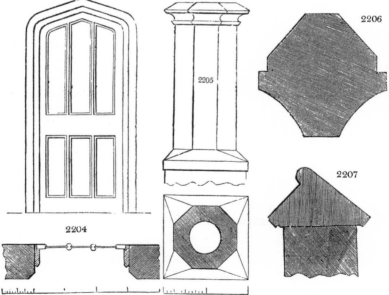

2206

2205

2207

2204

Fig. 2206. is a section of the window centre mullions, one third the full size.

Fig. 2205. shows a plan and elevation of the chimney shafts; the base and cap of which are of stone, and the shaft and plinth rising from the roof of brickwork; the diameter of the flues, nine inches.

Fig. 2207. is a section of the stone coping for parapets, to a scale of an inch to a foot.

Fig. 2208. is an elevation of part of the verge-board of the east, west, and south gables, showing also sections, to a scale of one inch to one foot.

Fig. 2209. is an elevation of part of the verge-board of the north gable, to a scale of one inch to one foot.

Fig. 2210. is a section of the architrave for the doors, one half the full size.

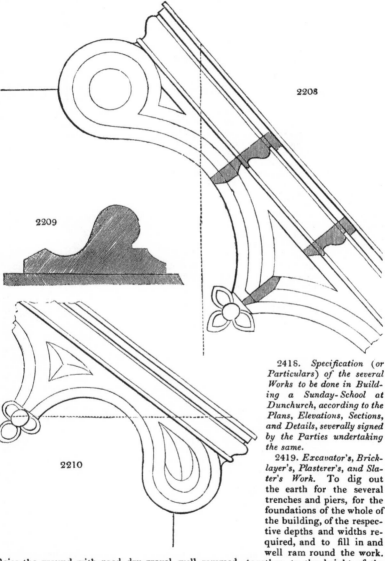

2208

2209

2210

2418. *Specification* (*or Particulars*) *of the several Works to be done in Building a Sunday-School at Dunchurch, according to the Plans, Elevations, Sections, and Details, severally signed by the Parties undertaking the same.*

2419. *Excavator's, Bricklayer's, Plasterer's, and Slater's Work.* To dig out the earth for the several trenches and piers, for the foundations of the whole of the building, of the respective depths and widths required, and to fill in and well ram round the work. Raise the ground with good dry gravel, well rammed together, to the height of the several floors, and back up and well cover over the arch over the moat under the girls' school, to a uniform level with the boys' school, ready to receive the floors. Level the ground all round the buildings, and clear away any rubbish that may accumulate during the execution of the work, and leave the same in a clear and perfect manner. Lay drains from the rain-water spouts all round the building, and thence conduct the water into a well on the west side of the building, with a drain tile set with compo on a brick laid flat, as in fig. 2211. Build the walls of the several dimensions and thicknesses, and with proper footings, as set forth and described on the plans, sections, &c., with good, sound, and hard, well-burnt bricks, and mortar composed of well-burnt fresh Neobold lime, made up with sand, to be got on the ground or carted to the spot, in the propor-

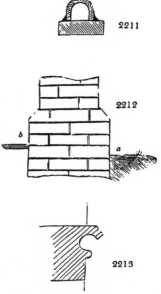

2211

2212

2213

tions of at least one part lime to two parts sand, and work all the walls above the surface with a neat flat joint, jointed and struck (struck with lines between the bricks, by an instrument called a jointer) on both sides. Lay two courses of eighteen-inch work for the foundations of the main building, and two courses of fourteen-inch work to the walls where nine-inch work is intended above. Set over, fourteen inches below the surface of the ground, two inches and a quarter for a plinth to the main building, on both sides of the walls; the outer side, *a*, to be carried up one foot above the surface to form a plinth, and the inner side, *b*, to be carried nine inches above the floor to form a skirting, both to be neatly jointed, and to finish in again to the fourteen-inch work with proper plinth bricks made for the purpose, with the upper angles taken off, as in fig. 2212. No plinth is requisite for the privy, yard, and mound walls, which are to be carried up with nine-inch work from within six inches of the foundations, the latter consisting of fourteen-inch footings; these walls to be covered with proper coping tiles, made for the purpose. The window jambs and arches to be built and turned on both sides, within and without, with splayed bricks; as also the inner and outer side jambs and arches to all the doors and openings, with projecting bricks round above the arches on the tops of all the window openings, to form a label to be worked in compo, as in fig. 2213. Put a rubbed and gauged fourteen-inch brick arch over the opening in the east porch. The whole of the external walls of the main building to be faced with picked white bricks, and all the piers and chimney shafts to be built octagonal shape, with bricks to be made on purpose, the bases and caps of which to be worked in Attlebury stone (see § 2420., Stonemason). The pediment of the porch on the east side to be carried up six inches above the ramp of the slates, and coped with stone. To pave the porches on the west side, also the privies and shed, with seven-inch square paving quarries, set in mortar and jointed. The school floors and east porch to be laid with nine-inch red and blue Newcastle quarries, bedded and jointed in mortar, and laid diagonally. No part of the walls, while building, to be carried more than four feet above the other, but the whole to be carried up in a regular, uniform, and equal manner. To fix all the wooden bricks and bed all the plates, bond timbers, and lintels in mortar. To cut all the rakes and splays, and all chasings required for lead flashings, and to make good and stop the same with Roman cement; to bed and point the door and window frames in lime and hair, and underpin all the sills. Colour all the internal walls and roofs of a neat drab colour. To cover the whole of the roofs with the best countess slates on ⅜-inch deal laths, and nailed with copper nails; the ridges to be covered with the blue Newcastle tiles, and the whole to be done with particular care, so as perfectly to exclude the snow, rain, and wind. The fillets, listings, and vergings, to be of Roman cement. The bricklayer to find all materials, ropes, boards, tackle, tools, centres, scaffolding, workmanship, and iron-work for the completion of his work (exclusive of the carriage of the bricks, slates, and quarries only), and to do the whole in the best and most workmanlike manner. To do all the beam-filling and wind-pinning required, and the whole to be done subject to the provisions of the general particulars at the end hereof. The plasterer to lath, lay, float, set, and whiten the ceilings to the porches and privies. The inside of the school walls to be left neatly pointed down in brick, and coloured over with a drab or stone colour.

I, the undersigned, hereby undertake to perform the foregoing bricklayer's, slater's, plasterer's, and excavator's work, for the sum of three hundred and fifty-nine pounds eight shillings and fourpence.

(Signed) W. S.

2420. *Stonemason.* To put Yorkshire stone steps and riser to the entrance of the east porch, and to provide and set seven Attlebury stone window-sills, according to the enlarged drawing. To put moulded caps and bases to the two chimney shafts, and two octagonal stone caps to piers ; also one date, one shield, and one inscription stone, as in the drawings. To put York stone slabs to cover privy wells, and Attlebury stone coping to the pediment of the east porch, with one projecting stone at gable, and key-stone to the gauged arch in east porch. The contractor to find all materials, work-manship, and carriage, and setting the same in a workmanlike and satisfactory manner.

I, the undersigned, hereby undertake to perform the foregoing stone-masonry, for the sum of seventeen pounds two shillings and one penny.

(Signed) E. A.

2421. *Carpenter and Joiner's Work.* The whole of the materials to be sawed out square, free from waste, and of the several scantlings and thicknesses herein specified ; to be carted to the spot by the contractor, and to consist of the best yellow Dantzic or Memel fir. The whole of the carpentry is to be framed in a workmanlike manner, according to the drawings ; the carpenter finding labour, nails, and tools, and all kinds of iron-work required for the purpose : the whole to be done subject to the general particulars at the end hereof. To frame and fix a span roof, with four sets of prin-cipals, braces, strutts, purlins, rafters, ridge-pieces, gutter-planks, wall-plates, &c., of the several scantlings set forth in the plans and sections. The purlins to be let into the principal rafters, so as to admit of the common rafters lying flush with them on the upper side. All the timbers and scantlings to the internal part of the roof to be neatly wrought and chamfered on the edges, and the principals ornamented with noggings spiked on, and neatly wrought down to form one uniform appearance, according to the section produced. A three-inch diameter staff-bead, neatly wrought, to be put round the internal walls, to hide the intersection of the wall-plate with the rafters. The wall-plates to be dove-tailed and bolted together at the angles, with three-quarter-inch bolts, nuts, and screws. Proper lintels to be provided, and put over all the openings for windows and doors, and wood bricks built in, as the building proceeds, for fasten-ing the door-jambs, architraves, &c. Provide and fix four-inch diameter cast-iron spouts round the eaves, supported from every other rafter by a wrought-iron bracket, or holdfast, as shown in the section of eaves, with four upright cast-iron wall-spouts, and heads properly fastened and connected with the spouts, and connecting with a shoe to the drains. — Scantlings of timber. Principal beams, ten inches by eight inches ; principal rafters, nine inches by seven inches and by five inches ; purlins, six inches by five inches ; king-posts, seven inches by five inches ; strutts, four inches by five inches ; ridge-piece, eight inches by one inch and a half ; wall-plates, nine inches by three inches ; valley planks, nine inches by two inches and a half ; common rafters, three inches by two inches and a half. The lintel over the folding-doors to be ten inches by eight inches, and to have a bearing of at least nine inches at each end, with an inch bolt through the middle, and keyed up to the arch. To put inch yellow deal gutter-boards round all the eaves and chimney-shafts, &c.

2422. *Joiner's Work* to be done according to the several drawings and details. All the stuff to be of the best yellow deal, listed free from sap and shakes ; the whole to be neatly wrought and finished off in a workmanlike manner. To put four two-inch paneled doors according to the drawings, with 4½-inch rebated and headed frames, to be built in as the work proceeds. Two one-inch six-paneled doors, made with one fold each, to turn back into the recesses between the two schools, each seven feet six inches wide, by ten feet high (the openings being ten feet by fifteen feet), hung to two-inch rebated jambs beaded on edge, and finished round on both sides with an architrave, as shown by the drawings. To put one-inch ledge deal doors and frames with oak sills between the boys' and girls' yard, and in the yard dividing the boys' yard and church-yard. No doors are required for the privies. To frame five window-frames with square heads and chamfered edges, of well seasoned yellow deal, with middle mullions and Gothic heads to oak sills ; and two frames with pointed heads, as shown by the drawings : these are to be set and built up with the brickwork. To put 1½-inch well-seasoned yellow deal carved verge-boards, with crown mouldings and cham-fered edges, to all the gables, with carved pendants of oak, as expressed by the drawings. To put ¾-inch soffits to all the eaves and gable-hangings, with 1½-inch staff-moulding in the angle against the wall. The carpenter and joiner to find all materials, tools, labour, nails, glue, and every description of ironmongery, locks, bolts, bars, hinges, and fastenings, and the carriage and fixing thereof, and every thing required for the completion of his work in the best and most workmanlike way ; and to prepare and fix all manner of beads, stops, fillets, grounds, linings, and backings, required for the perfect execution of the work, whether the same may or may not be minutely specified in this particular; and the whole to be done subject to the general particular at the end hereof.

I, the undersigned, hereby undertake to perform the foregoing carpenter's and joiner's work for one hundred and ninety pounds thirteen shillings and seven-pence.

(Signed) W. L.

2423. *Plumber, Glazier, and Painter's Work.* To put flashings of milled lead, eight inches wide and five pounds to the foot superficial, chased into the brickwork, and fastened with wall-hooks to each of the chimney-shafts, and where the roofing abuts against the buildings and front parapet of porch. To put milled lead, fifteen inches wide, to all the gutters and valleys. To glaze all the windows with second Newcastle crown-glass in diagonal shape, properly leaded, and neatly pinned at convenient distances to cross-bars of iron; with an iron casement in each window, to swing on a centre, complete with staples, cords, and hooks. Paint all the woodwork, within and without, of a drab colour, twice in oil. To put a lead pump, with pipe and all complete, to the soft-water cistern in the back yard, and leave all the windows, &c., in a perfect and complete state.

I, the undersigned, hereby undertake to perform the foregoing plumber's and painter's work for the sum of thirty-seven pounds ten shillings and three-pence.

(Signed) G. K.

2424. *General Particulars.* The contractors to find all and every kind of material, labour, and workmanship, scaffolding, and carriage, &c. (except such as hath hereinbefore been specified to the contrary), necessary, proper, and requisite for the due execution of all and every part of the works. And if any alteration shall be made in any part thereof, by direction of the employer, during the progress of the works, it shall not vitiate or annul the contract; but the value of such alteration shall be ascertained according to the annexed schedule of prices; and if to such other portion of the work to which the annexed schedule does not refer, then according to the customary prices of the neighbourhood, by the architect, whose decision between the parties shall be final.

The whole of the works must be executed of the best materials of their respective kinds, and in the most substantial and workmanlike manner; and the rooms to be scoured, and the chimneys cored, the windows cleaned, and the whole building left clean and complete on or before the 10th day of October next.

Dated, Rugby, Aug. 5., 1837. (Signed) Fred. Wood, Architect.	(Signed) { W. S. W. L. E. A. G. K.

Recapitulation.

	£	s.	d.
Excavator's, bricklayer's, plasterer's, and slater's work (§ 2419.)	359	8	4
Stone-mason (§ 2420.)	17	2	1
Carpenter and joiner (§ 2421.)	190	13	9
Plumber, painter and glazier (§ 2423.)	37	10	3
Actual cost	604	14	3

2425. *Remarks.* The architect's fees are not included in the above sum. In moderate foundations the above estimate would be less 70*l.* at least, the site of this school being peculiarly situated over an old moat, the foundations consequently were bad, and had to be laid at a great depth, and arched over, as expressed in the section of the foundations.

Schedule referred to.

	s.	d.	
Nine inches reduced brickwork	4	6	per yard super.
Paving with seven-inch red quarries	3	0	do.
Do. do. nine-inch red and blue Newcastle quarries ...	4	4	do.
Tile drain on brick flat set in compo	0	6	per yard run.
Coping to nine-inch walls, with tiles	0	2	per do. do.
Ridge coping with Newcastle tiles	0	10	per foot
Lath and plaster to ceilings	1	6	per yard
Stucco on walls	1	1	do.
Countess slating on long ⅝-inch laths and copper nails	36	0	per square
Paving with brick flat	1	10	per yard.

Design III.—*A Union Workhouse.*   By C. Eales, Esq., Architect.

2426. *Description.*   This design was prepared and submitted to the guardians of the Horncastle Union, Lincolnshire, in the early part of the last year, for their proposed workhouse, in accordance with the terms of an advertisement which appeared in the daily papers; viz. to accommodate two hundred inmates; the expense not to exceed £2,800. The drawings (figs. 2214. to 2218.) are accurately reduced from those sent in, which, however, were not adopted.

Fig. 2214. is the elevation of the principal front of the main building.

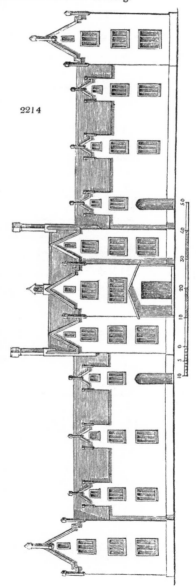

2214

Fig. 2215. ground plan of the workhouse. The first building, forming the gate-house, is two stories in height, and comprises on this plan every convenience for the officers of the establishment; viz. *a*, porter's room; *b*, relieving office; *c*, waiting-room for the poor; *d*, searching-room, together with a staircase leading to the board-room on the story above. A water-closet for the use of the guardians is intended under these stairs. Right and left of this building are the various offices and receiving wards for the use of the girls and boys, women and men's wards, and general purposes; E, work-rooms; F, receiving wards; G, baths; H, washing-rooms, fitted up with troughs; I, privies; K, refractory cells; L, coal-house; M, wood-house; N, bakehouse; O, flour and mill room; P, bread and potato stores; Q, laundry; R, ashes. The main building upon this plan comprises, S, chapel. It is proposed, as the service will be attended by the inmates on the sabbath only, that during the week it should be appropriated for the purpose of the girls' and boys' school and dining-rooms, which could be conveniently done by movable partitions on the dotted lines, at the same time reserving ample space for the performance of daily worship should it be necessary. On either side of the chapel, T and U are women's and men's dining-rooms, classified, each of which have staircases, V, conducting to the dormitories on the stories above; W, staircase to master's and mistress's rooms, each of which have separate access to their respective departments; X, store-rooms, kitchen, scullery, and larder. Considering it most essential, in an establishment of this nature, to keep the sick in as isolated a situation as possible, particularly in case of an epidemic or contagious fever, the building containing the infirmary has been placed at the back of the premises, forming a separate structure, and contains, on this plan, Y, dead-house for each sex; Z, staircases for men and women to infirmary, &c.

Fig. 2216. Plan of the first Story. The gate-house comprises a spacious board-room, A; clerk's office, B; strong room, C. In the main buildings, D is the master's bed-room; E, master's parlour; F, mistress's parlour; G, women's and men's dormitories, classified, each of which have

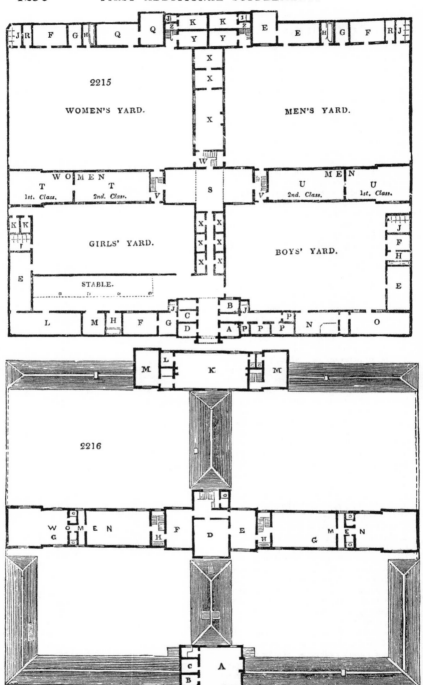

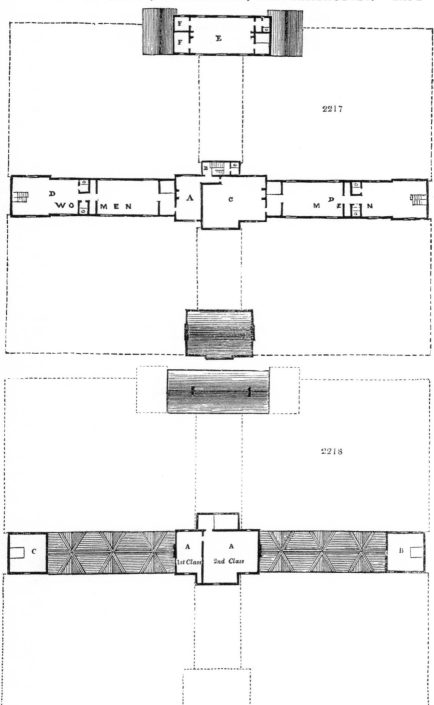

staircases, H, conducting to the dormitories on the stories above.   Two water-closets and washing-troughs are provided in each dormitory. I, staircase and water-closet for master's apartments; K, women's ward, and women's sick and lying-in ward; L, surgery; M, wards for the insane of each sex, with separate staircases and water-closets.

Fig. 2217. Plan of second Story.   The main building comprises, A, mistress's bed-room; B, staircase and water-closet; C, boys' first class dormitory; D, women's and men's dormitories, classified, as in the story beneath.   In the wings are staircases communicating with the story above; E, men's sick ward, with separate staircase, water-closet, and washing-trough: F, nurses' rooms.

Fig. 2216. Plan of third Story: the main building.   A, girls' bedrooms, classified; B, boys' second class dormitory; C, nursery.

Summary of Accommodation.

	1st Pair.	2d Pair.	3d Pair.	Total.
Men	40	40	—	80
Women	40	40	—	80
Boys	—	14	12	26
Girls	—	—	30	30
				216

Design IV.— *The Almshouses at Oving.*   By John Elliott, Esq., Architect.

The elevation is shown in perspective in fig. 2220., and the ground plan in fig. 2219. This plan is shown in isometrical perspective with the walls raised the height of four feet, a mode which renders plans much more easily understood, and consequently more interesting than the ordinary mode.

2427. *Accommodation.*   The dwellings at the two ends of this line of building are larger than the others, and consist of a living-room, twelve feet by fourteen feet, *a*; scullery, twelve feet by ten feet, which contains a stair to two bed-rooms, *b*.   The other dwellings, of which there are four, are smaller, and each of them consists of a living-

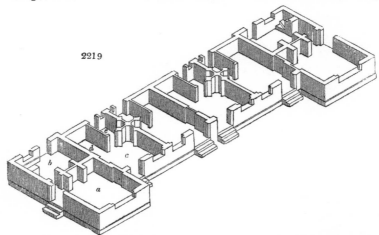

2219

room, twelve feet by ten feet, *c*; a bed-room, six feet by seven feet, *d*; and a scullery, five feet six inches by six feet six inches, in which there is a stair to two small bed-rooms over *e*.   Behind each dwelling is a small garden; and there is also in front a narrow slip of ground, neatly laid out and planted with shrubs and flowers.   The situation is on a bank or ridge along the public road, and separated from it by a small watercourse. The cost of these six dwellings was about £650.

2428. *Remarks.*   These almshouses were built for Miss Woods of Shopwyke, the proprietress of the village of Oving, near Chichester.   This village she has greatly improved, by rebuilding most of the cottages from designs by Mr. Elliott, adding large gardens to them, and charging a rent for each cottage which does not pay more than between 2 and 3 per cent on the capital employed.   The church of Oving has also been repaired

2220

and restored by Miss Woods; and the churchyard we have noticed in the *Gardener's Magazine* for 1841, p. 591., as reformed in the very best taste, under the care of the rector, the Rev. G. H. Langdon. Miss Woods has also built a commodious school at Oving, from the designs of Mr. Elliott, which, like all that gentleman's designs that we have seen (and they are numerous), is in excellent taste. We regret much that time and space prevent us from taking advantage of Mr. Elliott's kindness in offering us the use of any of his designs for publication in this Supplement.

Design V.—*A Public-house.* By I. W. Wild, Esq., Architect.

The elevation is shown in fig. 2222., and the ground plan in fig. 2221.

2429. *Accommodation.* The plan shows a porch, *a*; lobby, *b*; kitchen, *c*; parlour, *d*, with a bay, *o*, which may be separated in the winter season by a screen of glass, so as to form a small greenhouse; an open veranda, *e*, with seats for smoking and drinking, the liquor being served out through the small window shown at the bottom of the staircase; *f*, the staircase, over which there is a pigeon-house, and from which the sign is projected; *g* is the back-kitchen; *h*, the pantry; *i*, the dairy; *k*, water-closet; *l*, open porch; *m*, cow-house; and *n*, dotted lines, showing in what manner the bay of the parlour may be extended, so as to afford a larger space when partitioned off as a greenhouse.

2430. *General Estimate.* The cubic contents are 18,583 feet; which, at 6*d*., amounts to £464 14*s*. 6*d*.; at 4*d*., to £309 14*s*. 3*d*.; and at 3*d*., to £232 7*s*. 3*d*.

2431. *Remarks.* The walls of this cottage are supposed to be covered with stucco between the principal timbers of their construction; thus being divided into panels, which, again, may be ornamented with patterns stamped by plates of wickerwork upon the stucco while yet moist. The impression would resemble interlacing basket-work, according to the disposition of the wicker, of which there may be many beautiful patterns. Some of the panels might be ornamented with initial letters, appropriate devices, foliage, &c., easily executed and of good effect; as in ancient plastered houses in many parts of this country. Perhaps the most beautiful example in the world, of

2222

elaborate ornament in stucco-work, is the Moorish palace of the Alhambra in Granada. In this building there is an endless variety of patterns, many of them so complicated as to have three planes of ornament, one overlying the other, yet each perfectly distinct; others, again, are simply formed by the intersection of geometrical patterns, in lines slightly engraven in the stucco. This building, so elaborately illustrated by Owen Jones, is a complete encyclopædia of ornament, and deserves especial attention when the subject of enriched stucco is considered. The practice of covering walls with cements has been condemned by some architectural writers, but upon insufficient grounds. The material, particularly, is of the greatest value, as it enables us to make a thin wall more weather-proof than one much thicker and more costly without it. When used externally it should be protected by projecting eaves.

Design VI. — *The Hand and Spear Hotel, at Weybridge, Surrey.*

2432. A perspective view of this very picturesque hotel is shown in fig. 2223. We have not given the plan, because there is nothing remarkable or characteristic in the arrange-

2223

ment; in short, it is merely an old public-house with some additional rooms. The whole, however, is commodious and comfortable. The elevation, as it appears in the figure, was designed by the Honourable Peter John Lock King, the proprietor of the estate on which the inn is built, who, with his brother, the Earl of Lovelace, appears to inherit a taste for architecture from their ancestor, Mr. Lock of Norbury Park, in Surrey. (See Gilpin's *Cumberland.*) The view shows the inn as seen from the South-ampton Railroad.

CHAP. V.

Details of Construction applicable to Cottages, Farm Buildings, Villas, &c.

As many of these details are alike applicable to several classes of buildings, we have, for more convenient reference, brought them all together. We shall begin with foundations, and take, in succession, walls, roofs, interior arrangements, and miscellaneous matters.

SECT. I. *Foundations and Walls.*

2433. *Concrete.* The use of this mixture of lime, gravel, and sand, in foundations, and for floors of sheds, and even of cottage dwellings, is now very general. In using it

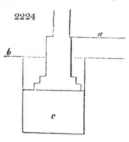

in the foundations of a house, a trench is dug out about eight inches wider than the lowest course of brickwork or masonry, and to such a depth as is necessary to arrive at firm soil. This is shown in fig. 2224., in which *a* is the floor line; *b*, the ground line; and *c*, the concrete. When the trench is made, coarse and fine gravel are thrown into it, just as they come from the pit, to the thickness of about four inches; it is then grouted with thin hot lime, just enough to bind the gravel together, and afterwards rammed quite hard. Course after course must then be laid, and so treated till the mass reaches within about eighteen inches of the ground line. The proportion of hot lime to the gravel is about one eighth part only. Others use lime in the proportion of one to five of loamy gravel. In countries where gravel is not common, dry brick rubbish, broken stone, flints, or any material that will bind into one mass, will answer. Carter informs us that the foundations of Westminster Abbey, erected in 1245, consist of flints, irregular stones, rubble, and mortar, forming an almost impenetrable body. In many of the ancient castles, particularly in Kent, the foundations are thus made. (*Arch. Mag.*, i. 248.)

2434. *Preventing Dampness in Foundation Walls.* Fig. 2225. represents the section of a wall built on a concrete foundation, *c*, formed within a trench, the sides of which

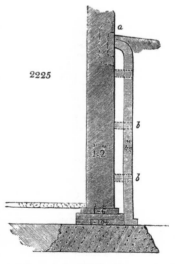

are pared down inwards, so as slightly to increase the base. Around all the walls of the foundation against which ground will lie a dry area should be formed, in order to prevent dampness within the building. This may be done with a half-brick wall, placed at a little distance from the part to be protected, as represented by the annexed sketch. The space thus enclosed must be arched over at the top, just below the level of the ground; and if iron air-bricks, or small gratings communicating with the dry area, be introduced, wherever open areas are formed, around windows or elsewhere, a free circulation of air will be obtained. Should no open areas occur in the basement story, small flues, or throats, may be formed at certain intervals within the wall, terminating just above the ground, to receive an air-brick, as shown at *a* in the figure. The wall of the dry area, although under ground, should not be carelessly executed, as it must necessarily be subjected to considerable pressure, and the workmen should be directed to put in whole headers at certain distances, that is, bricks placed lengthwise in the direction of the thickness of the wall, as at *b b*, so as to stiffen it.

2435. *To prevent Damp from rising in Walls*, a vacuity may be left in the centre of the wall just above the surface of the ground as at *a*, in fig. 2226., laying over it slabs of stone or slate, chamfered off so as to form a neat finish to the plinth round the outside of the building. At various intervals, small openings, communicating between this channel and the interior of the building, should be made as at *b*, so that a current of air may be driven through the vacuity and openings under the floors, in order to ventilate them. (*A. M.*, i. 233.)

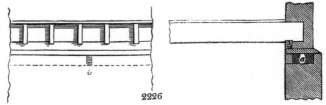

2226

2436. *To prevent Damp from ascending the Walls of a House already built,* introduce
a water-proof medium through the wall, just above the level of the ground, in the
following manner : First, make a hole through the wall, over the ground course, taking
out two courses in height, and two bricks in length ; consequently, the hole will be six
inches high and eighteen inches wide.   Then fill up half this hole, at one end, with two
courses of sound bricks, laid in Roman cement.   It is clear that the operation could
not injure the wall, the width of eighteen inches not allowing of any settlement.   Two
courses more, of nine inches in width, are next removed, making the hole again eighteen
inches wide ; the half of which is then filled up with bricks and cement as before.   The
operation is to be repeated until the whole of the walls of the house are underpinned by
two courses of hard bricks and three joints of Roman cement ; constituting a water-
proof septum, through which the damp cannot rise.   (*A. M.,* i. 123.)

2437. *Brick Walls.*   In addition to the various modes of building hollow walls shown
in the *Encyclopædia,* we give the following mode of building a wall fourteen inches in

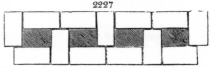

thickness, with only a small additional
quantity of bricks to what are required
for a nine-inch wall.   Fig. 2227. shows
the plan, or first course of bricks, of
such a wall, and all the rest is mere repetition.   Walls built in this manner
may be carried to the height of ten or
twelve feet, without any piers, and hence they are suitable both for the walls of cottages
and gardens.   For the latter purpose two courses of cross bond may be left out, on a
level with the surface of the ground, in order to leave room for a hot-water pipe, which,
in consequence of the vertical vacuities, will heat the whole wall.   If we suppose
that only half the amount of cross bond is used, then the saving of bricks will be
still greater.   A rod of solid nine-inch brickwork requires 4,500 bricks; a rod of hollow fourteen-inch brickwork, such as fig. 2227., requires 3,600 bricks; and a rod
with only half the amount of cross bond shown in fig. 2227. requires 3,200 bricks.
If the whole of the brickwork were set on edge, then, for a common nine-inch wall,
hollow, the number of bricks required per rod will be 3,000; for a fourteen-inch
wall, hollow, on the principle of fig. 2225., but with bricks on edge, the number
required per rod will be about 2,800; and for a wall, brick on edge, with only half
the cross bond shown in fig. 2227., the number per rod required will be about 2,500.

2438.   It is evident that hollow walls might be made eighteen inches or two feet in
thickness, either with brick in bed or brick edgewise, on the same principle as fig.
2227.; and if such walls were filled in with concrete, they would form excellent walls
for cottages.   When cottage walls are built hollow, it is necessary to have solid piers
to the doors, and to have a space carried up solid from the foundation to each window,
the jambs of which, like those of the doors, must of course be carried up solid.   In
brick-on-edge work the solid parts must still be built with all the bricks set on edge,
but no bricklayer will find any difficulty in effecting this object.

2439. *Brick Walls, seven inches and a half thick,* and fair or smooth on both sides,
are convenient, not only for partitions, but even for the outside walls of sheds and
other buildings, and for garden walls.   A common nine-inch wall, as every reader
of any experience in building knows, can only be built fair on one side, unless built
hollow, as in the one in the preceding paragraph, but $7\frac{1}{2}$-inch walls having no bricks
which pass right through the wall, the attention of the bricklayer is only required
to one side at a time.   These $7\frac{1}{2}$-inch walls are formed of bricks of the common size,
and of bricks of the same length and thickness, but of only half the width of the common bricks, by which means they can
be " worked fair " on both sides.
These are laid side by side, as in
fig. 2228. ; in which *a* represents the
first course, and *b* the second course.
The bond, or tying together of both

2228

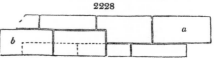

sides of the wall, is not obtained by laying bricks across (technically, headers), but by the full-breadth bricks covering half the breadth of the broad bricks, when laid over the narrow ones, as shown at *b*, and in the vertical section, fig. 2229. Besides the advantage of being built fair on both sides, *there being no headers, or through and through bricks,* in these walls, the rain, when they are used as outside walls, is never conducted through them, and the inside of the wall is consequently drier than the inside of a wall nine inches in thickness. These walls are adapted for a variety of purposes in house-building and gardening. The only drawback that we know against them is, that the narrow, or half-breadth, bricks must be made on purpose.

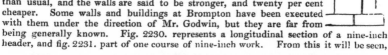

2229

2440. *Hitch's Patent Rebated Brickwork.* The bricks are much larger than usual, and the walls are said to be stronger, and twenty per cent cheaper. Some walls and buildings at Brompton have been executed with them under the direction of Mr. Godwin, but they are far from being generally known. Fig. 2230. represents a longitudinal section of a nine-inch header, and fig. 2231. part of one course of nine-inch work. From this it will be seen,

2230

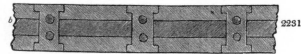

2231

that the headers and stretchers are rebated together, and form two external faces of brick-work enclosing a hollow space, or series of hollow spaces. Each of the headers has two dowel-holes through it, in the direction of its height, and is hollowed out on the under side as shown in fig. 2230.; so that these spaces communicate with one another, by means of the dowel-holes, throughout the whole extent of the wall. Now, into these chambers, as each course is laid, a concrete, properly compounded of gravel and lime, is introduced; and the whole, when finished, is thus rendered a solid and well-combined mass.

The appearance presented by walls built in this manner is uniform and bold (each brick being five inches high, and proportionally long): very little mortar is required for laying the bricks; so that, if affected by frost, the work may be repaired at small cost. Again, the importance of giving to the bricks the perfect shape of the mould entails the necessity of previously well kneading the clay, and, when moulded, the form of the brick allows full effect to the fire while burning; so that, in composition also, these are generally superior to common bricks: and, notwithstanding all these supposed advantages, brickwork can be executed in this manner twenty per cent cheaper than by the ordinary method. A variety of other bricks, besides those we have mentioned, are used in this system of construction, such as bat-headers, closers, reveal-headers, and angle-headers; and this slight complexity seems to be the chief objection to its general adoption, as common workmen are unable to execute it without some little previous instruction on the subject. In thick walls, for the interior of which the patentee uses what he calls a "clenched core-brick," to tie the whole together, and prevent the walls from splitting. almost any degree of strength may be attained; and here, inasmuch as a greater proportion of concrete is employed, a much larger saving than that mentioned above may be effected; probably as much, in some cases, as 40 per cent. For arches, Mr. Hitch has made wedge-shaped bricks of various radius, by means of which the larger mortar joint occurring when common bricks are employed for this purpose is avoided; and ordinary vaults may thus be formed of five-inch "arch bricks," having over them a thin layer of concrete, for about 5s. per yard superficial. Several small bridges have been successfully built with them. For garden walls, bricks are especially made with merely two dowel-holes in them; so that iron rods or oaken stakes may be passed through, thus stringing them together, the interstices being filled up with concrete. Fig. 2233. shows the plan of one of these bricks; and fig. 2232. exhibits a section of garden walling constructed with

2232

a

2233

them, under Mr. Godwin's direction, in several places. A footing of concrete, about twelve inches in thickness, is first thrown in. Upon this is laid one course of nine-inch work, and one course of splayed bricks, made for the purpose, from which commences the six-inch walling of doweled bricks, terminating with a bead-brick and coping of the same material, set in cement.   At certain intervals angular piers are formed, to strengthen the wall; and iron rods, as before mentioned, are introduced in various places.   One of the latter is shown in the engraving, passed through the bottom courses into the concrete.   The cost of a wall thus constructed, with six-inch bricks, including the coping and piers, but exclusive of the concrete footing, is about 5s. per yard (being little more than the price of wooden fencing, which constantly requires repairs, and is, therefore, a continual source of expense); and a similar wall may be built with four-inch bricks for 4s. per yard.   For horticultural purposes the patentee has occasionally glazed the face of his bricks: this is the case with a garden wall in the garden at Hampton Court Palace, built by him several years ago. (*Arch. Mag.*, vol. i. p. 581.)

2441. *Hitch's Brick Drain*, for which he has a patent, is of simple but excellent construction, of which fig. 2235. represents a section. Each brick is about thirteen inches long, segmental, and wedge-shaped; and is rebated at the ends (as shown by fig. 2234., which is a longitudinal section of a single brick), so as to fit together accurately without much cement.   On the top of each two indentions are formed, in order to lessen the quantity of earth required for making them, and afford a handle to the workmen. Four bricks form a nine-inch drain, as represented by the sketch, which can be executed complete for $11\frac{1}{2}d$. per foot running; and six of them, having a slightly different radius, make a twelve-inch drain, costing 1s. $4\frac{1}{2}d$. per foot: in both cases exclusive of digging.   The bricks themselves cost about 17s. per hundred, and the amount of labour and cement required is very small.

2234

2235

2442. *Bricks may now be made of ornamental Forms*, or coloured, on payment of double duty, which it is to be hoped may lead to the revival of brick cornices, architraves, &c., such as were in use till ornamental bricks were heavily taxed.   The fine effect of coloured bricks is admirably shown in the Lombardo-Venetian church, recently built from the design of Mr. Wild, at Streatham.   How the colouring of bricks is effected in the manufacture has been shown by John Dobson, Esq., in the *Proceedings of the British Association* for 1838.

2443. *Building Cottage Walls of Clay Lumps*.   John Curtis, Esq., of Rougham, informs us that he has built cottages, barns, and farm-yard walls, with what are called clay lumps.   They are, he says, more durable than any thing except stone, very dry, and from 600 to 700 per cent cheaper than bricks.   "I have built the walls of a farm-yard one foot thick with clay lumps; and, when at the desired height, made a coping for it of a frame-work of boards one inch and a half thick, and six inches wide.   These, nailed together with cross pieces at every four or five feet's distance, are laid on the top of the wall, which thus forms the eaves, by projecting two inches on each side of the wall; the outer edges of the boards being beveled or sloped off to facilitate the drip of the water from the wall, similarly to a drip brick.   The coping is then finished by covering it with worked clay, in the state that it is when ready for making lumps.   This, with a little occasional repairs, will last for many years."

2444. *To make Clay Lumps*.   Three loads of soft tender clay, which should be yellow, not blue, the latter being too strong, will make one hundred lumps; which, when dry, will weigh six stones, of fourteen pounds each.   The three loads should be put into a heap, all large stones being carefully picked out, and soaked with as much water as the mass will absorb; then tread it with one or two horses, and, as it is trodden, mix as much short old straw as can properly be mixed with it, by adding more water as may be required.   The edges of the mass should be turned into the middle of the heap from time to time; and the horses should be kept treading it till all the clay is thoroughly broken, and mixed so as to become like stiff mortar.   All the secret depends on well mixing the clay with plenty of straw.   It should not be made too thin. As soon as this quantity is properly prepared, men should be making it into lumps, which is done by putting sufficient clay into a mould of wood, of the following dimensions: eighteen inches long, twelve inches wide, and six inches deep, no bottom.   The mould, when well filled, by the men putting in the clay with a spade, and pressing it with the foot, the top being smoothed with the back of the spade, should be lifted up, and the lump will then be left perfect.   Wet the mould with a wisp of oat straw, to prevent the clay hanging to it, and place the mould about two inches from the first lump, and fill as before; then wet the mould and place it about two inches off, and proceed as before. This filling of the mould is best done on level grass ground.   As soon as the lumps get a little stiff, that is, just enough to admit of handling them, they should be set on one edge, and as they dry be turned; and in doing this, place the wet side to the sun.   The

rough edges must be trimmed with a spade, or any edged tool, as they become dry
enough to be haled (that is, built up in rows about three feet high, one brick wide, and
the lumps one or two inches apart at the ends, as new-made bricks are before they are
burned), so as that the wind can pass between each lump. Winter is the best time to
get the clay into heaps, that the frost may pulverise and mellow it. In March, as soon
as the severe frosts are over, begin to work the clay and make the lumps, and, if the
weather is favourable, they will be fit to build with in three weeks or a month.

2445. *To build a Cottage, Barn, or any Building, with Clay Lumps*, the foundation must
be good; that is, built with brick or stone at least eighteen inches above the surface of
the ground. The larger the building, the higher the foundation should be; say three
feet; and it should be two inches wider than the lumps, so that one inch of plaster may
be put on each side of the wall; the width of the walls being according to the size of
the building. Of course lumps can be made to any size, according to the building intended. The expense of building the walls (which are eighteen inches thick) is 6*d*. per
yard; and 1*d*.per yard, covering each side of the wall with cement, which is only common
clay mixed well with very short straw, being very particular in picking out every stone,
and treading it more than usual. Let it lie in the heap till the autumn, and then (in
October) apply it to the walls as a coat of plaster is applied to any common wall. —
J. C. Feb. 3. 1842.

The only objection that we see to these walls is, that they do not appear to admit of
finishing with common lime plaster within; but on writing to Mr. Curtis on the subject, he informs us that he has no doubt lime plaster will adhere equally well with
plaster of clay. It does so in the pisé walls of France.

SECT. II. *Roofs and Floors.*

2446. *Terrace Roofs* have of late years become very general in and about London.
They are formed of thin arches of tiles and cement, supported on cast-iron bearers or
ribs, which are placed about three feet apart. The arch is composed of three courses
of common plain tiles, bedded in fine cement without sand. In laying the tiles, laths
or small slips of wood are used, resting on temporary bearers between the iron ribs;
the laths being shifted as the work advances, in the course of about half an hour after
the tiles are laid. Particular attention is required to bonding the tiles both ways; and
they are rubbed down closely upon each other, much in the same manner as a joiner
glues a joint. Mr. Fowler covered a wing of his house with a roof of this kind, over
which he laid a bed of coarse gravel, and on that nine inches of soil, so as to form a
terrace-garden : he also covered the roofs of two taverns in Hungerford Market in this
manner, and found it a more agreeable surface for walking on than lead, both as to
texture, and from being a non-conductor of heat. Where a covering or roof of tiles
and cement is not intended to be walked on, two courses of tiles are considered sufficient; but where it is liable to be loaded by persons standing on it in crowds, three
courses should be used. Two courses of tiles on iron joists amount to one third less
expense than covering with "eight-pound lead" and fir joists. (*Trans. Inst. Brit. Arch.*,
vol. i. p. 48.) This covering has the advantage over one of asphalte, in not being liable
to be softened by the heat of the sun; but asphalte, being much lighter, may be laid on
wooden joists, covered with boards, in the same manner as if lead were to be used.

2447. *Asphalte* is one of the most remarkable introductions for building purposes
which has taken place since the publication of the Encyclopædia. Asphalte had been
in use in France for many years, but was comparatively neglected there till the
stimulus given to improvement by the Revolution of 1830. It is now in very general
use in France for foot-pavements, flat roofs, and lining water-cisterns; and in England
it has also been a good deal used for the same purposes, and for flooring to barns. We
are not aware that it has been used as flooring for cottages, but we know of no objection
to it, at least for rooms on the ground floor in which there are no fireplaces. Asphalte
is found in a natural state in the Ohsaun and other parts of France; but it may be
formed artificially in every respect equally good, and in England much cheaper. A
very good recipe is: eighteen parts of mineral pitch, and eighteen parts of resin, put in
an iron pot, and boiled for a little; after which, sixty parts of sand, thirty of small
gravel, and six of slacked lime, are to be added. The foundation being rendered dry,
and being brought to a level with gravel or small stones, the mixture is taken out of
the pot, or caldron, in which it was boiled, with an iron shovel, in a boiling state, and
spread evenly over the prepared surface about the thickness of two inches for ordinary
pavements, and about a third part thicker for barn floors and flat roofs. According to
Dr. Ure, boiled coal-tar, mixed with powdered chalk or bricks, will make as good
asphalte as the natural kind. (*Dict. of Arts, &c.*, Bitumen.)

2448. *Pocock's flexible Asphalte Roofing* is intended to supersede the use of slates, tiles,
zinc, thatch, &c., in the covering and lining of farm buildings, sheds, cottages, and other

erections; and, from its durability, lightness, and economy, it is in very general use. The weight of this manufacture being only sixty pounds to the square of one hundred feet, the walls and timbers to support it are required to be but half the usual substance; it is also a non-conductor of heat, impervious to damp, and will bear a heat of two hundred and twenty degrees without injury. Several architects and railway engineers have already adopted the asphalte roofing for sheds and other buildings; it has also been used instead of mats or boards for covering glass frames in gardens. The materials of which this roofing is composed are the refuse felt of hatters, and natural or artificial asphalte, mixed together and compressed into thin plates.

2449. *The new French Roofing Tiles* (fig. 2236.) were introduced from Paris by Sir John Robison in 1840. These tiles are square in form, about nine inches or ten inches

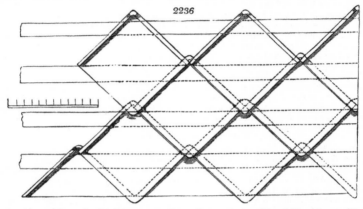

2236

on the side, with a raised ledge on two sides. They may be either laid with or without mortar or cement, but they are better with a little, by which they effectually exclude water. The boundary lines of the tiles being all diagonal, the rain-water tends to run to the lower points (instead of hanging in the joints by capillary attraction), where the nosing on the lower angle of the tile, shown in the section (fig. 2237.), conducts the

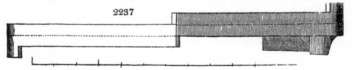

2237

stream or drops, on to the flat part of the next tile below it. To finish the roof at the ridge half tiles are placed there, analogous to those placed at the eaves, but having a raised ledge along their upper edge, over which edge a peculiarly shaped ridge-tile is inverted to complete the whole. These tiles are lighter than pantiles, in the proportion of sixty-eight pounds to one hundred and ten pounds per square yard, which is the usual weight. The general aspect of roofs covered with them is agreeable, and the cost will be evidently much less than that of any description of tile roof at present in use. The Highland Society is endeavouring to introduce the tiles into Scotland, and we have sent drawings of them to Mr. Varden, at Worcester; Mr. Elliott, at Chichester; and Mr. Wilds, at Hertford.

2450. *Cubitt's Improvements in Roofing* are of a very ingenious character, and though confessedly not adapted to first-rate or other houses requiring roofing of a permanent and perfectly weather-tight description, will be found, nevertheless, of very extensive application. Wherever quickness of construction, lightness, and cheapness are objects of importance, and no more is cared for than protection overhead during ordinary states of the weather, as in the case of colonnades, verandas, penthouses, drying-houses, tool-houses, summer-houses in gardens, boat-houses, workmen's sheds, railway stations, &c., these improvements will be found of great applicability and value. (*Mech. Mag.*, vol. xxxiii. p. 210.) It would occupy too much space to describe this mode of roofing, which will be found illustrated with engravings in the work quoted. We shall only add, that its appearance is very light and elegant, but that it could not be executed without the aid of the circular saw.

2451. *Suspension Roofs.* The principle employed in suspension bridges is beginning to be applied to roofs both in France and England. In the back premises of Messrs. Gillow, the extensive upholsterers in Oxford Street, part of a roof was suspended by a chain in 1840, under the direction of Messrs. Abraham, architects; and Mr. Hansom of Foley Place, architect, proposes a roof of this kind for the Metropolitan Music Hall, now in contemplation, which, if carried into execution, will be the largest room in the world. The four angles of the building are proposed to be carried up a sufficient height to form the fulcrums for the suspension chains, which may, perhaps, be most advantageously applied in the manner adopted by Mr. Dredge of Bath, in his suspension bridges. (See *Mech. Mag.*, vol. xxxiii. p. 500.)

2452. *Sunk Wooden Eaves-Trough for Cottage Roofs*, figs. 2238—2240. This finish to the eaves of a roof has now become very general for country-houses, and deservedly so; being the neatest, cheapest, and most durable of any, and adapted to the humblest cottage as well as to the elegant villa. In order to obtain a fall in the old metal troughs, they are obliged to be fixed a little slanting, which adds to the otherwise unsightly appearance of them; they are also liable to be crushed in by the weight of ladders, &c. placed against them, as well as to a sagging or dropping down between the several iron brackets which support them, and the water from time to time lodging in these parts very soon renders them useless. This is made of the best clean seasoned fir timber, with as few joints as possible, the mitred joints at the angles put together with a copper

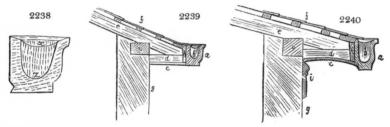

2238   2239   2240

tongue and white lead; about four inches by four inches, more or less, according to the character of the building. It is fixed perfectly level, the fall being within itself, which is obtained by hollowing out the middle, beginning at *x* in fig. 2238., the highest part of the fall, and proceeding gradually deeper to *z*, the lowest; thus, a trough of this description may be fixed along a front of forty or fifty feet in length, the fall being given from the centre to the right and left. It requires no lining, but a thorough good painting, which should be repeated every three or four years. A large moulding being wrought on the front, it is thus made to represent the crowning member of a cornice. Fig. 2239. represents the application of it to a cottage; where *a* is the moulded front of the eaves-trough; *b*, the hollow; *c*, the plastered soffit; *d*, bearer; *e*, rafter; *f*, slating; *g*, front wall of house; *h*, fascia; *o*, wall-plate. Fig. 2240., the same with a higher style of finish. The same letters of reference answer: in addition, *i* shows a lead moulding and fascia in cement, and the plancier, *c*, is curved. It may be finished in a still more elaborate style, with dentils or cantilevers, if required. — *W. Wilds, Architect, Hertford.*

2453. *Cast-Iron Gutters to Roofs*, as a substitute for leaden ones, are found economical and effective. Fig. 2242. is a section of a gutter between two roofs, in which *a a* show the gutter, with a flange, *b b*, for joining the different pieces together; *c c*, the slates; *d d*, the rafters; and *e*, the gutter-beam. The fall requisite to carry off the water is found to be from a half to three quarters of an inch in the yard, and this necessarily occasions the plane of the roof to rise towards the centre of the building, as shown in the section, fig. 2241., in which the rise is indicated by the dotted lines *f f f f*.

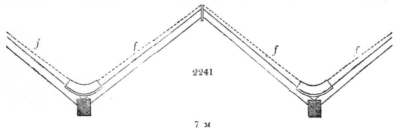

2241

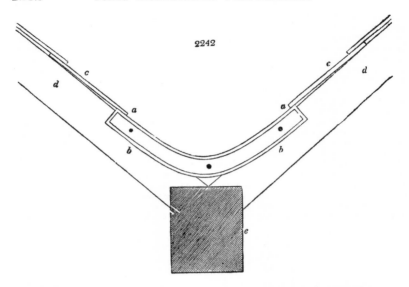

2242

All the care that this requires in slating or tiling is, to bring the upper edge of the lower course of tiles to a level, as indicated in the longitudinal section through the gutter, fig. 2243.; in which *g* is the gutter; *h*, the lower course of tiles; *i*, the gutter-

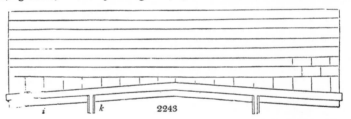

2243

beam; and *k*, the hollow posts for supporting the gutter-beam, and serving as pipes for conducting away the water from the gutter.   Cast-iron gutters of this sort will be found peculiarly adapted for ridge and furrow hot-house roofs.

2454. *Roofs of native Scotch Fir.*   The Closeburn method of preserving the durability of timber consists in first cutting it to the size required, and then steeping it in a pond of limewater for a fortnight, or, more or less, according to the dimensions of the pieces.   It is found that the acid contained in the wood is crystallised, by combining with the alkali of the lime.   Sir Charles Menteath has now some farm buildings on his estate, the timber in the roofs of which is the common young Scotch fir; but, having undergone the limewater process, it is as sound after a lapse of forty years as the day it was put up.   The same timber, under ordinary circumstances and in similar situations, would rot in from three to seven years. (*Mech. Mag.*, vol. xxxi. p. 105.)   Notwithstanding this statement, the preservative effect of limewater is denied by some, but there can be little doubt that sulphate of copper would be effective.

2455. *Thatch may be rendered comparatively incombustible*, by soaking it in whitewash made of lime, or whitening and size, in the usual way, to every four gallons of which has been added one pound, or rather more, of alum.   Alum would suffice by itself but the rain would wash it off.   The lime and size form a film over every straw, insoluble in water. (*Mech. Mag.*, vol. xxxvi. p. 106.)   If the interior of a thatched roof be kept dry, it will last as long as the timber which supports it.   Possibly something might be gained by covering a thin layer of thatch with Pocock's asphalte roofing.

2456. *Martin's Fire-Proof Cement* has been used in various cases by Mr. Cubitt as a substitute for boards in flooring, and it is said Mr. Barry intends to use it in the new Houses of Parliament.   Applied to floors, stairs, and partitions, even though only as a covering to boards, it would go far to render private houses fire-proof. (*Mech. Mag.*, vol. xxxvi. p. 85.) The principal ingredient in this cement is gypsum.

2457. *Cement Floors for Cottage Bed-rooms* have been strongly recommended for their durability, and as, in some degree, rendering cottages fire-proof. They are common in Italy, and to be found in some parts of France and Germany, but they are comparatively rare in England. The best that we know of are at Houghton, in Norfolk, which we examined upwards of thirty years ago, and through the kindness of John Curtis, Esq., who sent us the information respecting building walls with clay lumps (§ 2440.), we are enabled to give the following account of them :—

2458. *The Cement Floors* at Houghton Inn, and in some of the farm-houses on the Houghton estate, are thus formed. The floor joists are laid in the same manner as if for boarding, but well stiffened by what is locally called bridging, which consists of pieces mortised into each joist, as shown in fig. 2244., in which *a* is the plan and *b* the section. But as this mode weakens the joists by cutting into them, a better one would

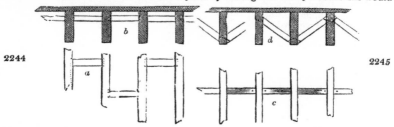

2244   2245

be, to use cross strutts in the usual manner, as shown in fig. 2245., in which *c* is the plan and *d* the section. Some floors are first laid with reeds, so as to bear the cement on a floor of reeds ; and others (which is the better way) are covered with double laths, but the ends of these laths should only just meet in the middle of the joists. The cement is then laid on, half an inch or two inches thick, and the floor must not be left by the workmen till it is quite finished ; that is, they must keep beating and smoothing it over, night and day, till it is completely set, in order to prevent its cracking. This can only be done by having a swinging scaffold from the ceiling for the men to work from. The cement must be laid on directly it is made ; therefore, while some persons are making it up, others must be laying it on. The cement is commonly called red plaster, which is red gypsum. It is burnt for this purpose, by making a fire with small billets of wood, and mixing small lumps of gypsum with the wood, and then covering the whole with turves to prevent the fire escaping, in the same manner as billets are covered when they are made into charcoal ; or a better way is, to grind the gypsum in the flour stones of a mill, and then bake it in an oven, before mixing it into a cement, which should be done with the iron dust which falls from a blacksmith's anvil, and not with the smithy ashes ; the scales of iron being so much harder and better for the purpose. Chalk and lime are both unfit for the purpose, though ground floors for cottages and barns are frequently made of these materials, well beaten together.—*J. C.*

2459. *Bed-room Floors, formed of two Courses of plain Tiles laid in Cement,* resting on joists lathed over in the manner described, would, we should think, make very good floors ; but, unless they came cheaper than boards, it would scarcely be worth while adopting them. Cottages might be roofed with semicircular arches of tiles, laid in cement, and covered with turf or creeping plants or ivy, so as to render them warm as well as durable.

2460. *Equal Parts of Lime, Sand, and Cinder-dust,* worked up well together, make very good malting-floors ; but, as in the process of malting they are occasionally moistened, this composition may not be so well adapted for the bed-room floors of cottages.—*S. T.*

2461. *Clay Floors,* that is, floors formed of a mixture of clay and marl, were formerly a good deal used in Norfolk for barns, malt-houses, hay-lofts, cottages, &c. They are composed of clay and marl mixed with chopped straw, well trodden by horses, and mixed together in the manner clay lumps are to be made (§ 2444.); and, when the mixture is to be used for malt-floors, bullock's blood is added. Much of the excellence of these floors depends on the thoroughly mixing and working of the material.— *W. T.*

Sect. III. *Windows and Doors.*

A great drawback to the improvement of cottages, both in Scotland and England, hitherto has been the expense of the windows ; but these are now manufactured of cast iron at so moderate a rate, that the expense can no longer be an object of solicitude.

2462. *Windows* having been generally among the worst constructed parts of Scotch cottages, the Highland Society offered a premium for the best cottage window, which was awarded to Messrs. M'Culloch and Co. of Glasgow, for the form shown in figs. 2246. to 2248. This form, of the dimensions shown in the figure, viz., three feet three inches by two feet, without the wooden frame, costs, in cast iron, only 5s., and the glass for such a window may be purchased at 2¾d. per square. This kind of window admits of being formed of any size, and is equally adapted for work-shops, farm buildings where glass windows are required, and cottages.

The dimensions that have been recommended for the windows of ordinary cottages are, thirty-nine inches for the height, and twenty-four inches for the width, within the wooden frames. The size of glass required for these frames is seven and a quarter inches by five and a quarter inches. The sash is divided into two unequal parts, the lower part having three squares in height, and the upper part two. The lower part is permanently fixed, while the upper part is constructed to turn in the vertical direction on pivots, which are situate in the line of

its middle astragal; and both parts are set in a sub-stantial wooden frame, which may be either built in while the wall is erecting, or may be set in afterwards in the ordinary way, with or without checked rabbets (§ 911.), according to the taste of the proprietor. The window, and its arrangements, will be better understood by reference to the annexed figures.

Fig. 2246. is an inside elevation, fig. 2248. a plan, and fig. 2247. a vertical section, in each of which a portion of the wall is exhibited, and the same letters refer to the corresponding parts in each figure; *a* is a portion of the surrounding wall; *b*, the wooden frame of the window; *c*, the lower sash, which is dormant; and *d*, the upper and movable sash.

In fig. 2247. the upper sash is represented as open for ventilation; when shut, the parts of the opening-sash cover and overlap the fixed parts in such a man-ner as to exclude wind and water; but, when venti-lation is required, the arrangement of the parts which

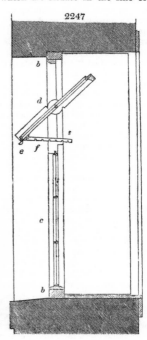

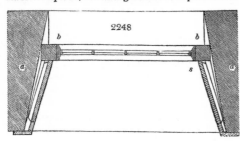

produce this is such as to enable the housekeeper to admit air to any extent. For this purpose the notched latch, e, is jointed to a stud in the edge of the sash ; a simple iron pin or stud is also fixed in the wooden frame at s, and the notches of the latch being made to fall upon this stud at any required distance, the requisite degree of opening is secured, and when the sash is again closed, the latch falls down parallel with, and close to, the sash. To secure the sashes when shut, the T bolt, f, in the middle of the meeting bars, has only to be turned one fourth round, and the movable sash is held fast in close contact with the other. The figures represent the window as finished up with single dressings, viz., plain deal shutters, facings, and sole, which, at a small expense, would give an air of neatness and comfort to the apartment, and promote a corresponding taste in the other parts of the cottage. Though the dimensions of the window here stated may be conceived sufficient for lighting an apartment of ordinary size, they can nevertheless be varied to suit every purpose. This may be done either by employing two such windows as above described, with a mullion of wood or stone between them, or the single window may be enlarged by one or two squares in width, or in height, or in both directions. " (*Highland Soc. Trans.*, vol. xiii. p. 541.)

2463. *The Belper Cottage Window* is formed entirely of cast iron, and has a compartment in the centre which opens. It differs from the Glasgow window in the nature of the fastening which keeps the window

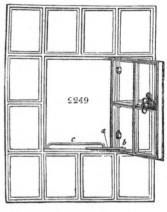

open or shut. To give an idea of the value of this fastening, it is necessary to observe that, in the latticed windows of cottages, there is very frequently either one entire frame, or a portion in the centre of one, which opens, and is kept open by an iron stay-bar, with an eye at one end which moves on a staple attached to the fixed part of the sash, and a hook at the other which drops into an eye in the part of the sash which is to be opened. Now, the objection to this hooked fastener is, that, as there is only one eye for the hook to drop into, the window can only be opened to the same width, whether the ventilation required be little or much ; and when the stay-bar is not in use, it hangs down and is blown about, and very frequently breaks the glass. The new stay-bar, on the other hand, opens the window or door to which it may be applied to various widths at pleasure, from an inch to the whole width of the window or door, and the stay-bar can never hang down, or run the slightest risk of breaking glass. The general appearance of the new stay-bar, supposing the window to be open to its full extent, is shown in fig. 2249. ; in which a is the stay-bar, which turns on the pivot b at one end, and slides along a horizontal groove under the guide-bar, c, at the other.

Fig. 2250. is a view of the stay-bar apart from the window, showing the eye, d ; the handle, e ; and the stud, f, which drops into holes in the horizontal groove, so as to keep the window open at any desired angle.

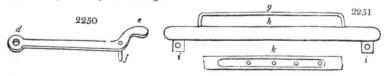

Fig. 2251. is a view of the groove and the guide-bar ; g is the guide-bar, or small rod, which is for the purpose of keeping the stay-bar in its place in the groove h ; i i are two plates with holes, by which the groove and guide-bar are riveted to the window ; k, vertical profile of the groove, the guide-bar being removed, so as to show the holes into which the stud of the stay-bar drops. The groove is of cast iron, and the guiding-rod is of wrought iron, let into it and riveted, and both are bolted to the bar of the window by means of the plates i i, which are of cast iron. Fig. 2252. is a section across the groove, the guiding-rod, l, and the bar of the window, m, to which the groove is bolted ; n is the handle of the guide-bar.

The window is cast in two pieces; the larger, fig. 2254., being two feet ten inches high by two feet one inch broad ; and the smaller, fig. 2255., being one foot four

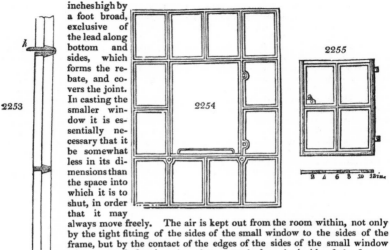

2253 2254 2255

inches high by a foot broad, exclusive of the lead along bottom and sides, which forms the re-bate, and co-vers the joint. In casting the smaller win-dow it is es-sentially ne-cessary that it be somewhat less in its di-mensions than the space into which it is to shut, in order that it may always move freely. The air is kept out from the room within, not only by the tight fitting of the sides of the small window to the sides of the frame, but by the contact of the edges of the sides of the small window with the heads forming the rebates attached to the inside of the frame;

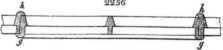

2256

and also by means of the contact of the beads, or rebates, of the small window with the edge of the sides of the large one, or frame, into which it shuts. In consequence of the sides never touching, the window moves with the greatest ease, whether expanded by heat in summer, or contracted by cold in winter, and whether painted and smooth, or unpainted and rusty. Fig. 2256. is a horizontal section across the small window and the two side bars, showing the outside beads at *g g*, and the inside beads at *h h*. Fig. 2253. is a vertical section through the small window and the top and bottom bars of the fixed frame, showing a weather-fillet, or weather-table, which projects half an inch from the general face of the window at *h*, and the stay-bar in the situation in which it rests when the window is shut, and also the groove and guiding-rod at *i*. The total weight of this window, before being glazed, is about 61¼lb., and the prime cost in Derby is 12s. 4½d., thus:—

		s.	d.
Two castings, 60lb., at 1½d.	- -	7	6
Iron-work, 1¼lb. at 1s. 1d.	- -	1	4½
Fitting-up, 6 hours, at 24s. per week	-	2	0
Scurfing castings, 4 hours, at 12s. per week		1	0
Priming window, 3d., and paint, 3d.	-	0	6
Prime cost -		12	4½

We can bear testimony to the excellence of this window, having seen it extensively in use at Millford and Belper, near Derby, where it was invented by Anthony Strutt, Esq.

2464. *A Cast-Iron Window and Wooden Shutter, adapted to Warehouses, Granaries, and other Farm Buildings.* The accompanying sketches, figs. 2257. to 2259., are of a cast-iron window and shutter, which, from the simplicity and security of the construction, appear to be worthy of imitation. Fig. 2258. is a section of the window, in which *a a* represent the shutter open; it being hung upon centres fixed to its two sides, and working in the outside frame. The outside, or top, of the shutter is the longer, and, consequently, the heavier, end; or the shutter may be kept open by a bolt or wedge under it, as at *b*. The sashes *c* and *d* are so far apart as to leave room for the shutter at *e* and *f*, when it is closed; and at *g* there is a fastening to secure the bottom of the shutter. Fig. 2259. is an elevation of the window, with the shutter in the position in which it is shown in the section fig. 2258.; and fig. 2257. is an elevation of the window when the shutter is closed; both of which are sufficiently explanatory to render description unnecessary. It will be seen that, by this mode of constructing warehouse or granary

windows, there is, when the shutter is open, excellent
ventilation and light, as well as perfect security. Bru-
met and Cope's Venetian blinds of wrought iron have
been very generally employed in London, as protective
shutters to the windows of dwelling-rooms and to shops.
The Duke of Wellington first brought them conspicuously
into notice by employing them to protect his first-floor
windows in Piccadilly. When not in use they are rolled
up, and sheltered from the weather by a hood; and, when
let down, they have rather an elegant appearance than
otherwise, from their resemblance to Venetian blinds.
They are commonly painted green; but this colour seldom
harmonises with exterior architecture.

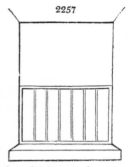

2465. *The upper Sashes of Windows should not be fixed*,
because, when this is the case, the room to which they give
light can never be properly ventilated (2475.). As an
additional argument against having the upper sashes of windows fixed, a practice common in the north of England and Scotland, the windows, whenever they are above

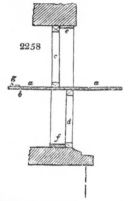

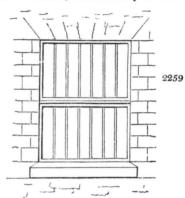

six feet high, cannot be cleaned, painted, nor a new pane put in, without the use of a
very long ladder. (*A. M.*, i. 247.) An apparatus for cleaning the outsides of lofty
windows of this kind is described and figured in *Arch. Mag.*, vol. i. p. 392.

2466. *Windows brought down to the Floor*, by reflecting light up to the eye, are much
less agreeable than those that do not come lower than the height of a chair back, and
they also give the worst light for displaying pictures. Nevertheless, windows down to
the floor are more cheerful where there is any thing near at hand worthy of being
looked out on.

2467. *A Door Stay-bar.* The Belper window stay-bar, it will readily be conceived,
may be applied to the opening of doors to any angle, or keeping them closely shut.
All that is necessary is to place the groove,
in which the bar works, against a wall or
other fixture, so that it shall stand horizontally at right angles to the door or gate.
Fig. 2260. represents a horizontal section
through a door, *a*; the wall of the hanging
style to which it is hinged, *b*; and the wall
against which it shuts, *c*. The gate or door
is supposed to be shut, and it is held in its
place by the stay-bar, *d*, which moves on a
stud at *a*, and at the end along a groove
from *f* to *g*. If we suppose the end of the
stay-bar at *f* secured in its place by a padlock, it will be next to impossible for house-
breakers to open the door, *a*; because they
could not by any means reach as far as *f*,
to pick the padlock. Other details of this
door stay-bar, and its application to various

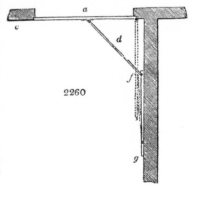

kinds of doors and gates, will be found by referring to the *Gardener's Magazine* for 1839, p. 440.

2468. *Cast-Iron Angles for outside Doors* would render them more durable. In fig. 2261., *a* is the upright style; *b*, the bottom rail; *c*, the horizontal section at *e*, *f* showing the top of the iron angle foot, and the section of the style. There would be much saving of labour and great durability in making door-frames in this manner.

2263

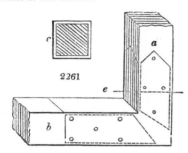

2261

2262

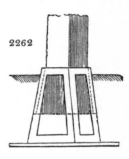

2469. *Cast-Iron Sockets to Wooden Posts*, fig. 2262., may be made very light, and being fitted to the part of the post to be inserted in the ground would render them much more durable, as well as much more architectural, since the posts would rise out of a proper base.

2470. *Doors to Rooms should be hung on the Side nearest the Fire.* First, then, I have observed that when doors are not hinged on the side nearest the fireplace, the smoke is drawn out every time they are used; secondly, I think I can account for this circumstance in a very simple way: the air that is displaced by the motion of the door is supplied by that which is near the fire; and, consequently, a vacuum is created, or the current of air that is feeding the fire is interrupted, and part of the air that had entered the chimney returns with the smoke to supply its place, or, in common parlance, it "puffs out." In the case of the door being hinged on the opposite side, the vacuum is supplied either by the expansion of the whole of the air in the room, or by some current, without disturbing the current of air that flows to the fire.—*T. W.*

2471. *To prevent the slamming of a Passage Door.* Fig. 2263. represents one side of the door-case. Instead of fixing the piece of wood which joiners call the check-plate on this, a similar piece is taken and prepared by being cut hollow on the edge *a*, which the door strikes on, and then cut down by saw-draughts (slits made by the saw), as represented by the lines *b b* in the figure, leaving a portion in the middle equal to one fourth or one fifth of the length uncut; it is then securely fixed by screws to the door-post, as shown in the sketch at *c*. The door, of course, first strikes against the top and bottom extremities of this check, and must press them back before it can reach the solid part of the plate in the middle. If, therefore, the plate of wood be made of such breadth and thickness as that the united resistance of its ten or twelve springs be a little greater than the force the door strikes with, it will never reach the solid part at all, and its slamming will be nearly inaudible, however strong the current of air may be. This has been proved to succeed perfectly, after all sorts of iron springs and checks have failed to remove the nuisance.—*J. R.*

Sect. IV. *Chimney-Tops and Smoky Chimneys.*

2472. *Every Chimney or Stack of Chimneys*, to be truly architectural, ought to be treated as a column, or as a group or series of columns; and as every column consists of three parts, a base, a shaft, and a capital, so ought every chimney-top. As an example of this we shall take fig. 2265., which is a column from a stack in Eastbury House, in Essex. It is entirely built with brick, and rises seventeen feet above the cornice of the base on which it is placed. In fig. 2264., *a* is the plan or horizontal section of one half of the shaft at *a* in fig. 2265.; and *b* in fig. 2264. is the plan of the upper member of the capital at *b* in fig. 2265. There is a stack of five of these shafts in the centre of Eastbury House; and by their beautiful proportions, and commanding height above the roof, they produce a strikingly grand and picturesque effect. There are many examples of brick chimney-shafts still remaining in the ancient mansions of England well deserving the attention of the architect; and as chimney-shafts form a principal feature in modern domestic architecture, their forms and situations cannot be too much studied.— *E. B.* Every person that has a house

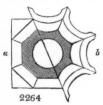

2264

designed for him ought to object to every chimney-top, whether Grecian or Gothic, that does not consist of an obvious base, shaft, and capital, and the base ought in general to be somewhat higher than the ridge of the roof. In general, all the upper terminations of a building ought to be bold and free; and this cannot be the case with chimney-shafts, unless they have a distinct base, a shaft of considerable length, and a capital consisting of several members according to the style of architecture employed.

2265

ft. in.
17.0

2473. *In Chimneys of Cottages built in Woods,* and where overhanging branches of trees may prevent the egress of smoke, care should be taken to contract the smoke-flue or vent, in an ordinary-sized room, to seven inches square, at about eighteen inches above the grate, gradually widening it to ten or eleven inches square. The heat forces the smoke through the narrow aperture, and it increases in volume the farther it rises from the heat, as may be easily observed, as it ascends in curls, gradually increasing above the chimney-top. By attending to this simple rule, which was with some difficulty imposed on the masons who built Annat Cottage (§ 2360.), which is surrounded with lofty trees, the rooms are free from smoke.—*A. G.*

2474. *A Chimney-pot for preventing Smoke from being blown down a Chimney* has been in use at Poole Park,

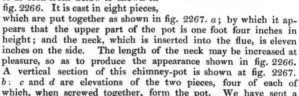

2266

near Ruthin, Denbighshire, for several years; and we are informed, by Lord Bagot's agent there, that it has answered, and continues to answer, in every instance in which it has been applied. It is formed of cast iron; and the appearance of it as seen from below is shown in fig. 2266. It is cast in eight pieces, which are put together as shown in fig. 2267. *a;* by which it appears that the upper part of the pot is one foot four inches in height; and the neck, which is inserted into the flue, is eleven inches on the side. The length of the neck may be increased at pleasure, so as to produce the appearance shown in fig. 2266. A vertical section of this chimney-pot is shown at fig. 2267. *b:* *c* and *d* are elevations of the two pieces, four of each of which, when screwed together, form the pot. We have sent a model of this pot, which was kindly forwarded to us by Mr. Turnor, Lord Bagot's agent at Poole Park, to Messrs. Cottam and Hallen, iron-founders and manufacturers, Winsley Street, Oxford Street, London; from whom pots

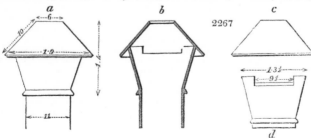

2267

of this kind may in future be purchased. Fig. 2268. shows the form of a cast-iron chimney-pot, in use in the neighbourhood of Barnsley, in Yorkshire; where it has been tried for a number of years, and is considered to be an effective cure for a smoky chimney, where the smoke is blown downwards by wind. Fig. 2269. shows the general appearance of a chimney-top furnished with pots of this kind. The usual form of this pot is that of a truncated pyramid, as in fig. 2268.; but it might easily be made to terminate in a Gothic pinnacle, or in any other ornament which was considered suitable to the style of the building to which it was to be applied. It might even be made circular, and used in the case of cylindrical chimney-shafts, built in the form of Grecian columns. Where the form is that of fig. 2268., the four sides are cast separately, and bolted together; and, where the pot is to stand alone, or with a short distance between it and other pots of the same kind, each side is fitted up with a hinged door, as shown in figs. 2268. and 2269.; but, where the pots are to stand close together, these hinged doors are only placed on the two exposed sides. The top, in either case, is closed with an iron cap. Each hinged door is connected with the opposite one by a rod of iron, about two inches longer than the diameter of the pot; so that, when the

2268

2269

weather is calm, the lower part of each of the four doors projects from the chimney-pot about one inch; while, on the other hand, when the wind blows, it closes the door on the side against which it strikes, and opens the door on the opposite side to the extent of two inches. It is evident that the same kind of doors might be introduced near the termination of each flue, in an architectural chimney-top without pots. Other modes of curing smoky chimneys by pots, either ornamental in themselves, or rendered so by architectural casings, will be found in the *Suburban Architect, &c.*, chap. i.

SECT. V. *Ventilation.*

2475. *Ventilation.* The following extract is from a work which ought to be in the hands of every individual, but especially in those of every architect, viz., Combe's *Principles of Physiology applied to the Preservation of Health*, third edition. " One of the evils of ignorance is, that we often sin and suffer the punishment, without being aware that we are sinning, and that it is in our power to escape the suffering by avoiding the sin. For many generations mankind have experienced the evil results of deficient ventilation, especially in towns, and suffered the penalty of delicate health, headachs, fevers, consumptions, cutaneous and nervous diseases; and yet, from ignorance of the true nature and importance of the function of respiration and of the great consumption of air in its performance, architects have gone on planning and constructing edifices and houses, without bestowing a thought on the means of supplying them with fresh air, although animal life cannot be carried on without it; and, while ingenuity and science have been taxed to the uttermost to secure a proper supply of water, the pure air, though its admission is far more essential, has been left to steal in, like a thief in the night, through any hole it can find open. In constructing hospitals, indeed, ventilation has been thought of, because a notion is prevalent that the sick require fresh air, and cannot recover without it; but it seems not to have been perceived, that what is indispensable for the recovery of the sick may be not less advantageous for preserving from sickness those who are well. Were a general knowledge of the structure of man to constitute a regular part of a liberal education, such inconsistencies as this would soon disappear, and the scientific architect would speedily devise the best means for supplying our houses with pure air, as he has already supplied them with pure water." (p. 236.)

Few modern practices in building are more absurd than that of making the doors and windows of rooms air-tight, and yet expecting that there can be a sufficient draught in the chimneys to prevent them from smoking. There ought to be a contrivance in the upper part of every door and window for admitting air, merely for the sake of supplying the chimney. (See Sir John Robison's House, § 2378.) In the case of doors, instead of having them to fit exactly at the top, we would leave from a fourth to half an inch, according to the size of the room; and, in the case of windows, we would leave that space in all those that fronted the points from which the wind was mildest, and half as much in the case of windows facing the north. The advantage of admitting the fresh air at the upper part of the room is, that it comes immediately in contact with the hottest air of the room, and is thus rendered temperate before it reaches persons seated in the middle of the room, or near the fireplace; whereas, when the air is admitted or drawn in by the bottom or lower parts of doors or windows, it slides along the floor towards the fireplace to supply the draught, at once cooling the feet of every one in the room, and leaving the great body of the air of the apartment entirely unchanged. It thus frequently happens that a person is seated in a room in which there is a brisk fire, with his feet and legs in an atmosphere of forty degrees of air continually changing, and consequently carrying off heat from him, and his head in an atmosphere of a temperature of sixty degrees, which, unless the door of the room is frequently opened and shut, or the breast of the chimney is higher than usual, is never changed at all, and, consequently, is breathed and rebreathed by the occupants. We have often been perfectly astonished at the ignorance of professional men on the subject of ventilation, and equally so sometimes at their speculative impracticable notions; such as ventilating by small tubes, &c. The only practicable mode of judiciously ventilating apartments in modern houses, without radical changes in construction, we venture to state is that above suggested: but even that simple mode will not be adopted till the occupiers of houses are aware of the importance of ventilation. One piece of advice we would wish to impress upon every reader, viz. never to take a lodging, or rent a house, in which the windows are not carried up as high as the cornice of the room. Unless this be the case, the ventilation, even by the mode we have suggested, must necessarily be imperfect; because the stratum of air between the top of the window and the ceiling will remain unchanged, and of no sort of use to the occupants of the room. Many hundreds of houses about London, which have a splendid appearance exteriorly, have this defect within. It will be found in the bed-room floors of most of the houses round the Regent's Park, and, indeed, more or less, in almost all the new houses everywhere, that have any pretensions to exterior architecture, and especially to a frieze and cornice. As these houses are generally built on speculation, by persons whose great object is to get them sold as soon as possible, this utter neglect of the health of the occupant is not to be wondered at, more especially as the occupant is generally too ignorant to detect the evil; but what excuse shall we find for architects who commit the same fault in the country-houses of wealthy noblemen? We could refer to many new country-houses where this is the case: we have in our mind's eye the state bed-room of a noble marquess lately married, in which the space above the windows is upwards of ten feet, and, the whole height of the room being twenty feet, it follows that exactly one half of the atmosphere of the room is rendered useless. The misery and suffering in cases of this kind, however, are nothing to that which must be endured by those who have no other room to live in but one, and that one perhaps not above seven or eight feet high. It is lamentable to think that this misery must be endured by the passing generation, and even by that which is rising to succeed it, till, as Dr. Combe observes, a general knowledge of the structure of man enters into a system of general education. There is no better substitute for this defect in our education, that we know of, than Dr. Combe's most excellent work.

2476. *Ventilation in Public Buildings* is most effectually obtained by having a fire in the upper part of the building, which can only be supplied by air drawn from the different rooms below by means of air-flues. In private buildings, instead of a fire, these flues may communicate with, or be carried up alongside of, the smoke-flue of a fire kept constantly burning, such as that of the kitchen.

2477. *Ventilation of Bed-rooms.* There should be a constant circulation of fresh air in bed-rooms. The lungs must respire during sleep as well as at any other time, and it is of great importance to have, when asleep, as pure an air as possible. It is calculated that each person neutralises the vivifying principle of a gallon of air in one minute: what havoc, therefore, must an individual make upon the pure air of his bed-chamber, who sleeps in a bed closed snugly with curtains, with the doors and windows shut, and perchance a chimney-board into the bargain. Our health and comfort depend more upon these apparently trivial points than most people are aware of. (*A. M.*, i. 87.)

2478. *Warming and Ventilating.* The objects to be aimed at are, pure and cool air to breathe, and radiant heat to warm the person. The evils to be avoided are, currents and draughts, whether hot or cold, and over-heated air for respiration. The larger and loftier the room, the more effectually can fresh air be introduced, without any rapidity of current. The impure exhalations rise to the ceiling, and their place is supplied by fresh air from below. In short, the upper part of a room may be considered as a reservoir of the impurities which are generated in the lower part by the persons breathing there. In ordinary houses, the simplest and best mode of warming and ventilating is to have some description of hot-air stove placed at the bottom of the staircase, which shall heat a current of air introduced from without, or, in small houses, drawn from the air within the lower part of the house. The heated air so generated will ascend the staircase, and, consequently, enter all the rooms which open into it. There are many different kinds of stoves that may be used for heating the air; one of the best is the invention of White of Haddington, of which there are various sizes, at different prices, from £3 10*s.* to £30 or £40. The smallest size will suffice for a house of ten or twelve rooms. (See next chapter.)

2479. *Cooling and Ventilating in warm Climates.* Captain R. Wainhope, R. N., has shown, in *Jameson's Journal,* Oct. 1831, that this may be easily effected by forcing in air through porous earthenware tubes, kept moist exteriorly. The great evaporation which will take place on the outer surface of the pipes will cool the air in its passage through them. If, by some similar process, the air charged with moisture in cold climates could be deprived of that moisture before it entered dwelling-houses, the benefit to invalids would probably be very great.

Sect. VI.   *Tanks and Cottage Privies.*

2480. *A Tank for Rain-water.* The ground having been taken out to the required depth, pave the bottom with one flat course of bricks grouted with cement, and on this set singly two courses of plain tiles in the same material   Form the sides each of two four-inch walls of bricks and cement, breaking the horizontal joints : and, when completed, render the whole of the interior with cement one inch in thickness. Turn a brick arch in mortar over the tank thus formed, leaving a man-hole, two feet square, with proper trimming stones, and a Yorkshire stone-paving cover ; or cover entirely with flag-stones. The suction-pipe of a pump placed within a few inches of the bottom, and a small drain introduced at the top of the tank, and communicating with a sewer or cesspool, to carry off the superfluous water, when there is any, are then all that are required to render the tank fit for use.

2481. *Filtering the Water from the Roof of a Cottage into a Tank or Well.* The well, of which *a* in fig. 2270. is a ground plan, is supposed to be formed adjoining the sink in the scullery, or partly within the scullery and partly without, as indicated in the model plan in p. 1148. ; and the filter, *b,* is supposed to be formed adjoining the wall, but outside the house : *c* is the situation of the pump, which ought to be such as to deliver the water into vessels held over the sink-stone. Fig. 2271. is a section of the

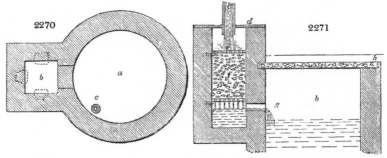

well and of the filtering apparatus ; the latter being placed close to the wall outside the scullery : *d* is the slate cover to the filter ; *c,* the tube which conveys the water direct down from the gutters to a plate of slate or zinc, *e,* pierced with small holes ; *f,* sand and charcoal, supported on a lower plate, also marked *e ;* the opening by which the water passes into the well is shown at *g ;* and the cover to the well, consisting of a Caithness flag-stone, at a short distance beneath the surface, is shown at *h.* The two plates of slate or zinc, *e e*, rest on pieces of slate which project from the sides of the filter-box, as indicated by the dotted lines at *b* in fig. 2270. The sand and charcoal can be taken out and cleaned at pleasure.

2482. *Constructing a Cottage Privy in Connexion with a Cesspool or Tank for Liquid Manure.* The privy may be either partially or wholly over the tank, which ought to be closely covered, on a level with the privy floor, by a flag-stone, as shown in fig. 2272. In this figure, *a* represents the seat, which is hinged, in order that when the slops of the house are being thrown in from a pail, or other large vessel, the seat, or pierced flap, may be lifted up, to keep it from being wetted (see page 1147. No. 11.); *b* shows the fixed and permanent seat, on which the moveable seat, *a*, rests; *c* shows the movable seat partially raised up; *i*, the flap or cover to the whole raised up; *d*, the basin of stone ware, cemented at *f* into a tube, *e*, also of stone ware, or it may be of wood or metal; *g* is the surface of the water in the tank, higher than which it can never rise, in consequence of a waste drain; and it will only fall lower than the bottom of the tube *e* when the tank is nearly empty; *h h*, the walls of the tank, and of the back of the privy.

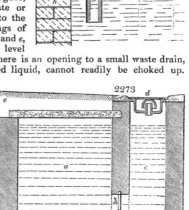

2483. *The Liquid-Manure Tank.* Fig. 2273. is a section of the liquid-manure tank, supposed to form also the tank for the privy. In this figure, *a* represents the liquid; *b*, a pierced slate or grating, through which the liquid filters into the well, *c*; *d*, a bell-trap to admit the drainings of the yard, and to prevent the rising of smells; and *e*, the covering of flag-stone and earth. On a level with the surface of the water in the well, *c*, there is an opening to a small waste drain, which, as it can only be entered by filtered liquid, cannot readily be choked up.

Wherever a proper value is set on liquid manure, however, the cesspool will never be allowed to overflow. The most convenient mode of taking out the water from the well, *c*, is by a pump; but where this is wanting, the cover, *d*, may be taken off, and a vessel dipped into it. It is unnecessary, after what has been stated in § 2408., to add, that the sides and bottom of the tank and well should be built in Roman cement; or that occasionally, perhaps every year or every two years, the tank will require to be cleaned out. Some recommend mixing powdered gypsum with the liquid, in order to neutralise the ammonia.

SECT. VII. *Construction and Arrangement of a Bath-Room.*

2484. *The Bath-Room, comprising a common and Shower Bath.* Invalids sometimes require to know exactly the quantity of water which forms the shower, as well as its temperature, and for this purpose there is a supply of both hot and cold water to the shower cistern. A gauge to indicate the quantity of water in the cistern and its temperature, and also the means of regulating them, is contrived in the following manner: The gauge consists of a tube as high as the cistern is deep, fixed on the outside of the cistern, and communicating with the bottom of the inside; in consequence of which, when water is let into the cistern, it rises to the same height in the tube. In order that the water may be seen, the front of this tube, which may be about three inches in width, and a foot in height, is formed of a narrow pane of glass, and one side of the case into which the glass is fixed is divided into equal parts, like the scale of a thermometer, each part or degree representing a pint of water. This tube is open at top, for the purpose of cleaning the glass, should it get dim, but chiefly for the purpose of putting in and taking out a thermometer with coloured spirits of wine, which shows through the pane in front the temperature of the water admitted into the cistern and rising into the gauge. There is a pipe of cold, and another of hot, water, communicating with this cistern; and each is closed or opened by a trigger-stopper, operated on by a cord ; and hence the temperature may be regulated by the thermometer at the pleasure of the bather.

Fig. 2274. is a plan of the bath-room, in which *a* is the door ; *b*, a window; *c*, the bath ; *d*, a chaise-percée, with a fixed waste-pipe ; *e*, a wash-hand stand, with a fixed basin, supplied with hot and cold water in the usual manner, with a waste-pipe for letting off the water ; *f*, two steps to ascend to the bath ; and *g*, a movable seat in the bath, formed of bars two inches broad, with intervals of two inches. The lateral dimensions of the room are about ten feet by twelve feet, and it is twelve feet high.

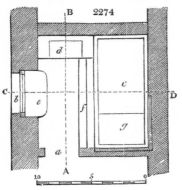 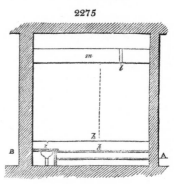

Fig. 2275. is a section on the line A B, in which *h* is the upper edge of the bath ; *i*, the chaise-percée ; *k*, the steps ; *l*, the glass front of the gauge of the shower-bath ; and *m*, the cistern of the shower-bath.

Fig. 2276. is a section on the line C D, in which are shown the bath with the stool, *n* ; the steps, *o* ; the chaise-percée, *p* ; the wash-hand stand, *q* ; the shower-bath cistern, *r* ; and the glass gauge, in which is also kept the thermometer, *s*.

2485. When a shower-bath is to be taken, the bather first pulls a string to admit the cold water into the cistern ; or, if it is to be slightly warmed, he pulls a second string, observing the gauge as to quantity, and the thermometer within it as to temperature. He then takes a small tray of sheet lead, about eighteen inches square, with the sides raised about two inches ; he sets this on the top of the seat, having previously moved it to the end of the bath from which the shower is to fall. He next draws some water from the cock in the wash-hand stand in a jug, and pours it into the tray, to prevent his feet from feeling the chill of the lead. He now ascends the bath, stands on the leaden

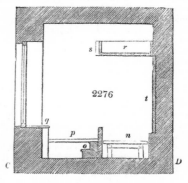

tray, having previously opened two doors, which, when closed, appear as part of the sides of the upper part of the bath, as indicated by the double lines at *t* in fig. 2276. These two doors, when fully opened, completely enclose the bather, who has only to pull a third string, which furnishes the shower. The doors may be kept in their new position by a fastening, which may be moved either from within or from without (the latter in case of accident to the bather); but this is only found necessary when the risk of the bather falling is apprehended from the violence of the shock. There are a great many different kinds of baths, portable and fixed, recommended by tradesmen, and, in consequence of ill health at various periods during the last forty years, we have had occasion to try several of them. We are compelled to acknowledge that most of the portable baths heated by small stoves with movable smoke pipes, the ends of which are inserted in the chimney of the bed-room to which the bath is brought, have, in our case at least, proved unsatisfactory, from the length of time required to heat the water. A good plan for small houses and ordinary establishments is, to have a bath-room on a level with the kitchen or scullery floor, and to have, when a bath is wanted, the water heated in the copper in the kitchen or scullery, and conveyed to the bath by pipes regulated by cocks. We are aware of a great variety of modes by which the water may be heated and conveyed to different parts of a house; but, except where such kitchen apparatus as that employed by Messrs. Steel and Co. is in use, or where there is a boiler in the attics (see § 1858.), they cannot, as we have experienced, be depended on.

This bath-room (described from one in a house in the neighbourhood of London) is on the bed-room floor, and supplied with hot water from a boiler in the floor above, which also supplies the nursery and all the other bed-rooms and dressing-rooms. The cold water is supplied from a cistern in the upper part of the house, which is completely excluded from the frost by a double roof. The cold and the hot water are incorporated by stirring with the pierced spatula, fig. 2277., in the usual manner; the round holes in the spatula having been made by a gimlet of large dimensions. There is ready access to the cistern by a door, by opening which heated air can be admitted at pleasure during severe frosts. From this cistern pipes are conducted in situations where they are secure from frost, and where they can be readily examined and repaired, to all the water-closets, and fixed wash-hand basins, &c. There are two water-closets on each floor, near the two extremities of the central passage, and there is a housemaid's closet on each floor, with a sink supplied with hot and cold water, immediately adjoining the servants' stairs. The roof of the main body of the house is of brick arches covered with lead; and that of the kitchen and other offices is formed of flat tiles and cement, in Mr. Fowler's manner. (§ 2446.) All the waste-pipes lead to a large cesspool in the yard, which has a man-hole for cleaning it out; and adjoining it is a well, into which the water overflows, and whence it can be pumped up at pleasure, to be used as liquid manure.

2277

SECT. VIII. *Gates and Fences.*

2486. *A Lodge-Gate Fastening.* Lodge-gates, when in one piece, or single, as the technical term is, are commonly hung at the side farthest from the lodge, with a view, it may be supposed, of bringing the latch as near the person who comes out from the lodge to open the gate as possible. But it must be recollected, that, after the latch is lifted, the operator (who is frequently an old person) must walk across the road, perhaps in the night when it is dark, or during rain or snow, and he or she (for this operation is generally performed by the female occupant of the lodge) must wait on the opposite side, " gate in hand," till the carriage has passed through. Sometimes also, when the horses are impatient in the day-time, or when it is dark at night, the gate-opener, while crossing the road before the horses' heads, is liable to be knocked down by them, or by the pole of the carriage. These and other inconveniences attending this mode of opening gates are avoided by hanging the gate on the side next the lodge, and by having a long horizontal rod, reaching from the latch to about the middle of the gate. The gate-opener advances only half across the road, pulls the rod to raise the latch, and walks a few steps backwards, opening the gate to its full width, and is at the same time protected by it. The application of the rod by which the gate is to be opened depends on the kind of fastening used. One of the simplest is, when the latch is retained in its place by a spring, and the rod being used to pull it back so as to open the gate; when the gate is again shut the latch returns to its place of itself. The rod may either be conducted along the top or the side of the upper bar of the gate, or under or along one side of a bar from three to four feet from the ground.

Fig. 2278. shows the mode adopted at Bridge Hill and Allestree, in which *a* is the latch, supported on a fulcrum at *b*, operated on by the S lever *c*, by means of the rod *d*

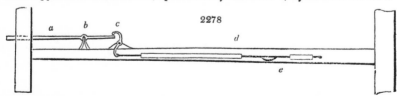

and the handle *e*. This handle serves both for pulling the rod backwards towards the hinges, so as to raise the latch, and for pulling the gate towards the operator, so as to open it by his walking a few steps backwards. For this benevolent invention the public is indebted to the late George Strutt, Esq., of Bridge Hill, Belper, near Derby.

2487. *Cast-Iron Heads or Hanging-Styles to Gates, and Wrought-Iron Rods as diagonal Braces*, are common in field and other gates in the neighbourhood of Derby. The cast-iron hanging-styles have mortise holes for the ends of the wooden bars, and these are made fast in a very simple but effective mode, which consists in having the mortise wider at one end than the other, as indicated in fig. 2279., in which *a* is a section of the mortise ; *b*, the end of the bar which is fitted into it; and

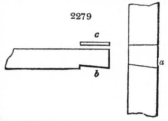

2279

c, a wedge, which, by keeping the tenon of the bar in its place, effectually prevents it from being drawn out. The hinges of such a gate are much less costly than the common ones, and the gate bars are preserved in their full strength at the tenons. Two wrought-iron rods pass from the bottom of the falling-style through the top of the hanging-style, where they are made fast by nuts on their screwed ends, by which nuts they can be drawn up as tight as may be desired. The wrought-iron rods at the lower end are passed through a thin wrought-iron plate, which forms a sort of shoe to the falling style.

2488. *Cottam's Iron Field Gate*, fig. 2280., has not been surpassed for strength of construction or durability of material. It is made of wrought iron, and the horizontal bars and braces are of flat bar iron, riveted together at every intersection, in order to prevent the swagging or sinking of the head. The cost singly is 26*s*.,

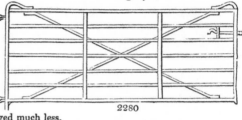

2280

but by the dozen it will be charged much less.

2489. *Buist's Fan Wire Gate*, fig. 2281., is at once light, strong, and economical. The wires which constitute the fan are fastened at their outer extremities by being

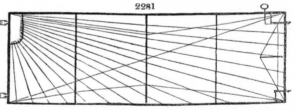

2281

driven up like nail heads ; and at the point of their convergence, at the upper hinge of the gate, they are screwed up tight by nuts. The gate is so close as to be nearly game-proof, and so strong, that one of the form shown in the figure, with a weight of eight hundred and sixty pounds at its extremity, after being made to swing for some time to and fro, did not undergo the slightest alteration in shape. The weight of this gate is from eighty-five pounds to ninety-five pounds, and its cost from £1 15*s*. to £2. The same principle is equally applicable to toll-bars as to park gates ; and, indeed, is the more important in its uses the more extended is the span of the gate. Fig. 2282. is a park gate with wickets on

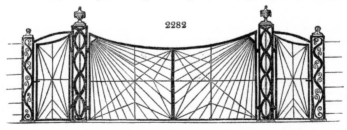

2282

this plan. The span of the gate is twelve feet ; the wickets are two feet and a half wide and six feet high. The supporters may be made of open iron castings. The wickets could be made for about 18*s*. a piece, the gate itself for £4 ; or £5 10*s*. in all : a very small fraction indeed of the price commonly paid for park gates of similar appearance and show. Much depends on the excellence of the workmanship of these gates, and Mr. Buist the inventor, now in Bombay, strongly recommends Mr. John Douglas, blacksmith, Cupar, Fifeshire. (See also *Gard. Mag.* for 1840, p. 193.)

2490. *A full-down Gate-stopper*, fig. 2283. Where double gates are used, the gate-stopper standing up in the middle of the road or walk is a great nuisance, both to men and horses, but, by having the stopper to work on pivots, as in the figure, it can be raised up when the gate is shut, as at *a*, and turned down when it is open, as at *b*. These stoppers are the invention of Messrs. Cottam and Hallen.

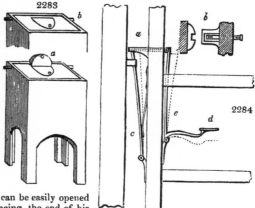

2491. *A Gate Latch*, which cannot be shaken out by cattle, is represented in fig. 2284., in which *a* is a side view, and *b* a transverse section. The upright latch, *c*, is held in the catch by a spring, so that it cannot easily be shaken out by the rubbing of cattle, or the shaking of boys or idle persons, while it can be easily opened by a person on horseback placing the end of his whip or stick in the hollow thumb-piece *d*, which, acting as a lever on the upright piece *e*, pulls back *c*, and compresses the spring, by which the gate is readily opened.

2492. *A Cap for the upper Rail of a Wooden Fence*, in which no nails are to be used, is shown in the section fig. 2285., in which *a* is the cap, having one end of a strong wooden pin, *c*, driven tight into it; *e e*, the angles of the cap, formed so as to drip the water clear of the rails; *d d*, the rails, overlaid and fastened in the post *b* by the pin *c*. The other rails need not have any fastening, further than being halved and overlaid, as the bottom end of the post is fast in the ground. Some very handsome designs for rustic fencing and gates, by Mr. Ricauti, will be found in the *Gardener's Magazine* for 1842; but more especially in Ricauti's *Sketches for Rustic Work*, now publishing.

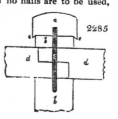

SECT. IX.   *Miscellaneous Details.*

2493. *To prevent Sash-Windows from shaking and rattling with the Wind.* This evil arises from the sashes not having been tightly fitted to the grooves, and is to be prevented by tightening them, which may be done in two ways. The most common is by a sash-fastener, fig. 2286., one part of which, *e*, is screwed to the side of the lower rail of the upper sash, and the other part, *b c d*, to the upper side of the upper rail of the lower sash. Then the part *a* being brought down over the part *b*, which travels backwards and forwards in the box *c*, is made tight by the thumb-screw *d*. In this way both sashes are drawn to press against the parting bead which separates the two sashes, and, in consequence, they are effectually prevented from shaking, or from

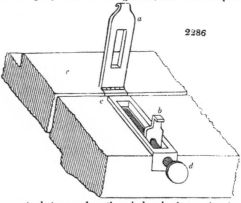

any lateral or perpendicular movement whatever, when the window is shut. Another mode of effecting the same object, and keeping the sashes from shaking, whether the window is shut or open, is by inserting a double bead of well-seasoned oak in the groove of the window case in which the sash moves up and down. This is shown in fig. 2287. at *a*; and, as the style of the sash moves up and down on this bead, it is kept firmly in its place, altogether independently of the parting beads or the outside beads. The situation of the outer sash is shown at *b*, and it works on a similar double bead; *d* is the boxed frame for the shutters inside the room; *e* is the box for the weights; *f*, the brick forming the outside jamb of the window; and *c*, the outside sill. This is a very effectual mode of preventing large old windows from shaking, whether open or shut, but it is rather expensive.

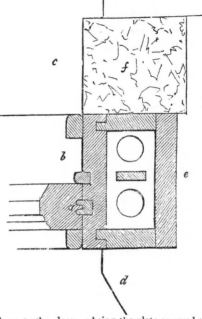

2287

2494. *A Hinge for a Jib-door.* A jib-door is a door which opens either by being pushed from, or drawn towards, the opener, and which, after being opened, shuts of itself. The action of these doors is founded on the construction and application of their hinges, and hence various forms have been adopted, aided by springs in some cases, and weights and pulleys in others. But the cheapest, and that which operates with the greatest ease, is the one which we are about to describe. The top hinge of the door is merely a pivot, which works in a projecting eye; and the folding-hinge is fixed on the lower part, or heel, of the hanging-style of the door.

Fig. 2288. is a general view of the folding bent hinge, before being screwed on to the door; *c* being the plate screwed to the jamb, and *b* that screwed to the style, both parts being connected by *a*. It may be made either of cast iron or of brass. Fig. 2289. is a horizontal section through the

2288

2289

2290

hinge when the door is shut, in which *l* is the jamb; *f*, the style of the door; *g g*, screws; and *h h*, parts of the folding hinge which project beyond the door on each side. Fig. 2290. is a horizontal section, showing the door partially opened.

2495. *Lath and Plaster Partitions*, when open from the bottom or from any floor of the house, admit of a current of air from bottom to top, and in the case of fire greatly accelerate its progress. It is, therefore, recommended to fill them in solid behind the skirtings of the rooms, which can readily be done by common mortar, with fragments of tiles or bricks, or by cement.

2496. *Fire-proof Floors and Partition Walls.* Much might be done to effect these objects by iron joisting, laid two feet or thirty inches asunder, and covered with Caithness flags, the flattest, the hardest, and the most tenacious of this class of stones. They are incapable of being cut by masons' irons, but they saw easily; and, being truly flat by nature, they require no farther dressing than being sawn square. They are found of all thicknesses, from a quarter of an inch to three inches and a half, and are so strong at two inches thick that no accident which can occur, in ordinary cases, could injure a square of thirty inches, or even three feet. If, therefore joists of iron, as shown in section fig. 2291. (in which *a* is the line of flag-stones forming the floor; *b*, the cast-iron

2291   *b*

c

joists; and *c*, the wrought-iron rod for stiffening them), were covered with these flags a substantial fire-proof floor might be made of any extent. In many cases, the natural surface of the stone may do; but, in conspicuous places, where neither carpet nor oil-cloth is laid down, the slabs may be polished by rubbing one against another, and, when finished in this way and oiled, they look as well as Tournay marble. Sir John Robison heated a portion of this stone red hot, and quenched it in water, without its cracking, or appearing to lose its peculiar tenacity. This stone may be had in London of Messrs. Freeman, Milbank Street, Westminster.

2497. Thin fire-proof partitions with Caithness stone, or with Arbroath stone, may thus be formed. Suppose a set of upright iron standards, like *a a* or *b b*, in the horizontal sections figs. 2292. and 2293., were erected, and stone slabs, grooved or plain

2292   *a*   *a*

(according to circumstances), were dropped into the spaces, a very firm partition might be built up, without requiring any fastening, except the top course, where, of

2293

necessity, there could be no feather or ledge, as all the stones would have to be let in there. Other and better forms would probably occur on further consideration. — *J. R.*

2498. *Windows in Roofs.* In introducing windows in roofs, care should be taken that the panes of glass are flat, and not in any way globular, like what are called bull's-eyes, it having been found that a house was set on fire by a bull's-eye being introduced in the roof, in order to light a garret. The bull's-eye concentrated the sun's rays on a muslin dress lying exposed on a large box beneath. From the flame communicating to the box, its contents were soon set on fire, and the flooring and rafters were in a short time completely in flames. This happened in the house of a gentleman on the Stroud road, near Gloucester. (*Scotsman*, Aug. 3. 1839.)

2499. *An Air and Vermin Trap for Drains.* In fig. 2294. *a a* represent the drain,

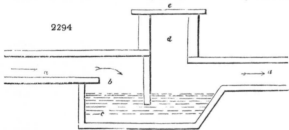

the bottom of which is straight or circular, as the case may be; but it projects at *b* over the water in the trap *c*, from three inches to six inches, which prevents the vermin from passing one way, as will be perceived. The level of the water in the trap is several inches below the under side of the bottom of the drain. (*A. M.*, iii. 192.)

2500. *To guard against Mice and Rats.* The aliment of mice and rats consists of nearly equal food and water. In farmeries the first cannot be withheld, but the latter may. All drains should be made of close-jointed stone, or of bricks, with properly constructed air-traps, see fig. 2295.; in which *a* is a stone, which is made to lift up, to clean

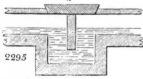

out the earth or other matter from the trap. Roof gutters, if any, should be made as inaccessible as possible; water troughs decidedly so. This is easily done. Project a wooden fillet, or frame, all round within the trough, making it project three inches or thereabouts into the trough, and keep the surface of the water about three inches below the frame. By this method no rat of the ordinary size can get a drop. To prevent them from getting up into the roof, let a flagstone be projected over each of the interior angles. No walls, especially of dry stone, should be allowed near the buildings; or, at least, to come in contact with them near the level of the walls.—*I. M.*

Sect. X. *Materials.*

2501. *Cements.* Various kinds of cements have been introduced since the Encyclopædia was published, but none surpass that variety of the old Roman cement called the Mulgrave Cement, and sometimes Atkinson's Cement. It is double the price of the common Roman cement, but it is proportionately superior in point of strength and durability.   As a proof, we may mention that houses built of stone in the neighbourhood of Whitby, and, among others, Mulgrave Castle, have been covered with it, to protect the stone from the effects of the sea air.   In our opinion, the walls of a house built of brick, and covered with good cement, are far stronger than walls of brick with outside casings of stone.   In all cases, therefore, where walls of great strength and durability were required, and where they could not be built wholly of stone, we should build them of brick, either laid in cement or covered with it.   The facility which cement affords of introducing architectural forms, such as architraves, cornices, &c., at little expense, requires no eulogium, since it has contributed more than any thing else to the present highly improved state of British architecture.   When plain walls are covered with cement, the surface ought always to be marked by lines, so as to give the expression of stone; and this imitation of stone ought not to be confined to stone with a smoothly hewn surface, as it generally is at present, but every manner of hewing stone ought to be imitated, including plain ashlar, tooled ashlar, random-tooled, chiseled, boasted, pointed, rusticated, frosted, scappeld, hammer-dressed, &c.

2502. *A Metallic Cement,* formed of powdered scoria from copper-works and stone lime, sets rapidly, and takes a fine metallic polish.   It is sold in powder, mixed in due proportions; price 9*d.* per bushel. (*A. M.,* i. 46.)

2503. *Asphalte, Caithness Stone, and Slate.* Asphalte, as a material of recent introduction, and its various uses, have already been noticed (§ 2447.), as has Caithness stone (§ 2496.).   Slate is coming into very general use for shelves to pantries, dairies, &c. ; for kitchen tables, for panels to doors, for flooring to rooms, and for a great variety of other purposes.   A layer of asphalte in a wall is found as effective in preventing the rising of damp as a course of slate or flagstone, or a layer of Roman cement.   Caithness flagstone is at last acknowledged by some of the first architects, both in Scotland and England, to be superior to all others for works in the open air.   " As regards strength and hardness, it is not to be equalled by any paving-stone used in London : it completely resists the action of the severest frosts; it neither scales, flakes, nor becomes slippery ; and, from not being porous, it dries rapidly after rains : in fact, none of the objections so common to the Yorkshire paving, or any other freestone, seem to apply to the Castlehill Caithness paving.   The method of squaring the stone, with sawn joints, is also of great advantage, by securing a close joint, and thereby contributing to the solidity and ornament of the work."

2504. *Cylindrical Earthenware Tubes for Flues* are in general use in building all good houses in the North of England and in Scotland.   The cylinders are about ten inches in diameter, one foot in length, and an inch in thickness; one end of every cylinder being rectangular, and the other oblique, in order to admit of building the flues either straight or curved at pleasure.   When they are to be built curved, the oblique ends are joined to straight ends, and when they are to be built straight, the oblique ends and straight ends are put together alternately.   The great advantage of this kind of flue is, that it is easily swept by machinery, and that much less soot adheres to the sides than in square flues.   A series of bricks of different forms, for effecting the same purpose, has lately been invented by Mr. Welch, architect, Liverpool.

2505. *Sheet Glass for Windows,* and especially for sashes for greenhouses, has recently come into use.   This glass is thicker than common crown glass, though not much dearer, and it can be obtained in panes of any length under six feet, and of any breadth under two feet.   It has been extensively used at Chatsworth, both in the roofs of hothouses and in the windows of cottages.   Its great advantage for hothouse roofs, and sashes for garden frames of every kind, is, that very few joints are required, and hence the heated air within is prevented from escaping, and the rain from being driven in.   In short, the introduction of this glass into hothouse buildings is one of the greatest improvements that have been made in their construction since the substitution of roofs of glass for roofs of opaque materials.   Where the ridge and furrow mode of forming hothouse roofs is adopted, there need not be a single glass joint in the entire roof.   Verandas may be glazed without joints, by using panes of the full length, and the advantage, both in point of beauty, admission of light, and saving of breakage, is incredible, as we have proved in our veranda here.   This glass is manufactured by different persons, and we can very strongly recommend Messrs. Claudet and Houghton, Holborn.

2506. *Plate Glass,* when it is to be ground on the surface, may be obtained of the manufacturers at a very moderate rate, because the slightest defect in the material unfits it for being polished, but is no drawback to its being ground.   The ceilings of lobbies, passages, and all rooms having skylights, may be finished with this glass below the skylight with admirable effect, as may be seen in the houses of various gentlemen in Newcastle, Liverpool, and Edinburgh.   The same damaged glass, without being ground, is admirably adapted for cottage windows, not only because it is not easily broken, but because from its thickness it is a very bad conductor of heat, and might almost serve as a substitute for window-shutters.

2507. *Preservation of Wood.* Sulphate of copper, which abounds in the mineral waters of the mines in Cornwall and Anglesea, has been proved to be an excellent preservative of timber which has been immersed in it. (See *Mech. Mag.*, vol. xxxiii. p. 568., and *Gard. Mag.* for 1842, p. 174.)

In the last work the following recipe is given for preparing the composition: — Take fifteen pounds of sulphate of iron (7*s.* 6*d.* per hundredweight); twelve pounds of sulphate of copper (45*s.* per hundredweight); twenty-four pounds of sulphate of zinc (45*s.* per hundredweight); one quart of sulphuric acid (3*d.* per pound). The sulphates to be well pounded, and dissolved in hot water; and then the sulphuric acid to be mixed in the solution, and well stirred up with a scrubbing-broom. The above, added to thirty-six gallons of water, is ready for the tank. Time of saturation: for one-inch board, three days; three-inch plank, or scantling, seven days; five-inch to six and seven inch scantling, all twelve to fourteen days; large timber, twelve inches to fourteen inches square, will require twenty-one days.

Creosote has been employed for ages in the preservation of animal structures for anatomical purposes, and is found also the most effective in preserving timber. Mr. Bethel's mode of preservation consists in impregnating the wood to the centre with this substance. (*Mech. Mag.*, vol. xxxi. p. 309.)

2508. *Ironwork coated with Gas Liquor, Tar, or Pitch,* is found to be far less durable than when painted with lead and oil in the usual manner. The oxidation is greatly accelerated in a damp situation, but it takes place even in coal-scuttles kept in dry rooms: of course this does not render gas liquor, tar, or pitch, less fit for preserving wood. (*Gard. Mag.*, 1840, p. 514.)

CHAP. VI.

Fittings-up, Finishing, and Furnishing.

SECT. I.   *Modes of Heating.*

2509. *Many different Kinds of Stoves* for heating the general air of a house have been invented or brought into notice within the last seven years. Among these, the more remarkable are Arnot's and Joyce's stoves. The latter needs only to be mentioned to be avoided; since, in effect, it is nothing more than burning charcoal without a flue to carry off the fumes, the deleterious effects of which are so frequently exemplified in the case of suicides. Arnot's stove is unquestionably the best apparatus of the kind that has yet appeared, since the quantity of heat produced is regulated with the greatest nicety; the fuel, in consequence of being burned in an enclosure of fire-brick, is thoroughly consumed, and, by regulating the supply of air, but a small proportion of heat is allowed to escape with the smoke. For the halls or passages of small houses, and for large rooms, in addition to open fires, Arnot's stove is therefore one of the best; but it must be borne in mind that it introduces no fresh air, and is therefore altogether unsuitable in cases where ventilation is to be combined with warming. For this purpose it is essential that a stream of fresh air should be introduced from without, as in Strutt's stove (§ 2530.), and be heated by the stove before being allowed to escape into the apartment. This has been effected by many different stoves, and with Arnot's stove, by a modification introduced by Mr. Jeakes. An excellent ventilating stove, combining an open fireplace, has also been invented by Mr. Jeffery, the inventor of the respirator, and may be seen in action at No. 148. Regent Street. The stoves of Mr. White, already mentioned (§ 2478.), are calculated either to heat the air of the apartment, by passing it through a flue or case, or to heat the external air by the same means. There are various other stoves; such as the Chunk stove, Kirkwood's stove, the Vesta stove, Brown and Green's ventilating stove, the Olmsted stove, &c., but the three which deserve the preference, in our opinion, are: Arnot's stove, alone for a small house, or with Jeakes's improvement for a larger house; White of Haddington's warm-air stove, and Jeffery's warm-air stove, where it is desired to combine an open fireplace. The price of one of White's stoves of the smallest size is £3 10*s.*, which is about the same price as Arnot's stove without Jeakes's improvement: Jeffery's stove is much dearer. The great merit of Dr. Arnot's stove consists in the saving of fuel; but, as ventilation by this stove depends solely on combustion, it is diminished in proportion to the saving. It can never, therefore, be recommended as the sole means of warming living-rooms; but for halls and staircases, or small houses where outer doors are being constantly opened, it will be found more economical than any other. To derive the full benefit from Arnot's stove, the outer casing ought to be of sheet iron, in order to disperse the heat generated as rapidly as possible; for, when cast-iron casings are used, great part of the heat is carried up the chimney. In large houses, we repeat, White's stove deserves the preference. It may be some recommendation of this stove, to mention that it is the only one introduced into his new buildings by Mr. Burn, the most extensively employed architect in Scotland. Much discussion on Dr. Arnot's stove, and on the others mentioned, will be found in the *Architectural Magazine.*

2510. *Heating the general Atmosphere of a House by Hot Water* is occasionally resorted to, as producing a more agreeable heat, from the moisture it contains, than dry air, which, when too dry, abstracts moisture from the skin, and also as not admitting of overheating the air by the apparatus. This mode of heating is variously effected, but the best apparatus for the purpose, in our opinion, is that of Price and Manby of Nelson Street, Bristol, and of Chester Place, London. The air is heated in a cellar by a series of shallow flat closed vessels, or cases, of hot water, and rises through a trunk or flue in the same manner as by Mr. Sylvester's mode (§ 2379.). As the air by this mode can never be heated much above 100°, the risk of fires from the apparatus is much less than by any mode of heating by a stove or cockle.

Sect. II. Interior Fittings-up and Finishing.

2511. *Fittings-up of Cottages.* It has been suggested by the Highland Society, that, if doors, shelving, and other wooden work for cottages, could be manufactured in the

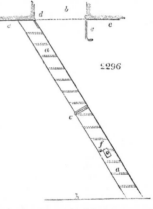

wholesale way, like M‘Culloch's windows, it would materially lessen the expense. We have suggested in the *Gardener's Magazine* the idea of manufacturing cottage fittings-up and furniture in Norway, and importing them in a state fit for use. Were there a sufficient demand, the manufacture would be carried on as regularly as that of Norway battens, and the saving to the builders and occupiers of cottages would be very great.

2512. *A Fold-up Step-Ladder* is often a convenient substitute for a stair in cottages. Fig. 2296. shows a ladder of this description hinged at *d*, and with a joint at *c*. When folded up it has the appearance shown in fig. 2297., there being a stud at *f* which rests on the hook *e*.

2513. *Cowell's Sash-Suspender* enables sash-windows to be cleaned, painted, or repaired, without the operator's going outside for these purposes. The line by which the sash is suspended, instead of being nailed to it, is secured in a socket provided with a hook. To this is fitted a plate or eye, which is let into the sash, so that it can be attached or detached in an instant, and with the greatest ease. A complete set of the brass suspenders, including an ingenious brass bolt for fixing the bead, instead of nailing it, costs only 3s. 6d. (See the figures of this invention, and farther details, in *Arch. Mag.*, vol. iv. p. 72.)

2514. *The Rollers of Window-Blinds,* formerly made cylindrical, are now made octagonal or polygonal, which is found to give them a better hold of the blind or other material to be rolled round them than cylindrical rollers. A pulley-rack for blinds, invented by Messrs. Loach and Clarke, is considered a very great improvement, as is a wedge-fastener by the same party. We have tried both, and consider the pulley-rack very superior to that in common use.

2515. *Preserving the Tapes of Venetian Blinds from the Sun.* This object is attained by two slips of wood the length of the blind, connected as a parallel ruler, and screwed within the frame of the blind upon both sides. When the blind is about to be let down, the preserver is drawn out, and the slip of wood covers the whole of the tape, which would be otherwise exposed to the action of the sun. By this simplest of all contrivances, the durability of the blind is insured for a considerable period.

2516. *Venetian Blinds made of Glass instead of Wood* have recently been invented, and may come into occasional use in dwelling-houses, water-closets, &c. (*A. M.*, iv. 206.)

2517. *The Poor Man's Window-Blind.* The simple homely furniture of the poor cottager requires to be protected from the scorching rays of the noonday sun as much as the more elaborately finished articles which occupy the apartments of the citizen and tradesman; but the expense of the roller, the pulleys, the trap-rack or slide, the stretching-rod and line, as well as the holland (cotton cloth not being capable of being rolled evenly), places that description of window-blinds which is generally used beyond the means of the poor labourer; therefore a simple window-blind may be made as follows. After a piece of cheap thin calico of the proper size has been hemmed, attach a few small rings to the upper edge; fix a nail on each side of the window case at the top, and extend a strong piece of cord across, on which the blind is to be hung in the manner of bed-curtains. A small string is then attached to the last ring on the left side, and hanging down on the same side, to pull the curtain on the window; and another string is to be fixed to the same ring, but passing through all the other rings, and hanging down on the right side, to pull the curtain off. Each of the two strings to have a small ring fixed at the ends, by way of finish to them; and if the labourer has a tidy wife, she will not fail to make a little frill or vallance, with a loop at each end, to hang upon the nails, so as to hide the working of the rings. The whole would not, for an ordinary-sized cottage window, cost above 10*d.* — *S.*

2518. *Painting and Papering, as Modes of Finishing, compared, with Reference to Salubrity.* Of all the arts connected with domestic comfort, there is scarcely one on which so little has been written, and consequently of which so little is known, as housepainting. It is well understood that the ceilings and walls of all the apartments of dwelling-houses and other buildings, in this country, are now almost uniformly finished in plaster; and the nature and properties of this composition are also well known. One of these properties is its power of absorbing moisture, or, in other words, its facility in attracting and imbibing dampness. Consequently, when an apartment is left for any length of time without the benefit of a fire, or of heated air supplied by other means, the plaster will continue to absorb a portion of the dampness from the atmosphere with which the room is filled; and it is natural to suppose that, when a fire is put on, or heated air is otherwise admitted, this dampness will be gradually given out by exhalation from the plaster. This process of exhalation must affect the durability, not only of the plaster itself, but of the woodwork under it, and must also render the apartment much less comfortable than if it had been rendered incapable of such absorption. It therefore becomes an enquiry of some interest, whether painting or papering (the two methods by which the walls of our apartments are usually decorated) is the better adapted to counteract these disadvantages.

2519. *The Process of painting Plaster-work* is as follows. White lead and linseed oil, with a little litharge to facilitate the drying, are mixed together to about the consistence of thin cream; a coating of this being applied, the oil from it is sucked into the plaster in the course of a few hours, leaving the white lead apparently dry upon the surface. In the course of a day or two, when this coat has sufficiently hardened, another is given a few degrees thicker, the oil from which is partially absorbed according to the nature of the plaster. In the course of a few days more a third coat is applied. This coat is made pretty thick; and, if the absorption of the oil from the second coat has not been great, about one fourth of spirits of turpentine is added; but when the absorption has been great a less proportion of the spirits of turpentine is employed. Into this coat are put the colouring ingredients, to bring it near the shade intended for the finishing coat. Should the plaster now be thoroughly saturated, the flatting or finishing coat is applied; before this is done, however, a fourth coat, thinned with equal portions of oil and spirits of turpentine, is generally given, particularly when the work is wished to be of the most durable kind. The flatting, or finishing coat, is composed entirely of paint; that is, of white lead, and the colouring ingredients mixed together, and ground in oil to an impalpable paste. This mixture is of a very thick consistency, and must be thinned with spirits of turpentine until it will flow easily from the brush. The spirits of turpentine, being very volatile, evaporate entirely, leaving the surface of the paint of a very compact and hard nature. By this process, the plaster is rendered incapable of absorption; and the surface of it is hardened by the oil which it has sucked in from the first and second coats, and is thereby rendered less liable to breakage, with the great advantage of being washable.

2520. *Paper-hangings.* It now remains to be seen whether paper-hangings are equally well adapted to the comfort, cleanliness, and durability of the generality of apartments, as a decoration for plastered walls. Every one knows that paper is more or less absorbent, according to its quality. When it is manufactured into paperhangings, it is washed over with a coating of size colour, equally absorbent with the paper itself, upon which a pattern is stamped with the same material. To prepare the plaster for papering, it receives a coating of a weak solution of glue in water; and the paper, as every one knows, is fixed on the wall by paste. Paper-hangings, therefore, cannot be considered, in a general point of view, as being so well adapted to plastered

walls as paint; and there are particular situations in which serious disadvantages
attend paper, which a short explanation will make apparent to every one.   Take a
dining-room for example.   The papered wall has nothing in it to resist the absorption
of the steam of the dinner, or breaths of the large parties by which it is often crowded:
the glue and paste used in paper-hanging must be thereby softened, and the moisture
absorbed must, of course, be afterwards gradually given out in connexion with the
natural effluvia of these, the former of which all know to be extracted from animal
substances, not of the most cleanly nature, until the wall be again thoroughly dry.
Besides, a papered wall is liable to be injured past remedy by so common a casualty
as the starting of a bottle of table-beer, champagne, or soda-water.   Lobbies and staircases are sometimes papered, although the practice is not very common in Scotland.
This is very objectionable, as the condensation of the atmosphere, which always takes
place upon the walls of such apartments on a change of temperature, from cold to
warmth, must be absorbed, and again given out as before explained.   They are likewise very liable to accidental injuries, and should therefore have the hardest and most
impervious covering.   In regard to drawingrooms and bed-rooms, these particular
objections to paper-hangings do not apply, yet there are modes of painting drawingrooms superior, not only in point of utility (to which for the present these observations
are confined), but also in effect.—*D. R. Hay.*   Mr. Hay is at the head of his profession
in Scotland; and we are happy to be able to state that Mr. Moxon, who has been for
several years in Mr. Hay's establishment, and is equally enthusiastic in his art, has recently commenced business in Bury Street, St. James's, London.   Mr. Moxon is the
author of the *Grainer's Guide*, folio, £2 2s., a work by far the best of its kind which has
yet appeared.

2521. *Principles of papering Rooms.*   The following remarks are by Mr. Pugin.
" I will commence with what are termed Gothic pattern papers, for hanging walls, where
a wretched caricature of a pointed building is repeated from the skirting to the cornice
in glorious confusion; door over pinnacle, and pinnacle over door.   This is a great
favourite with hotel and tavern keepers.   Again, those papers which are shaded are
defective in principle; for, as a paper is hung round a room, the ornament must frequently be shadowed on the light side.   The variety of these miserable patterns is quite
surprising; and as the expense of cutting a block for a bad figure is equal, if not greater,
than for a good one, there is not the shadow of an excuse for their continual reproduc-
tion.   A moment's reflection must show the extreme absurdity of repeating a perspective
over a large surface with some hundred different points of sight: a panel or wall may
be enriched and decorated at pleasure, but it should always be treated in a consistent
manner.   Flock papers are admirable substitutes for the ancient hangings, but then they
must consist of a pattern without shadow, with the forms relieved by the introduction of
harmonious colours.   Illuminated manuscripts of the thirteenth, fourteenth, and fifteenth
centuries would furnish an immense number of exquisite designs for this purpose." —
Pugin.

2522. *Carpets.* These observations will apply to modern carpets, the patterns of which
are generally shaded.   Nothing can be more ridiculous than an apparently reversed groining to walk upon, or highly relieved foliage and perforated tracery for the decoration of
a floor.   The ancient paving tiles are quite consistent with their purpose, being merely
ornamented with a pattern not produced by any apparent relief, but only by contrast of
colour; and carpets should be treated in precisely the same manner.   Turkey carpets,
which are by far the handsomest now manufactured, have no shadow in their pattern, but
merely an intricate combination of coloured intersections.

2523. *Curtains.*   Modern upholstery, again, is made a surprising vehicle for bad and
paltry taste, especially when any thing very fine is attempted.   To arrange curtains
consistently with true taste, their use and intention should always be considered: they
are suspended across windows and other openings to exclude cold and wind, and, as they
are not always required to be drawn, they are hung to rings sliding on rods, to be
opened or closed at pleasure : as there must necessarily be " a space between this rod and
the ceiling, through which wind will pass, a boxing of wood has been contrived, in front of
which a valance is suspended to exclude air.   Now the materials of these curtains
may be rich or plain, they may be heavily or lightly fringed, they may be embroidered
with heraldic charges or not, according to the locality where they are to be hung, but
their real use must be strictly maintained.   Hence all the modern plans of suspending
enormous folds of stuff over poles, as if for the purpose of sale or of being dried, is quite
contrary to the use and intentions of curtains, and [therefore] abominable in taste; and
the only object that these endless festoons and bunchy tassels can answer is, to swell the
bills and profits of the upholsterers, who are the inventors of these extravagant and ugly
draperies, which are not only useless in protecting the chamber from cold, but are the
depositories of thick layers of dust, and in London not unfrequently become the strong-

holds of vermin. It is not less ridiculous to see canopies of tomb and altar screens set up over windows, instead of the appropriate valance or baldaquin of the olden time. It is proper in this place to explain the origin and proper application of fringes, which is but little understood. Fringe was originally nothing more than the ragged edge of the stuff, tied into bunches to prevent it unravelling further. This suggested the idea of manufacturing fringe as an ornamental edging, but good taste requires that it should be both designed and applied consistently.

1. In the first place, fringe should never consist of heavy parts, but simply of threads, tied into ornamental patterns.

2. Secondly, a deep fringe should not be suspended to a narrow valance.

3. Thirdly, no valance should be formed entirely of fringe, as fringe can only be supplied as an ornamental edging to some kind of stuff.

4. Fourthly, fringe should not be sewed upon stuff, but always on the edges. It is allowable at the very top, as it may be supposed to be the upper edge turned over." (*Pugin's Christ. Arch.*, p. 29.)

2524. *Metal-work.* The Gothic architects, Mr. Pugin informs us, suited the design to the material with which they worked; and instead of concealing construction, they avowed and decorated it, whether in the elevation of a house, or in the smallest article of furniture. Hinges, locks, bolts, nails, &c., which are always concealed in modern designs, were, in pointed architecture, rendered rich and beautiful decorations, not only in doors and fittings, but in the smallest cabinets. The hinges, in former times, covered the whole face of the doors with varied and flowing scroll-work; and such hinges were not less beautiful in design than they were practically good, by extending the whole length of the door, and being bolted through it in various places. Stock-locks were also avowed, and rendered very ornamental, but now they are concealed, by being let into the styles of doors, which are often cut more than half through to receive them. " A lock was a subject on which the ancient smiths delighted to exercise the utmost resources of their art. Keys were also highly ornamented with appropriate decorations referring to the locks to which they belong." (*Pugin's Christ. Arch.*, p. 21.)

2525. *Cast Iron-work*, when viewed with reference to mechanical purposes, Mr. Pugin observes, " must be considered as a most valuable invention, but it can but rarely be applied to ornamental purposes. Iron is so much stronger a material than stone, that it requires, of course, a much smaller substance to attain equal strength; hence, to be consistent, the mullions of cast-iron tracery might be so reduced as to look painfully thin, devoid of shadow, and out of all proportion to the openings in which they are fixed. If, to overcome these objections, the castings are made of the same dimensions as stone, a great inconsistency with respect to the material is incurred; and, what will be a much more powerful argument with most people, treble the cost of the usual material. Moreover, all castings must be deficient of that play of light and shade consequent on bold relief and deep sinkings, so essential to produce a good effect. Cast iron is likewise a source of continual repetition, subversive of the variety and imagination exhibited in pointed design. A mould for casting is an expensive thing; once got, it must be worked out. Hence we see the same window in greenhouse, gate-house, church, and room; the same strawberry-leaf, sometimes perpendicular, sometimes horizontal, sometimes suspended, sometimes on end; although, by the principles of pure design, these various positions require to be differently treated. Cast iron is a deception; it is seldom or never left as iron. It is disguised by paint, either as stone, wood, or marble. This is a mere trick, and the severity of Christian, or pointed, architecture is utterly opposed to all deception; better is it to do a little, substantially and consistently with truth, than to produce a great but false show: cheap deceptions of magnificence encourage persons to assume a semblance of decoration far beyond either their means or their station, and it is to this cause we may assign all that mockery of splendour which pervades even the dwellings of the lower classes of society. Glaring, showy, and meretricious ornament was never so much in vogue as at present; it disgraces every branch of our arts and manufactures, and the correction of it should be an earnest consideration with every person who desires to see the real principles of art restored." (*Pugin's Christ. Arch.*, p. 30.)

2526. *The Manner in which Fenders are fitted to Fireplaces* is almost everywhere unarchitectural; and there is not a single feature in the interior of living-rooms that is more in want of reformation. The meagre iron or brass rim of the fender abuts abruptly against the marble plinth of the chimney jambs, sometimes against the middle of the plinth, and sometimes against one side. There is nothing either in the jambs or in the fender to show that they are intended to be joined together; nothing to indicate whether the rim of the fender should abut against the jamb of the grate, middle of the plinth, or its outer edge; or whether it should not abut on the front of the grate within the jamb altogether. It is astonishing that so glaring a defect in the adaptation of furniture should so long have escaped the notice of architects, and that it should still

prevail in some of the most magnificent houses in Britain; for example, in Windsor
Castle and Hamilton Palace, in both of which the principal rooms have lately been
newly fitted up and furnished in the most splendid style.   There are various ways in
which this evil might be remedied.   1. The fender being of metal, might be so contrived as to fix into and connect architecturally with the grate, as being also of metal.
2. Grooves or recesses may be made in the plinths of the jambs, into which boxings of
metal might be fixed, and into these the fender might be made to drop, and be taken
out at pleasure; or projections from the jambs might be made, either in marble or
metal, extending on the hearth as far as might be necessary, and between these the
fender might be dropped in.   An idea of this mode may be formed from fig. 2298.   In

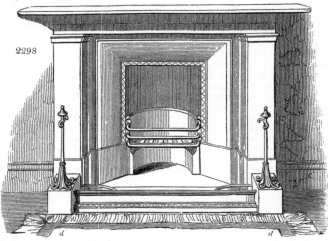

this figure the two projecting blocks may be of marble, stone, or of cast iron, hollow;
and they may be attached to the hearth by two wooden pins in the under sides of
the blocks, which should drop into two small holes in the hearth.   On the blocks
might be raised the supports to the fire-irons, as shown in the figure.   Some further
discussion on the adaptation of fenders to fireplaces will be found in the *Suburban Architect and Landscape-Gardener*, p. 125. to 127.; and we would strongly recommend
the subject to the attention of architects, convinced that, if they were to see this deformity in the light we do, the evil would soon disappear, at least in first-rate houses
and palaces.

2527. *Cornices, Ornaments in Papier-Maché, and various Architectural and Sculptural
Details*, are now very generally introduced in interior finishing.   The principal manu-
facturer is Mr. Bielfield of Wellington Street, who has published several books of
cornices and ornaments, and other details, from which selections may be made.

2528. *The Italian Mode of excluding the common House-Fly from Apartments*, and
which is as old as the time of Herodotus, is simply to cover the openings of the windows
by a net of white or light-coloured thread.   It is remarkable that the meshes of this
net may be an inch or more in diameter, so that there is actually no physical obstacle
presented to the entrance of the flies, even with expanded wings.   The flies seem to
be deterred from entering from some inexplicable dread of venturing within the net-
work.   It is even found that " if small nails be fixed all round the window-frame, at
the distance of about an inch from each other, and threads be then stretched across
both vertically and horizontally, the apparatus will be equally effectual in excluding the
flies."   It is essential, however, that the light should enter the room on one side of it
only; for if there be a thorough light, either from an opposite or side window, the flies
pass through the net without scruple.   (*Trans. Ent. Soc.*)

Sect. III. *Kitchen Fittings-up and Furniture.*

2529. *Various Ovens and Kitchen-Ranges* have been brought into notice since the Encyclopædia appeared; but no oven has equalled that of Count Rumford as modified by
W. Strutt, Esq., a man of most extraordinary genius (§ 1503.), and no cooking and
warming apparatus for cottages has been produced that at all approaches the Bruges
stove (§ 594.).   Nevertheless, some good kitchen-ranges have been invented, the most

complete of which is one by Messrs. Steel of Edinburgh, adapted for first-rate houses, and described in the *Repertory of Arts,* vol. xiv. p. 159. There are also three different ranges of recent invention, each of which has a closed fireplace, and consequently not only cooks very economically, with great cleanliness and with much less trouble or excessive heat to the cook, but is an effectual cure for a smoky chimney. The most complete of these is Braithwaite's, price £13; and the most economical, Brown's of Luton, price between £6 and £7. We shall first give a description of Mr. Strutt's oven, next of an improved Bruges stove, and lastly of one of the closed kitchen-ranges.

2530. *The Roasting-Oven* which has been in use in the kitchen of Joseph Strutt, Esq., of Derby, for upwards of thirty years, is represented by two sections and a plan, figs. 2299. to 2301. The front section, fig. 2299., shows the interior of the oven (the door

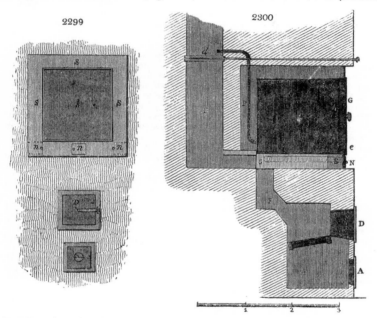

being removed), and also the cavity surrounding the oven. The oven rests upon bricks placed edgewise along each side, which forms a cavity under the oven, similar to that seen on the top and its other sides in the above figure. An opening into this cavity is seen at E, in the side section, fig. 2300. The fire, which is introduced at D, it will be seen, does not immediately act upon the oven: the flame branches on each side along the flues F F in fig. 2301., and then ascends perpendicularly, enveloping the back, the two sides, and the top of the oven; it is not, however, allowed to escape till it descends to E in fig. 2300., there being a similar hole on the other side. It is now compelled to pass under the oven, and thence into the chimney c, so that the bottom of the oven, which is generally the hottest part in other ovens, is the coldest in this; since the hot vapour does not reach it until it has given the greatest part of its heat to the top and sides.

In the front section, fig. 2299., is an opening, o, which indicates the mouth of a tube fastened into an iron plate, which is seen to close the front of the under cavity. This tube proceeds in a straight direction under the bottom of the oven, the whole length; it then turns with a curve, and comes back on the opposite side, where it terminates in the bottom of the oven, which communicates with the cavity, as seen in the side section, at c. This cavity is formed of sheet iron, similar to that of which the rest of the roaster is formed, and screwed to the door G. Towards the top of this cavity in the door is an aperture, h, opening into the oven. The tube F communicates with the oven and the chimney above the damper d. Now it will be evident that, when the door of the roaster is shut, a current of cold air will enter at o in the front section, and will become heated in passing along the curved tube under the oven; it will then enter the cavity c in the door G, and pass out at the hole h into the roaster, and thence through the pipe p into the chimney, to the draught of which it owes its motion.

2301

This contrivance has two great advantages: its heat is sufficient to have a great effect upon the substances to be baked or roasted, and the constant change of the air contributes to the crusty brown so generally liked. Its greatest advantage, however, consists in carrying off the disagreeable smell complained of when meat is roasted in a common oven.

A is a register-door, opening into the ash-pit; D, the door for the fuel: beyond this is a second door, which opens by a hook attached to the first door.

Opposite to the cavity on each side and the cavity under the roaster are three small doors, n, n, n, which are opened occasionally for raking out the soot and ashes. This last operation is not required very often. The top and sides, which will soon become clogged with soot, are raked very frequently by another contrivance, which we can better describe than represent in the drawing. In the front section, fig. 2299., suppose the dark space, s, which surrounds the roaster to be a piece of sheet iron capable of being moved backward and forward, by means of a rod of iron fastened into the middle of that part which fits the cavity at the top of the roaster, and projecting to the front, like the rod of the damper, d, in the side section; then it will be evident that a rake of this form will, by its motion, completely scrape the top and sides of the roaster; an operation frequently necessary. This rake brings the soot to the bottom of the cavities; and when it is accumulated there to a certain extent, it requires to be withdrawn from the openings, n n n.

The above description was sent to us by Mr. Joseph Hunt, ironmonger, Derby, who put up Mr. Strutt's oven, and who informs us that one similar to that above described may be fitted up complete in Derby for £10 10s.

Mr. Strutt has two of these ovens in his kitchen; one similar to that described for common use, and another about twice the size for extraordinary occasions. Nothing has been roasted before an open fire in Mr. Strutt's kitchen for upwards of thirty years. To the excellence of Mr. Strutt's table all who have enjoyed that gentleman's hospitality will bear testimony.

2531. *The Bruges Stove*, as improved by Messrs. Cottam and Hallen, figs. 2302. to 2304., appears to be better adapted both for warming a common cottage and cooking at the same time, than any other either of British or foreign invention. The Flemings are a rigidly economical people, and therefore whatever is in use among them deserves serious consideration. This led us to figure and describe this stove in the Encyclopædia, p. 285., and we have now to present an improved form of it as exhibited in the figures referred to. It will, no doubt, be extremely difficult to get a British cottager, with all her prejudices for an open fire, to use this or any other cooking stove; nevertheless, we cordially agree with Mr. Cottam, that this stove will do more with a given quantity of fuel than any other stove or fireplace whatever. It has the means of stewing, boiling, broiling, roasting, and baking, at one and the same time, with a small quantity of coke or cinders from any other fire. It is simple in form, and there is not the slightest difficulty in its use. The holes in the top may be arranged as is found most convenient for the situation in which the stove is to be placed, either in a line, as in fig. 2300., or in the form of a triangle. One thing is indispensable for the proper action of this stove, and that is a good draught. It must therefore have a separate flue.

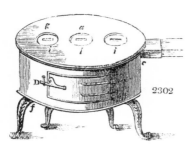

2302

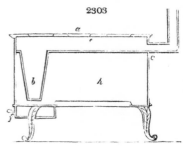

2303

As it stands quite detached, heat is radiated from it on every side, and only that small portion is lost which goes up the chimney. In the figures, *a* is the top of the stove; *b* is the fire-pot; *g* is the lid of the hole for feeding the fire-pot; *f* is an ash drawer; *c* is the flue; *d* is the oven door; *h* is the oven; *e* is a space for the fire to pass to the flue, *c*, and for heating the whole of the top plate, any part of which will produce sufficient heat for culinary purposes; *i i i* have lids, which may be taken off, and the battery of stew-pans or boilers will then be in contact with the flame. A gridiron fits on any of these

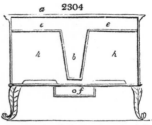

openings, which has the advantage of not smoking the article broiled, the draught being downwards. (*Arch. Mag.*, i. 77.) Unfortunately, the cost is between £6 and £7.

2532. *Brown of Luton's improved Kitchen-range*, fig. 2305., is founded on the principle of economising fuel. Its appearance is that of an ordinary range with oven and boiler,

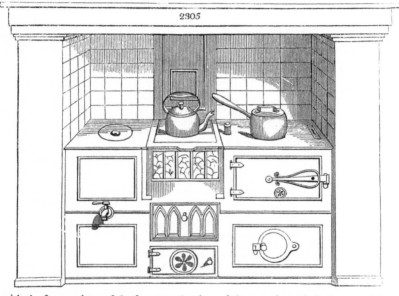

with the front and top of the fire-grate shut in, and the space beneath the bottom of the grate also partially enclosed. The fireplace is cased with fire-brick on the back and sides, and an iron plate forms the front, which, becoming red hot, supplies the heat necessary for roasting; when not in use for that purpose, it is screened by an outer plate sliding in groves on either side : a portion of the top plate is removable at pleasure, to afford an opportunity of boiling, frying, broiling, &c. The fire plays round the oven, and partly under the boiler, and the vapour escapes by a pipe into a chimney or other flue. The top forms a hot plate. The space under the grate-bottom in front is enclosed in part with talc, and the drawer for receiving the ashes occupies the remainder. There can be no doubt of the improvement effected in this range in the avoidance of smoke and dust, economy of fuel, &c., over the common range; the oven and boiler appear to act well in every respect; and the inventor states that he had roasted a leg of mutton by the red-hot plate of nineteen pounds and a half weight. This range is made in different sizes, and sold at from six to ten guineas each, at Luton, in Bedfordshire, and at 34. Gracechurch Street, London. Stoves very similar to that of Brown's are manufactured by Braithwaite, White Lion Court, Cornhill, at nearly double the price ; by Wright of Arthur Street, London Bridge, by Nicholson at the Baker Street bazaar, and by E. Brown of Birmingham. They are all excellent in principle, cleanly, economical, and effectually cure a smoky chimney ; and Mr. Brown's of Luton has the merit of being the cheapest.

2533. *Saul's improved Cottage Fireplace.* On the grate, fig. 2306., is placed a cast-iron plate, with a circular aperture in the centre at *a*.   It is eight inches and a half in diameter, which just takes a

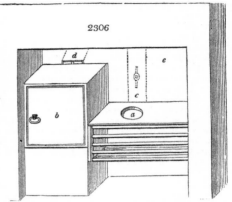

2306

common tea-kettle, and answers well for other-sized pans, as it is of no moment if the pan is larger than the aperture.   By this plan the heat is confined in the grate ; and, by several experiments, it has been proved that any thing will much sooner boil in this closed grate than in an open one: and it also throws out a greater heat in the room, and prevents smoke ; and, when the fire is not wanted for cooking, there is a plate to cover the aperture.   It also consumes less fuel, and is a sure remedy for a smoky chimney.   When an oven is also made in the same fireplace, as seen at *b*, the whole heat is made to pass under the oven by turning the damper in the flue *c*, which is behind the iron plate, when the smoke is carried up the oven flue, *d*.   When the oven is not wanted, the flue *d* is closed with the damper, and then the smoke rises through the flue *c*.   A small aperture is made on the top of the iron plate at *e*, to admit any smoke that may arise when putting on the fuel, or changing the kettles or pans.   This plan may be adapted to any grate now in use.   It is only necessary to get a cast-iron plate the size of the grate.   It is to rest upon the top bar of the grate, and on the brickwork on the back ; and a small aperture is to be made for the smoke to escape, and an iron plate fixed in front, to prevent the smoke from entering the room. (*A. M.*, v. 226.)

2534. *A portable Roaster*, formed of tin, is considered a most useful and economical apparatus for roasting meat before an open fire.   The ordinary size of this roaster is about three feet long, two feet high, and one foot deep ; but some are made nearly twice as large.   The front which faces the fire is open, and the back and sides are of tinned iron.   The spit is let into notches in the ends, and is turned by a small wind-up jack.   The American oven is formed of tinned iron, and when used is set before the fire, the heat of which it receives directly in front, and by reflection from the inside of the bottom and top, which slope, the one upwards and the other downwards, at an angle of about 40°.   The editor of the *British Farmer's Magazine*, speaking of this oven says, " it is one of the most valuable inventions of the kind we know, and ought to be in every farmhouse and every cottage in the kingdom.   Our own family bread is chiefly baked in one of these ovens placed before the fire, and better bread there cannot be from any oven whatever.   For roasting (not baking) small joints, we know nothing equal to it." (*Brit. Farm. Mag.*, new series, vol. vi. p. 98.)   Another very economical oven is thus formed.   A circular bottom of sheet iron, eleven inches in diameter, has a rim raised round it one inch and a half deep.   To this bottom there is a cover four inches and a half, or at most five inches deep, which fits easy within the rim of the bottom.   This forms the oven ; and it only requires a handle by which to suspend it over the fire, which handle must be sufficiently high to allow of taking off and putting on the cover without inconvenience.   There is a movable small hoop of sheet iron, about five inches in diameter and three inches and a quarter deep, to put the dish upon, and keep it from the bottom to prevent burning.   The cost is about 3*s*., and it bakes meat or bread well.   A figure of this oven is given in *Mech. Mag.*, vol. xxxiii. p. 569.   To these kitchen apparatus we must be excused for adding Platow's automaton coffee-pot, which is universally allowed to be by far the best utensil for making coffee that has hitherto been invented, price from 4*s*. upwards.

2535. *An economical Hot Closet* may be formed at very little expense, by taking a common hastener for placing before a kitchen fire when meat is roasting, and closing up the front, or side next the fire, with black sheet iron, forming a door at the back for putting in and taking out the articles to be kept hot.   Black iron absorbs the heat powerfully ; and the heated air within not being allowed to escape, becomes very hot.   When it is desired to use this hot closet as a hastener in roasting meat, it is only necessary to hang in front, before the black iron, a covering of tinned sheet iron, which may be in two or more plates, according to the size of the hastener, for convenience of lifting on and off.   Fig. 2307. is a back view of such a movable hot closet, with the door open, showing the shelves, &c.   It is scarcely necessary to observe that white sheet iron will, in many cases, be preferable to black iron ; because, while it reflects the heat and hastens the meat, it will conduct and radiate quite enough into the hot closet; and what is collected there will not be so easily radiated through the tin as through the black sheet iron.

2536. *Fuller's Ice-Box.* This box is one of the most ingenious and useful inventions that have been introduced into the domestic economy of the wealthy classes for many years. It may be described as one box within another, the inner box being six inches apart from the outer box on every side, and at the top and bottom. The space between the outer box and the inner box is filled up with burnt cork in a state of powder, as being a better nonconductor of heat than powdered charcoal of common wood. The lid is double like the sides, and the vacuity filled with charcoal in the same manner, to prevent the possibility of air getting in to the contents of the box when it is shut. The lid has ledges which project downwards into a gutter

2307

containing water, so as to render the junction airtight. The ice is contained in the well or space thus enclosed and protected, which is lined with cork; and which will keep the rough ice for three, four, or five weeks, in the hottest weather of summer. Mr. Harrison's box is three feet five inches by two feet eight inches, and three feet five inches in depth, outside measure; and the well, or inner box, will contain three hundred pounds of rough ice. The cost of a box of this size complete is £25 4s. The cost of the ice which is required to fill it, and which is supplied by a large wholesale dealer in that article at Southgate, Mr. Symonds, is about 15s.; the price per cwt. varying from 4s. to 6s., of three sorts, sweepings, mixed, and pure, at different prices. The box three times filled will serve an ordinary family a whole season. When we consider the expense of building an ice-house; the uncertainty of its answering the end proposed; the expense of filling it annually with ice, and of taking out a portion every two or three days, or in the hottest weather every day; the saving by the use of the ice-preserver must be obvious. In fact, there are few families who have an ice-house, who would not save a considerable sum every year by it, and be much more certain of always having ice when they wanted it. The box is the invention of Mr. Fuller, No. 60. Jermyn Street.

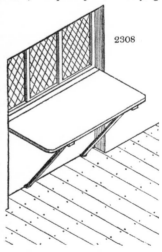

2308

2537. *A temporary Table or Ironing-board.* It is a matter of some difficulty, in small cottages, to place the shutters to the windows on the ground floor in such a manner as to answer the purpose, and yet be out of the way. The following plan has been adopted in some buildings of that description which have been lately erected. The shutters in fig. 2308. are hung on hinges in such a manner as to fall down into a recess below the window during the day time; and, consequently, they are quite out of the way when not wanted for shutting up the house, or for temporary purposes. The idea suggested itself, that shutters might be occasionally used as a table or ironing-board; and, to effect this end, two movable bars, as supports, were let into mortises in the floor, and made to abut against similar mortises made in the ledges on the under side of the shutters. The two cornices were slightly rounded, and the upper surface was left plain, without paint. Two swing iron or wooden brackets might be used, instead of the two wooden bars, as they could be folded back into the recess also. (*Arch. Mag.*, v. 75.)

SECT. IV.   *Bed-room Furniture.*

2538. *An Improvement in the Box Bedsteads used in Scotch Cottages,* made by Dr. Wilson of Kelso, is shown in fig. 2309. It consists of a curtain-rod and curtains, which may be drawn out about three feet from the front of the bed, so as to form sufficient space between the curtain and the bed to serve as a dressing-room.   Some of the Leith and London steamers had the berths in the ladies' cabins fitted up in this way some years ago.   Another improvement, introduced by Dr. Wilson, in these beds, consists of the hinging of a part of the roof of the bed so that it may be opened like a trap-door, at pleasure, for ventilation ; and the hinging of boards at the foot and at the back, for the same object, and for giving access to a medical attendant.   These improvements, we trust, form one step towards getting rid of box bed-steads altogether.   They may be very desirable in the wretched hovels in which they are generally found, but in comfortable cottages they are neither favourable to health nor to habits of cleanliness.

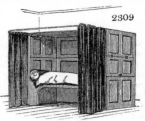

2309

2539. *Concealed Washhand-stand.*   In a room which serves both as a sitting-room and bed-room it may often be desirable to have a concealed wash-stand.   The recess by the side of the chimney is often enclosed as a cupboard by a door in the usual manner ; against the inside of this door may be screwed a common wash-stand, having its legs cut short enough to pass over the wash-board of the room without throwing the basin too high for comfortable use.   When the door is shut the washing apparatus is in the cupboard, but when the door is open the means of washing are in the room in a most convenient situation.   This contrivance, and a sofa bed, together, afford the economist the uses of a bed-room without the appearance of one. — *J. I. H.*

2540. *An oval Hip-bath*, made of tin or copper.   The depth of this bath, inside measure, is twelve inches ; the base on which it stands is three inches ; the length of the bath is thirteen inches and a half at the top, and nineteen inches at the bottom ; its breadth, twenty-inches at the top, and twelve inches and a half at the bottom ; the shoulder-piece is eight inches deep.   This bath may be used as a child's bath, hip-bath, foot-bath, spunging-bath, or even as a washing-tub.   A circular piece of oil-cloth, at least three times the diameter of the bath, having the edges turned up over a piece of rope, so as to form a water-tight rim, receives any splashings from the bath, and saves the carpet or the floor.   When not wanted, this oil-cloth saucer goes into very little bulk.

2541. *A cheap portable Shower-bath*, manufactured by Milne and Son, Edinburgh, is described in the *Architectural Magazine*, vol. v. p. 468.

2542. *A Dressing-table with a Bag Drawer*, fig. 2310., is a most useful piece of bed-room furniture.   It is three feet seven inches long, two feet seven inches high, and two feet six inches wide.   There are two upper drawers, and a frame resembling a drawer externally, of the length of the table beneath.   To this frame a bag of fluted silk is attached, tapering downwards, and reaching within six inches of the floor, leaving just enough of space to allow room for the feet and knees when the lady is sitting before the table.   The bag pulls out like a drawer, and has a wooden bottom, to which may be fixed stands (fig. 587. in p. 304.) on which to place bonnets ; and

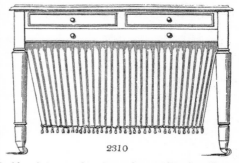

2310

hooks may be attached to the inside of the wooden frame from which the silk bag hangs, on which to place caps. — *Selim.*   (The author of the " Beau Ideal of an English Villa," in p, 790.)   Every lady will see at once the saving of room that this kind of dressing-table is calculated to effect.

SECT. V.   *Furniture for Living-Rooms.*

2543. *A handsome Architectural Commode* is shown in fig. 2313. ; the top may be a marble slab, and the panels of the doors filled in with green silk, protected by gilt wire.

2544. *Drawingroom Seats.*   Fig. 2316. is an hour-glass seat; fig. 2318. p. 1294. a reading seat ; and fig. 2321. a circular Ottoman sofa.   The last, besides its use in the drawingroom, may be made of straw; or, in some countries of heath, and appropriately placed in the centre of a large rustic summer-house. The reading-seat, fig. 2318., is by no means elegant in form; but we can assert, from experience, that it is exceedingly comfortable to sit on; not only the back, but the head, being supported

2313

by the peculiar form of the upper part of the end, or support for the back.   A footstool is shown in fig. 2314.

2545. *A Card-Table*, fig. 2315. The concave curve at *a*, as contrasted with the convex curve at *b*, has a good effect. The scroll foot, exhibited at *c*, is rather plain, and

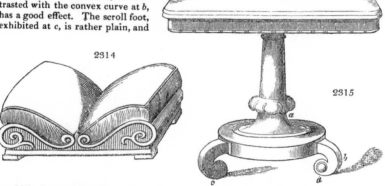

2314

2315

would be improved, as it appears to us, by some such addition as we have shown at *d*.

2546. *An occasional Table in the Elizabethan Style* is shown in fig. 2317.   It is very

2316

2317

handsome, and highly expressive of the most cultivated variety of that manner of architectural design.

2547. *Poys, or supported Tea-Chests*, are shown in figs. 2319. and 2320.; both handsome.   In the *Architectural Magazine*, a great many other handsome pieces of furniture, including sideboards, dinner waggons, desks, bookcases, ladies' work-tables, &c., will be found figured and described.

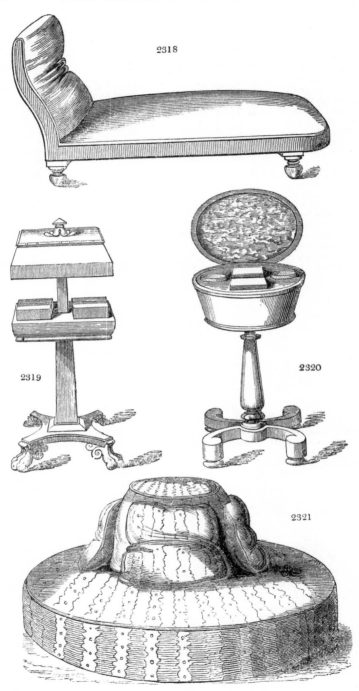

2318

2319

2320

2321

CHAP. VII.

Hints to Proprietors desirous of improving the Labourers' Cottages on their Estates.

2548. *On estates of moderate extent*, where the proprietor looks into every thing himself, much may be done by his personally examining, along with his carpenter, the *Labourers' Cottages* already existing, and ascertaining their present state with reference to the list of essential requisites in p. 1140. This being done, the next step is to devise improvements: — by draining; by additions of garden ground; by putting the garden and the cottage, if practicable, in a ring fence; and by such alterations and additions to the cottage as may appear necessary for health and comfort. To assist in this manner of improvement the following particulars may be found useful.

2549. *Situation.* It ought to be constantly borne in mind, that the main object in building a cottage is to produce a comfortable dwelling; and that for this purpose a dry airy situation, in which, if possible, the ground falls gently from the cottage on every side; an aspect that will allow the sun to shine on every side wall of the cottage a portion of every day in the year; thick walls, and thick or double far-projecting roofs of high pitch; are most desirable requisites. Whether the front, the end, or one side of the cottage is parallel to the adjoining road, ought to be considered a matter of no consequence; indeed, so far from a parallel position being desirable, an oblique one is in general preferable, as we have shown § 2237.

2550. *Garden.* The garden ought always, if possible, to surround the cottage, and it ought never to be less in extent than a sixth of an acre; but as in cottages already existing it may often be found impracticable to surround the cottage with its garden, the next best arrangements are, to have the garden before, or behind, or on one side; or partly before and behind and partly on one side. If the main body of the garden must of necessity be separated from the cottage, then there should be a direct communication with it by a path, so as to diminish as much as possible the inconvenience and discomfort of an isolated garden. Cottage allotments, by which are to be understood portions of ground in a field allotted to cottages at some distance, are much better than no gardens at all; but they are far from producing the comfort and enjoyment of a garden in close contact with the cottage to which it belongs.

2551. *Materials.* When the walls are of pisé, mud, cob, clay lumps, or any other description of consolidated earth, the thickness of two feet may be obtained in solid materials; and this may also be the case where stone is abundant: but where brick must, of necessity, be used, the thickness of eighteen inches or two feet is to be attained most economically by building the walls with brick on edge hollow, and filling them up with concrete. By this means we form a mass of solid material, which will, of course, have a greater capacity for heat than a hollow wall, and consequently give out more when it is wanted for heating the air of the rooms. The advantages of thick walls, and of thick or double roofs, of high pitch, and projecting at the eaves, with reference to retaining heat, are greater than can well be conceived by those who have not dwelt in a cottage. A high and dry floor is essential, whether this be obtained by placing the cottage on a terrace, as in the model cottage No. I. in p. 1141.; or by raising the floor inside, and ascending to it by outside steps, as in the mechanic's model cottage in p. 1145.

2552. *Designing Cottages.* In page 1140 we have summed up the essential requisites for a labourer's cottage, with a view to convenience, comfort, and other directly useful properties. The following Rules are to be considered as additional to those given in the page referred to, and as having for their object to superadd to comfort and convenience, Architectural Design and Taste.

1. Every exterior wall should show a plinth at its base, and a frieze or wall-plate immediately under the roof. In the case of earthen walls, the plinth should be of brick or stone, and the wall-plate of wood. The stones of the plinth should be larger than those used in the plain parts of the wall which are above it; and the upper finishing of the plinth may be the outer edge of a course of slates, flagstone, tiles, or bricks, laid in cement, extending through the entire thickness of the wall, in order to prevent the rising of damp; the appearance of the edge of this course as a moulding or string course crowning the plinth, will, therefore, be highly expressive of utility: or the entire plinth may be built in cement, which will be equally effective in preventing the rising of damp, as well as expressive of that important use.

2. The pitch of the roof, whatever may be the material with which it is covered, should be such as to prevent snow from lying on it; and for this purpose the cross section should generally be an equilateral triangle. Cottages which form gate-lodges in the Grecian or Italian styles form exceptions to this rule; but such lodges never ex-

press the same ideas of comfort as high-roofed cottages, with high and bold chimneys. Such lodges, indeed, are commonly called "boxes;" and in fact many of them are so deficient in height, and in every other dimension, that they give rise to ideas the very opposite of those of freedom and comfort.

3. When the wall is built of rubble-work small stones or bricks, a framing or casing of larger stones as quoins to the exterior angles, and jambs lintels and sills to the doors windows and other openings, seems to add to the strength and security of the wall, by preventing the small stones or bricks from being loosened by the weather or by accident, and so dropping out. Hence all doors and windows in such walls should be surrounded by facings of some sort, or have the jambs sills or lintels splayed. Hence, also, the propriety of quoin-stones at the angles or corners, of coping-stones to the gables, of cut and dressed stones to the chimney-tops, and of larger stones to the plinths than those generally used in the plain parts of the wall above them. In the case of earthen walls, the jambs may be splayed, or both jambs and lintels may be faced with boards or formed of brick carried up from the plinth.

4. Every stack of chimneys should consist of four parts: a plinth, which should be distinctly seen above the roof; one or more base mouldings, or splayed weatherings resting on the plinth; a shaft rising from the base mouldings, of analogous proportions to the doors and windows; and a capital or cornice moulding and cap or blocking, as a termination to the shaft. The materials of the chimney-tops ought in general to be superior in quality to those of the walls; for example, if the walls are of rubble stone, the chimneys should be of stone squared and dressed. When the walls are of earth the entire stack of chimneys will, of course, be built of brick or stone.

5. When the flues of the chimneys are carried up in the outer wall, there ought always to be a projection outwards in that wall, beneath the chimneys, carried up from the ground, so as to give the necessary space for the flues, the strength of a buttress to the wall, with a sufficient breadth for supporting the chimney-tops, and the architectural expression of all these purposes.

6. Eaves-gutters, and ridge and hip coverings, with similar details essential as "finishings," as well as for habitableness and comfort, should never be omitted. The eaves-gutters should be properly supported by brackets, these being of stone or brick, except in the case of earthen walls, where they ought to be of wood.

7. Over the front door or porch of every cottage, there ought to be a worked stone, on which should be cut the name of the cottage, the initials of the first occupant, a number, a sign, or some distinctive mark of the cottage, by which it may be registered in the Book of the Estate. See § 2327.

8. In rendering cottages ornamental, the most important parts and members of structure are those on which most decoration should be bestowed; such as the porch, entrance door, window of the principal room, upper parts of the gables, chimney-tops, &c.: and, in ornamenting each particular part, the most important details of that part should receive the highest degree of decoration; for example, the hinges and latch or lock of a door should be made richer than the muntings and styles, and the muntings and styles richer than the panels; and, hence, a door in which no ornament is bestowed on the latch or the hinges ought not to have the muntings, styles, or panels, studded over with ornamental nail heads as is often done.

9. Nothing should be introduced in any design, however ornamental it may appear to be, that is at variance with propriety, comfort, or sound workmanship.

2553. *For the Labourers' Cottages on Estates managed by Agents*, we would recommend a tour of inspection by a competent person, and a Report drawn up on their present state, and on the means of their improvement. The Report should include the character of the surface soil and subsoil on which each particular cottage stands; the state of surface and underground drainage; the aspect of the different sides of the cottage, and its shelter or exposure; the sources of water and of fuel; the state of the back-yard, &c., if any; the state of the garden; and the connexion of the cottage with the nearest public road. The cottage itself ought next to be examined as to plan and accommodation, height of the side walls, thickness of the walls, roof and gutters, floor, windows, stair, fireplace, bed-rooms, exterior appearance, &c. The Report should then point out the additions and alterations necessary to render the cottage what it ought to be, illustrating these by plans, sections, and sketches, and giving lists of fruit-trees and shrubs, where these are wanting for the garden. Would that we could hear of some of the first landed proprietors in the country having such Reports made on the labourers' cottages, and the school-houses, on their estates! The practice would soon after become general, and the good that would ultimately result to the cottager and his children, and the accession of beauty, and appearance of comfort, to rural scenery, would be immense.

GENERAL INDEX.

₊ *Where the letter* p. *does not occur,* § *is to be understood.*

A.

House, Sir John Robison's, Randolph Crescent Edinburgh, 2378.
House, circumstances which influence the position of a, 1642.
Houses for horned cattle, 756 ; for working oxen, 764 ; for sheep, 766.
Houses, half-timbered, 2279.
House-fly, the Italian mode of excluding it from apartments, 2528.

I.

Ice-box, 2536.
Ice-house, 736 to 738.
Implements for a cyder-press, 1312.
Implements of a barn, 1402.
Infant schools, models of, 1512, 1523, 1614.
Inlaid floors, 2010.
Inn, design for, in the Italian style, 1422, 1438, 1450 ; in the Gothic style, 1426 ; in the Italian Gothic Manner, 1434 ; in the old English style, 1442 ; hedge alehouse, 1446 ; in the Swiss style, 1452.
Inns and public-houses, principles for designing, 1413.
Inns, appendages to, 1417 ; garden, 1417, 1423, &c. ; skittle-ground, 1429 ; bowling-green, 1430 ; tea-garden, 1431.
Inns, finishing, fittings-up, and furniture for, 1460 ; general store-room, 1460 ; larders, 1461 ; napkin-press, 1460 ; cast-iron wine-bins, 1462 ; bottling and corking machine, 1463 ; Mallet's air-peg for ale and beer-casks, 1463 ; washing and wringing-machine, 1464 ; drying-closet, 1466 ; water-closet, 1467 ; cleaning-shed 1468 ; heating-stove, 1471 ; apparatus for lighting by gas, 1472 ; system of bells and speaking-pipes, 1473 ; descending table, 1474 ; system of distributing water, bath, 1476 ; Anglo-American stove, 1477 ; chairs of cast and wrought iron, 1477 ; benches and tables, 1477 ; other articles, 1478 and 1479.
Inns, fittings-up and fixtures for, 1443 ; bar, counter, beer, and spirit apparatus, 1443 ; gas cooking-apparatus, 1445 ; water-closet, 1453, 1467 ; for the bar, 1456 ; rising cupboards, 1457 ; folding register-grates, 1458 ; sinks, 1459 ; side-tables and dressers, 1459 ; for the store-room and larder, 1460, 1461 ; cellars, 1463 ; washing and wringing-machine, 1464, 1465 ; for the laundry, 1466 ; cleaning-house, 1468 ; baths, 1470.
Inns of Germany and other countries, 1410 ; of recreation, 1410 ; model designs for inns, 1413 ; accommodations for the house, 1414 ; of the bar or office, 1415 ; of the stable-court, 1416 ; of the grounds, 1417.
Inns, situations for, 1419 ; style of, 1420.
Interiors of rooms in the Grecian style, 2091, 2103, 2131 ; in the Gothic style, 2157, 2161, 2165 ; in the Elizabethan style, 2173.
Interior composition, suitableness of pointed architecture for, 1874.
Iron-boards and fixed flaps for cottages, 613.
Irregular buildings, beauties of, 117, 119, 120, 2208.
Iron bedsteads, cast, 1407.
Iron hand-mill for cottages, 612.
Iron sheep-rack, 1393.
Iron, preventing rust in, 2508.
Iron roofs for cottages, 419 ; corrugated, 420.
Italian architects worked on the principles of the painter, 1121.
Italian villas, 1659.
Italian architecture, observations on, by Mr. Lamb, 1918 to 1932.
Italian villa, 2391.
Italian styles, design for a cottage in the modern, 2294.
Italian style of architecture, characteristics of, 1933.
Italy, villas of, 1657 ; landscape architecture of, 1658.

J.

Jeakes, his mode of fitting up stewing-hearths in kitchens, 1501.
Jerningham, rich Gothic mansion at, 1865.
Joiner's and carpenter's work of a farmery, 852, 869, 919, 983, 989, 1064, 1100, 1207.
Joiner's work for a cottage, 239, 297, 445, 852, 983 ; for a school, 1584.

K.

Keeper's lodge at Bluberhouses, 2333.
Kilns for malt, 1262 ; for hops, 1270, 1272 ; for lime, 1281 ; for bricks or tiles, and other purposes, 1290.
Kilns for malt, 798 ; for hops, 799 ; for general purposes, 800.
Kinzigthal, cottages in, 205.
Kitchen-range in use near Leamington in Warwickshire, 2029.
Kitchen-ranges and cooking-apparatus for inns, 1481 ; for cottages, 592.
Kitchen-ranges with baking and roasting ovens, 1504.
Kitchens of inns, finishings, fittings-up, and fixtures for, 1480.
Kitchens of villas, fittings-up, and fixtures for, 2029 ; a kitchen, by Mr. Mallet, 2030.
Kitchens, principles and rules for fitting up, as laid down by Count Rumford, 1482 to 1500 ; practice usual in London, 1501.
Kitchen fireplace for cottages, improvements in, 2055.
Kitchen-garden of a villa, 1646.
Kitchen-range, improved, 2532.
Knife-board, 1384.

L.

Labourers' cottages, 334, 385.
Labourers' cottages in Bedfordshire, 2233.
Labourer's cottage, the essential requisites for a, 2242.
Ladder for cottage garrets, 180.
Ladies, how they may educate themselves in architecture, and influence which that will have on art, 1.
Lady's work-table, 2115.
Lancasterian schools, 1611.
Landscape architecture of Italy, specimens of, 1658.
Landscape drawing, the study of, p. 2.
Landscape-gardening, as connected with buildings, 9 ; how it may be acquired by an architect, 1674.
Land-steward's house, design for a, 2389.
Larder and pantry of farmeries, 719 ; of inns, 1461.
Latches, Chubb's patent, 1598.
Latch, a gate, 2491.
Lath and plaster partitions, 2495.
Laundry of farmeries, 726.
Laxton's cinder-sifter, 1385.
Laying out villages, 2347.
Library, interior of, 2161.
Library furniture for villas, 2092, 2158.
Library tables for villas, 2095, 2160.
Library, proper colouring for, 2020.
Lighting the rooms of villas by gas, 2055, 2381.
Lime-kiln, 802.
Lime-kiln, as improved by Menteath, 1282 ; other forms, 1289.
Limestone, modes of burning, 1281.
Liquid manure, tanks for, in a farmery, 825, 826.
Liquid manure tank, 2237, 2483.
Lithic paints for covering cement, 528.
Locality, what is to be understood by it, 1633.
Locks and other fastenings for cottages, 84.
Lodge, in the Swiss style, 2281.
Lodge, a turnpike, design for a, 2326.
Lodge, the Chequers Dairy, 2309, 2331.
Lodge at Bluberhouses, keeper's, 2333.
Lodge, design for a castellated, 439.
Lodges, entrance, designs for, 1987.
Lodging-places for animals, principles for designing, 745 to 749.
Loo-tables, 2118.

M.

Machine, barley-chopper, 1402 ; for filtering, 698, 2077.
Machines of a barn, 1402.
Machinery, gates to open by, 831 ; threshing, 1135.
Madras schools, 1530.
Maize, barn for, 782.
Mallet's cottage range, 593 ; apparatus for cooking by gas, 2044.
Malt-houses, 798.
Malt-kilns, designs for, 1262.
Mangers, 751 to 753.
Mangle, Baker's patent, 1381.

☞ *The Author may be consulted, either personally or by letter, on any of the subjects treated of in this Volume, at the rate of One Guinea per hour ; or, if required to go from home, at the rate of Five Guineas a day, with travelling expenses. The charge for Plans and Reports may be ascertained by previous agreement.*

THE END.

ERRATUM.

In p. 1162., in some copies, for " The Hon. Thomas Liddel," read " The Hon. Thomas Liddell."

LONDON:
Printed by A SPOTTISWOODE,
New-Street-Square.

Lightning Source UK Ltd.
Milton Keynes UK
UKHW012027270421
382751UK00001B/27